PERFORMANCE, COGNITIVE THEORY, AND DEVOTIONAL CULTURE

Cognitive Studies in Literature and Performance

Engaging Audiences
  Bruce McConachie

Literature, Science, and a New Humanities
  Jonathan Gottschall

The Public Intellectualism of Ralph Waldo Emerson and W.E.B. Du Bois
  Ryan Schneider

Performance, Cognitive Theory, and Devotional Culture
  Jill Stevenson

Performance, Cognitive Theory, and Devotional Culture

Sensual Piety in Late Medieval York

Jill Stevenson

PERFORMANCE, COGNITIVE THEORY, AND DEVOTIONAL CULTURE
Copyright © Jill Stevenson, 2010.
Softcover reprint of the hardcover 1st edition 2010 978–0–230–10319–1
All rights reserved.

The John the Baptist alabaster panel is reproduced by permission of the Burrell Collection, Cultural and Sport Glasgow (Museums).

All images from the Pavement Hours are reproduced by kind permission of the Dean and Chapter of York.

First published in 2010 by
PALGRAVE MACMILLAN®
in the United States—a division of St. Martin's Press LLC,
175 Fifth Avenue, New York, NY 10010.

Where this book is distributed in the UK, Europe and the rest of the world, this is by Palgrave Macmillan, a division of Macmillan Publishers Limited, registered in England, company number 785998, of Houndmills, Basingstoke, Hampshire RG21 6XS.

Palgrave Macmillan is the global academic imprint of the above companies and has companies and representatives throughout the world.

Palgrave® and Macmillan® are registered trademarks in the United States, the United Kingdom, Europe and other countries.

ISBN 978-1-349-28771-0   ISBN 978-0-230-10907-0 (eBook)
DOI 10.1057/9780230109070

Library of Congress Cataloging-in-Publication Data

Stevenson, Jill.
   Performance, cognitive theory, and devotional culture : sensual piety in late medieval York / Jill Stevenson.
      p. cm. — (Cognitive studies in literature and performance)
      Includes bibliographical references and index.

   1. Theater—England—York—History—Medieval, 500–1500.
2. Christian drama, English (Middle)—England—York—History and criticism. 3. Mysteries and miracle-plays, English—England—York—History and criticism. 4. English drama—To 1500—History and criticism. 5. York (England)—Religious life and customs. 6. Rites and ceremonies, Medieval—England—York—History. 7. Christianity and literature—England—York—History—To 1500. 8. York plays. I. Title.

PN2596.Y6S74 2010
792.1'60942843—dc22   2009041118

A catalogue record of the book is available from the British Library.

Design by Newgen Imaging Systems (P) Ltd., Chennai, India.

First edition: May 2010

10 9 8 7 6 5 4 3 2 1

Transferred to Digital Printing in 2013

*To many remarkable mentors and one in particular,
Professor John Steven Paul (1951–2009)*

Contents

List of Figures ix
Acknowledgments xi
A Note on Transcription and Translation xiii

Introduction: Devotional Modes of Becoming in Late Medieval York 1

One   Performance Literacy: Theorizing Medieval Devotional Seeing 15

Two   Material Devotion: Objects as Performance Events 45

Three   Claiming Devotional Space 67

Four   Devotion and Conceptual Blending 87

Five   Pious Body Rhythms 115

Six   Empathy, Entrainment, and Devotional Instability 133

Coda: Medieval Sensual Piety and a Few Twenty-First-Century Religious Rhythms 151

Notes 165
Selected Bibliography 227
Index 249

Figures

3.1 *Pricke of Conscience* window, All Saints North Street, York (*ca.* 1410). Photograph by author 73

3.2 Donor image in *Prick of Conscience* window, All Saints North Street, York (*ca.* 1410). Photograph by author 75

3.3 Head of John the Baptist, alabaster panel (*ca.* 1470–85). Cultural and Sport Glasgow (Museums) 83

4.1 Lifting Face of Christ insertion, folio 94r, *Pavement Hours* (*ca.* 1420). York Minster Library, York, England 107

4.2 Folio spread of St. Clare, three male saints, and IHC insertions, fols. 26v–27, *Pavement Hours* (*ca.* 1420). York Minster Library, York, England 108

4.3 Unidentified female saint insertion, folio 106r, *Pavement Hours* (*ca.* 1420). York Minster Library, York, England 109

4.4 Arma Christi insertion, folio 44v, *Pavement Hours* (*ca.* 1420). York Minster Library, York, England 112

Acknowledgments

This book began as a dissertation project and it is a pleasure to thank the many people and institutions that helped shape it into its current form. I am grateful to the following institutions for financial support: the American Society for Theatre Research; the Theatre Program of the Graduate Center, CUNY; the Medieval Academy of America and the Richard III Society; and Marymount Manhattan College for providing travel support, as well as a Sokol Award.

Thanks to the Centre for Medieval Studies at the University of York, and especially to Sarah Rees Jones and Richard Marks. A special thanks to Jeremy Goldberg who provided me with invaluable photocopies of his own research on Yorkshire wills. The archivists and librarians at the Borthwick Institute, the Museum of London, Jane Whannel at the Burrell Collection, and, particularly, Peter Young at the York Minster Library offered me tremendous help. Amelia Grounds was particularly generous in giving me a copy of her thesis on the Pavement Hours.

Many scholars offered me encouragement and advice during this project, particularly Glenn Burger, Mary Carruthers, Amy Cook, Rick Emmerson, Katherine French, Max Harris, F. Elizabeth Hart, David Morgan, Margaret Rogerson, Michael Sargent, and Anne Bagnall Yardley. Thanks to the Graduate Center's Theatre Program faculty, in particular to Judy Milhous (for so many layers of support) and Marvin Carlson, and to many graduate school colleagues, among them Susannah Crowder, Lyn Gibson, Amy Hughes, Thomas Meacham, Ken Nielsen, Jenna Soleo-Shanks, Christopher Swift, and, above all, Jen-Scott Mobley. I could not have completed this book without the encouragement I received from the entire Marymount community, and especially from Mary Fleischer, David Mold, and Kirche Zeile. I am incredibly indebted to various anonymous readers and Bruce McConachie, whose thoughtful and thorough feedback helped strengthen this book substantially, and to the editorial team at Palgrave Macmillan, particularly Brigitte Shull and Lee Norton.

To Pam Sheingorn, it is impossible to articulate my gratitude for all you have given me. You are an incredible mentor and teacher, and your extraordinary guidance brought this project to publication.

Thanks to my mom, dad, Sarah, Liam, David, Kim, Denise, Barb, and Erin. And finally, thanks to Kelly for getting me through countless pesky transitions.

A Note on Transcription and Translation

Throughout this book, all modernizations of Middle English are mine unless otherwise indicated. In general, I have not reproduced transcriptions of original Latin or Middle English texts when these are readily available in published editions. However, I have included transcriptions when the original word choice is significant to my argument, if published transcriptions are difficult to acquire, and when citing York's pageant texts. My source for the pageants texts is *The York Plays*, edited by Richard Beadle (London: Edward Arnold, 1982). My modernizations of the play texts were made using Beadle's extensive glossary. I also referred to Richard Beadle and Pamela M. King, editors, *York Mystery Plays: A Selection in Modern Spelling* (Oxford: Clarendon Press, 1984). Beadle's new edition of the plays is forthcoming. When citing evidence from the *Records of Early English Drama: York* volumes, edited by Alexandra F. Johnston and Margaret Rogerson, I use Johnston and Rogerson's transcriptions of Middle English documents and their English translations of Latin texts. I have included the page numbers of Johnston and Rogerson's transcriptions of Latin originals in parentheses in my citations.

Introduction

Devotional Modes of Becoming in Late Medieval York

I remember distinctly the experience that sparked my passion for theatre. I was ten years old and sat in the front row of the mezzanine at the National Theatre in Washington, D.C. During the performance, I leaned forward, my forehead pressed to the balcony railing and eyes glued to the stage. In the weeks that followed, despite repeatedly recounting in vivid detail all that I had heard and seen onstage, I felt incapable of expressing in words the show's powerful impact on me. Its narrative and main idea were not the source of pleasure; the spectacular set, make-up, and costumes were not the cause either. And although I am certain that I had seen other plays before this one, this is the production that stays with me even now. It was *Cats*.

Something happened at the theatre the night I saw *Cats*. The performance lodged itself inside my body and remained there in a visceral, tangible way. Trying to express this sensation in the weeks that followed, I recreated *Cats* in my family's living room, singing and dancing to the entire two-cassette soundtrack every night. This evening ritual was the only thing that I could do with the performance that lingered inside me.

We deem a play successful, pleasurable, or noteworthy for any number of reasons. It might provoke us to think in new ways, challenge our dramaturgical expectations, or entertain us. The text could be cleverly written, or the performance brilliantly acted, skillfully designed, and innovatively staged. But plays that transform us, that prompt us to commit ourselves to theatre, that we recall years later, not just mentally but also physically, these plays do something *to* us. Their performances certainly leave traces in our minds, but, more remarkably, they embed themselves inside our bodies in such a way that we carry them with us, not only to every future theatrical event, but also to our other encounters and experiences in the world. Many performances "move" us, but transformative theatrical events remain inside us, where they continue to affect us for years, and perhaps forever.

I interpret this kind of theatrical event as, in Aleksandra Wolska's words, a "mode of becoming." Wolska has argued that "in the criticism of performance, we have lost our theoretical hold on the rather obvious fact that theatre engages forces of becoming as well as those of vanishing." She therefore encourages scholars to study theatre as a mode of becoming that "does not stop with the fall of the curtain, but continues in the body and mind of the viewer."[1] This approach helps us to recognize how such a performance can emerge as "a field of activity that continues in the everyday."[2] In some respect, *Cats* still guides me to the theatre and directs my scholarship and pedagogy simply because it generated my belief in theatre's power and, with it, my initial interest in why performance can affect us so intensely. Moreover, this performance encounter lingers within me, a reminder that theatre truly, strangely, impacts the body.

Performance's ability to operate as a mode of becoming in this physical way makes it a particularly powerful medium for communicating ideology and belief and is perhaps one reason that communities throughout history have employed performance for religious purposes. This was especially the case in the Middle Ages, and, owing to this fact, many scholars have worked to understand how the visual and textual characteristics of sacred performances contributed to medieval devotional culture. A number of these scholars have investigated how bodies create meaning during religious performance events.[3] Most of this work has analyzed the actor's body, setting aside the ways in which spectators understand theatrical events through their own bodies. In this project, I examine how the medieval spectator's unique visual, and therefore physical, encounter with a play may have impacted the ways in which he or she derived ongoing religious meaning and value from that performance event.

My analysis situates medieval religious performance as one element in the larger network of visual devotion in the later Middle Ages. Theatre has not figured prominently in scholarship on the visual culture of religious belief.[4] I view this as a missed opportunity, since theatre challenges us to expand how we classify and examine visuality, and especially visual piety, what David Morgan defines as "the visual formation and practice of religious belief."[5] Rather than strictly visual encounters, performances create sensual encounters; therefore, performance suggests ways to think about how the sensual aesthetics of a visual medium impact the viewer's encounter with it and, consequently, how that bodily experience influences larger devotional patterns. My intention is to examine both how medieval performance functioned as a visual religious experience, and also how medieval spectators derived devotional meaning and understanding from that experience. In addition, I argue that lay Christians in the Middle Ages found other devotional phenomena spiritually efficacious, in part because, like my experience with *Cats*, their live encounters with these media lingered within the body as modes of becoming.

Performance and Visual Piety

By the later Middle Ages, medieval laypeople were expressing their religious impulses in response to and through a range of media—liturgy, texts, sermons, the sacraments, books, images, and objects. Many lay devotional practices involved physical rituals, such as processions or gestural interactions with small objects. In addition, laypeople sometimes responded physically to certain visual or aural cues.[6] We might interpret these practices, at least in part, as a reaction to the increased emphasis placed upon Christ's incarnation during the later Middle Ages. The incarnational theology espoused in this period accomplished a number of things, among them sanctifying the human body and sanctioning religious images. As Sarah Beckwith notes,

> Christ's willingness to be incarnated, his embodiment, is crucial because it is only this condescension to the flesh which will allow other images to signify...The material world becomes a text which may be interpreted, scrutinized, allegorized and investigated for the way it pointed to its exemplar and author: God. In this extraordinary renegotiation...there are new possibilities for the body as text and instrumental medium...Part and parcel of this renegotiation of the role of the body in worship, was a new appreciation and re-evaluation of the role of experience, affectivity and emotion.[7]

Many devotional genres, among them performance, reinforced incarnational theology's emphasis on the material world and the body's place within it.

The late medieval catechetical program supported this emphasis, while simultaneously directing laypeople in how they should appropriately use their bodies as part of their faith. Scholars locate the roots of this lay devotional program in the constitutions of the Fourth Lateran Council (1215), which strongly advocated more systematized pastoral care of lay souls (*cura animarum*).⁸ At the 1281 Council of Lambeth, the English church formulated this agenda into a comprehensive instructional system that included the Ten Commandments, Christ's decree to love God and one's neighbor, the Creed, the seven acts of mercy, the seven virtues, the seven vices, and the seven sacraments.⁹ Particularly troubled by what he saw as the laity's spiritual "ignorance," John de Thoresby, archbishop of York from 1352 until 1373, adapted, translated, and disseminated this devotional system in the *Lay Folks' Catechism*. Dated November 25, 1357, this text, originally issued in both Latin and English, outlines the various doctrines with which laypeople should be familiar, demands that parish priests provide more instruction to the laity in English, and offers an indulgence of forty days to all who try to learn the program.¹⁰ The *Catechism* repeatedly asserts the necessity of "good dedis" and proper conduct, admonishing those who "lead their lives as their flesh desires" [ledis thar lifs als thaire flesch yhernes] and arguing that one should "not live in pleasure nor in lust that the flesh desires, but instead gladly serve God by clean living" [ne lyue in lykyng ne lust that the flesh yernes, Bot gladly to serue god in clennesse of life].¹¹ The *Catechism*'s readers are instructed to follow the commandments in both bodily and spiritual actions, since there is no hope for eternal life "withouten gode dedis."¹²

Religious authorities, such as Thoresby, recognized that laypeople were increasingly moved to use their bodies as part of their devotional lives, and therefore they developed systems of piety that channeled these inclinations into "appropriate" activities and practices. The desire to regulate the physicality of lay piety is probably best illustrated by the frustration that many clergymen expressed when confronted with laypeople such as Margery Kempe. Kempe, an Englishwoman who lived during the late fourteenth and early fifteenth centuries, became infamous for how forcefully devotional experiences seemed to engage her body. Throughout her biography, the author repeatedly describes how Kempe weeps, often violently, at the sight of religious imagery and ritual, or even when she simply sees acts reminiscent of Christ's Passion:

> Then the friars lifted up a cross and led the pilgrims from one place to another where our Lord had suffered his pains and his Passion, every man and woman carrying a wax candle in one hand. And the friars always, as they went about, told them what our Lord suffered in every place. And this creature wept and sobbed as plenteously as though she had seen our Lord with her bodily eyes suffering his Passion at that

time. Before her in her soul she saw him in truth by contemplation, and that caused her to have compassion...And sometimes, when she saw the crucifix, or if she saw a man had a wound, or a beast, whichever it were, or if a man beat a child before her or hit a horse or other beast with a whip, if she saw or heard it, she thought she saw our Lord being beaten.[13]

Such accounts offer us detailed information about the clerically prescribed devotional activities in which laypeople participated and the critical role that visual images and objects had within these. But Kempe's devotional reactions also remind us—as they did the medieval clergy—that while it might be possible to contain some physical activities, one can never entirely supervise or control the body or the mind that functions as part of that body.

Examples such as Kempe's remind us that laypeople's physical interactions with visual culture were often accompanied by elaborate mental interactions and creations—the very activities that constitute visual piety. Visual piety involves the mental manipulation, combination, and erasure of images by the viewer in order to serve his or her needs. David Morgan contends that we assess the power of religious images based upon how well they help us solve problems or cope with problems that prove to be unsolvable.[14] Visual piety is, therefore, the way we make relevant and useful meaning from our experiences with the religious visual culture that surrounds us.

In an effort to better control lay visual piety, religious authorities in the Middle Ages wrote texts that were designed to direct laypeople's mental practices with images. Laypeople read or listened to others read from many different kinds of texts. Some of these, such as Nicholas Love's *The Mirror of the Blessed Life of Jesus Christ*, supplied the laity with specific ways to engage particular religious images.[15] For example, laypeople encountered images of the crucifix in a variety of public and private settings and were also encouraged to construct a mental crucifix as part of personal meditation.[16] But, as Kempe's biography illustrates, these mental activities could take on a life of their own. Consequently, texts such as *The Mirror* functioned on some level to constrain these meditative encounters by guiding the layperson in how to see and interpret the various details within an imagined scene.[17] Medieval religious performances were therefore embedded within a complex matrix of visual culture that included various modes of production, reception, and regulation.

Many scholars have examined the relationship between performance and other visual media during the Middle Ages. Early studies of this relationship focused on iconographic similarities between the two, often arguing that one genre's iconography served as the source for the other's visual design.[18] The founding of the Early Drama, Art, and Music project (EDAM) in 1976 signaled a more interdisciplinary, though still problematic, approach to research in art and drama. One of the project's goals is to contextualize drama artistically and geographically by creating localized catalogues of medieval art.[19] Although EDAM has immense value, and finding "origins" is not its explicit purpose, the project's philosophy is founded upon the notion that a high degree of representational similarity between medieval art and drama exists. Thus, intentionally or not, it promotes the idea that one artistic genre may have served as the visual "source" for the other.[20]

A more recent approach, foreshadowed by Pamela Sheingorn's work in the late 1970s and 1980s, situates art and drama within a common visual culture and interprets them as responses to the needs, desires, and anxieties of the people living within that context.[21] This scholarship examines religious art and drama as two participants in a larger visual discourse, repeatedly building on and reacting to each other and to other cultural forms. Visual culture theory can, as Sheingorn suggests, help us try to see what the laity saw,[22] but it also valuably directs our attention beyond strictly visual elements to other qualities, such as functionality and materiality.[23] Consequently, analyzing art and drama as elements in a common visual culture helps scholars to see not only *what* the laity saw, but also *as* the laity saw; the attention shifts from analyzing the visual image or object to analyzing seeing itself. In this project, I use a visual culture approach to explore how laypeople saw religious performances and how this "way of seeing" may have been triggered by or applied in other contexts of visual piety.[24] More specifically, I employ phenomenology and cognitive theory to analyze how the material reality of performance impacted the ways that spectators understood and used visual devotional media.

Theorizing the Lay Body

Throughout these chapters I refer to the medieval "layperson" as a coherent subject largely without making distinctions with respect to age, class, sexuality, or gender. Perhaps the most obvious trait that I neglect to address is gender. A great deal of excellent research has employed gender theory to examine women and female piety in the Middle Ages.[25] Caroline Bynum, in particular, has demonstrated the body's centrality in female spiritual discourse, while other scholars have investigated how lay women and lay men were taught to relate to their bodies differently—both in devotion and in everyday life.[26]

For instance, conduct literature contains important evidence of bodily discourse and practices among medieval laypeople. Books of conduct made explicitly for the laity began to appear in England in the thirteenth century, and, as Claire Sponsler notes, these regularly define the individual as in control over his or her own self-fashioning via the management of bodily impulses.[27] By examining the different tactics used in books directed at girls compared to those in books written for boys, scholars have suggested that women and men were taught to control their bodies in different ways. Anna Dronzek argues that authors of fifteenth-century texts on conduct not only assumed boys would encounter the material text visually (through reading) and girls aurally (hearing it read aloud), but "they also presumed that boys and girls would process information in two different ways."[28] The literature directed at girls uses a more experiential format than that created for boys, and Dronzek argues that this difference suggests that authors believed "that girls needed knowledge tied to the physical, to the world of the body that was at the very center of their nature."[29] Likewise, Robert Clark has analyzed how devotional guides directed at women construct the female subject by prescribing a program of physical attitudes and gestures.[30]

These examples demonstrate that certain elements within medieval culture promoted gender distinctions. But, at the same time, many of the examples that I use throughout this book indicate that late medieval piety emphasized and engaged all bodies. Therefore, although it is necessary to recognize that gender played a role in constructing medieval ideas about the body, vision, and devotion, differences in class, social status, age, and sexuality were equally important. A multitude of factors shaped how medieval laypeople saw and experienced religious performances and imagery—and these factors operated within and across gender, class, and age distinctions. My focus here is on how the concrete reality of live performances influenced the variety of ways that medieval laypeople experienced and consequently used these events to make religious meaning that served their individual devotional needs and concerns.

Phenomenology is an attempt to move philosophical inquiry from the abstract realm into the concrete, living world. This theoretical field is often interpreted as collapsing individual experience into homogeneity, and a number of theorists express frustration with phenomenological analyses for this very reason. By applying phenomenology to the medieval laity it might therefore seem that I am ignoring any notion of difference within individual devotional experience. But more recent applications of phenomenology demonstrate that this mode of theoretical inquiry can have quite the opposite effect. Instead of homogenizing experience, exploring the body's role actually exposes the personalizations, idiosyncratic possibilities, and negotiations involved in those experiences.

Furthermore, many scholars interested in bodily experience have turned to cognitive science as a way to supplement their philosophical inquiries, a trend particularly visible within theatre scholarship. Although we are currently witnessing a surge in interdisciplinary work that integrates cognitive theory into studies of theatre and performance,[31] for a number of years Bruce McConachie has argued that cognitive science holds tremendous value for the historical study of performance.[32] As McConachie contends, "The insights of cognitive science challenge some of the theoretical approaches now widely practiced," among them New Historicism, Saussurean semiotics, and aspects of deconstruction. As far as cognitive theory's relationship to phenomenology, McConachie notes that while certain concepts in these two approaches share common ground, the ways in which they are deployed in cognitive theory "depart from several of the assumptions and methods" of phenomenology and therefore "bear the potential to qualify them productively."[33] Recent work by Mark Johnson, Shaun Gallagher, Dan Zahavi, and Evan Thompson has effectively illustrated the value of integrating these two approaches. In *Mind in Life*, Thompson "maintains that mind science and phenomenological investigations of human experience need to be pursued in a complementary and mutually informing way." He thus situates his study as "contributing to the work of a new generation of phenomenologists who strive to 'naturalize' phenomenology."[34] Similarly, Gallagher and Zahavi describe their project as developing "a *phenomenological* approach to the philosophy of mind...to explore how phenomenology can enter back into a communication with analytic approaches that goes beyond generalities."[35] I discuss these methodologies and their relationship to my project in greater detail in chapter one.

For theatre studies specifically, evidence from cognitive science has added texture to our interpretations of audience reception and helped reveal the high degree of interactivity involved in spectatorship. As McConachie explains, the model offered by cognitive theorists demonstrates how the actors or objects of identification onstage "push back" because "the specific content of the actor's presence—both his/her corporality and significance in the narrative—must both empower and constrain the kinds of identification and projection possible for spectators in the theatre."[36] Because this interplay is always "a local affair, difficult to generalize about," McConachie argues that cognitive theory may provide "a better foundation for historians interested in establishing the usefulness and legitimacy of experience in their work," because it does not ultimately universalize experience across time, place, or event.[37]

A phenomenological approach that incorporates evidence from cognitive science—a "naturalized" phenomenology—offers exciting possibilities for investigating how medieval spectators engaged and understood performance and other devotional media. As Naomi Rokotnitz reminds us,

> cognitive scientists are now claiming, human minds do not, strictly speaking, produce meaning but, rather, process relationships between brain and world. These relationships are not simple cause-and-effect connections or on/off functions but systems of implications... [that] differ from individual brain to brain because they are formed by active, creative—and thus personal—participation.[38]

The body is the primary medium of performance. In order to understand how spectators derive meaning from a theatrical event (in this study, devotional meaning specifically), we must investigate how the body's unique properties and modes of experiencing the world contribute to performance events. As I hope to demonstrate, cognitive theory offers evidence that substantiates phenomenological conclusions about medieval devotional spectatorship, while also validating conceptualizations of devotional seeing prevalent during the Middle Ages.[39]

York as a Subject of Study

In this project, I argue that the discourse and cultural phenomena surrounding laypeople in the later Middle Ages encouraged them to approach devotional seeing as an embodied, live encounter—no matter what medium they considered. In particular, I propose that laypeople used a strategy of seeing in which they derived devotional meaning from their rhythmic encounter with an image's material actuality, a strategy I call "performance literacy." As I will discuss, a variety of philosophical theories about the body's role in religious life and practice emerged during the late Middle Ages, and performance literacy suggests how this discourse may have influenced the way people arrived at and engaged in devotional art encounters. Consequently, although in this book I will apply performance literacy within the specific context of medieval York, I believe this theoretical concept offers us a way to consider late medieval devotional culture more widely. I focus on York because a rich body of evidence related to medieval devotional culture survives from this city. For example, a number of York's medieval parish churches are still standing, and York has the largest collection of medieval stained glass in any English city.[40] The city was also home to many artisans and craftsmen who produced devotional art during the Middle Ages. In addition, we have extant texts related to lay devotional instruction in York, such as the *Lay Folks' Mass Book* and *The Lay Folks' Catechism*. York serves as an ideal case study for my examination of performance literacy precisely because the physical spaces, material culture, and documents that survive allow me to investigate medieval performance within a specific cultural context, and therefore to suggest what kind of cultural work performance may have accomplished in the later Middle Ages.

Medieval drama in York has been a serious subject of study for over a century. E. K. Chambers's influential *The Mediaeval Stage* situated the dramatic cycle as the most prominent genre of English medieval drama, and York's cycle as its model.[41] Scholarship that investigated the English cycle as a genre[42] eventually led to research into the distinctions between the individual cycles,[43] and scholars now recognize the dramatic cycle as a northern English phenomenon that is in no way representative of medieval drama (English or continental). Scholars now recognize York's cycle as a cultural product responding to and reflecting its own unique context.[44]

A number of scholars, among them Alexandra F. Johnston, Richard Beadle, Peter Meredith, Clifford Davidson, Margaret Rogerson, Pamela King, and Meg Twycross, have produced an impressive body of scholarship related to York's dramatic activity, particularly its Corpus Christi cycle. The first volume of the *Records of Early English Drama* series, edited by Johnston and Rogerson, is devoted to York,[45] and a large percentage of the citations in J. W. Robinson's *Studies in Fifteenth-Century Stagecraft* are related to York. Because the city's topography maintains much of its medieval character, York also offers scholars a valuable opportunity to consider performance and city space in an immediate context.[46] Furthermore, at present the city mounts a production of selected York pageants every four years, with both the 2002 and 2006 productions staged on wagons drawn through the streets.[47]

During the Middle Ages, York's Corpus Christi cycle was performed on a processional route composed of between twelve and sixteen stations around the city. The cycle was comprised of around fifty individual pageants, each typically performed by a different guild or group of guilds, and, in its entirety, ran to around fourteen thousand lines of Middle English verse.[48] The first record of this event appears in a 1376 entry in the *A/Y Memorandum Book*, York's principal city register and one of three manuscript compilations that contain important civic and guild documents.[49] Designed to be amended and updated by civic officials over the course of generations, the *A/Y* reflects the city's dynamic past and contains many entries related to performance practices in York.[50] The 1376 entry refers to storage of the Corpus Christi wagons, the mobile stages on which the pageants were performed, and thus provides evidence of performance earlier than the extant text of the cycle, which is dated to between 1463 and 1477.[51] Each year around the time of Lent, York's city council met to determine whether to authorize a performance of the Corpus Christi cycle for that year. If they scheduled a performance, the mayor sent billets to the guild masters to notify them of this decision, and the masters assembled their guild members to "take order for their pageant and their light," the light being the torches they carried in the Corpus Christi procession.[52] The cycle was performed in the city on a more or less annual basis, with the last known premodern production taking place in 1569.

York's medieval performance tradition extended well beyond the annual Corpus Christi cycle. The city staged various royal entries, as well as Creed and Pater Noster plays. Although texts for these two plays do not survive, a significant number of records of their planning and performance exist.[53] Eamon Duffy notes, "whatever their precise content, these plays clearly involved a massive corporate effort by the laity of York to foster knowledge of the elements of the faith."[54] The Pater Noster guild was founded specifically to continue the production of its eponymous play. A 1389 return reads,

> It should be known that after a certain play on the usefulness of the Lord's Prayer was composed, in which play, indeed, many vices and sins are reproved and virtues commended, and was played in the city of York, it had such and so great an appeal that very many said: "Would that this play were established in the city for the salvation of souls and the solace of the citizens and neighbors."[55]

Likewise, the 1449–51 account rolls related to the Corpus Christi guild's Creed play specify devotional instruction as this play's purpose:

> [The Creed play] can be fittingly (done) openly and publicly through the city of York in various <places>, both to the praise of God and particularly to the educating of the people..., indeed, so that the Creed may be brought a little to the good of the ignorant of the city...and the honour and great merit of the present fraternity.[56]

Surviving civic records like these, which refer to the goals of York's public rituals, coupled with the extant texts for most of the city's Corpus Christi pageants, have enabled me to explore how performance functioned within a late medieval community, and also to imagine how other media may have, like performance, represented modes of becoming within the medieval layperson's devotional life.

Like Sarah Beckwith, I interpret York's performance events as community theatre that created theological meaning, defined civic space, expressed local tensions, and articulated social ideology. I find Beckwith's arguments about space compelling and I agree with her assessment that York's pageants held "fictive localities...in active tension with the public spaces of the city."[57] I also echo her assertion that these plays "remember and argue over memory."[58] Although Beckwith's approach to visual performance proved fundamental in inspiring this project, my goals differ from hers. She raises provocative questions about what bodies might signify in communal, religious performance, but she is not immediately concerned with the spectator's body and how that body both influences the individual spectator's viewing experience and contributes to embodied meaning creation during performances. Although Beckwith acknowledges the actor-audience relationship as crucial to the cycle's function, it was not her objective to explore how the material reality and actuality of that relationship shaped visual piety. In this project, I consider how medieval performance functioned *as* a religious experience, and, moreover, how spectators understood that experience by means of their live encounters with it.

I begin this study by introducing phenomenology and cognitive theory alongside medieval visual theory in order to demonstrate the connections between these approaches to perception, and to argue that late medieval culture promoted performance literacy. In chapters two through five, I use performance literacy to examine how medieval laypeople may have derived specific kinds of meaning from their physical encounters with objects, spaces, and bodies. As part of this analysis, I introduce the cognitive theory of conceptual blending and suggest that the material characteristics of devotional media sometimes prompted laypeople to "live in" specific sacred blends, an experience fundamental to performance literacy. I explore this mode of visual piety in the context of York's religious performance tradition and the city's larger material devotional culture; therefore, I examine such phenomena as funerals, donated images and objects, parish churches, Books of Hours, and domestic art alongside York's Corpus Christi cycle and the city's other public performance events. In chapter six, I consider performance literacy's potential instability, and how this might have been counteracted, by analyzing York's two crucifixion pageants. I conclude by briefly suggesting connections between these medieval devotional experiences and certain contemporary religious practices.

Performance has influenced visual culture throughout history and therefore the questions I raise in this book could be directed at other cultures and periods. As I propose in my Coda, religious imagery's unique ability to spark controversy, strengthen faith, and provoke anxiety is very much apparent today. However, late medieval culture had a particular relationship to public, corporate performance and to specific visual theories and traditions; therefore, I believe some of my conclusions are specific to the Middle Ages. This does not mean they have no relationship to pre- or postmedieval religious performance and visual culture—and I use such periodization cautiously. As Jeffrey Jerome Cohen and Bonnie Wheeler write, at stake when studying cultural phenomena of the Middle Ages is "the very pastness of the past, its placement in a temporal category that declares the past has already done its work, that we who study it merely trace its preeffects to posit cause."[59] We are surrounded by evidence of religious imagery's power to provoke passionate reactions—both sympathetic and censorious. Our conclusions about the Middle Ages may help us better understand and respond to the complicated ways in which that power operates today.

Chapter One

Performance Literacy: Theorizing Medieval Devotional Seeing

The Book of Margery Kempe offers ample evidence of imagery's prominent role within lay devotional practices. The book's author suggests that religious images frequently triggered Kempe's powerful physical reactions:

> this creature saw a beautiful image of our Lady called a pieta. And through looking at that pieta her mind was wholly occupied with the Passion of our Lord Christ and with the compassion of our Lady, St Mary, by which she was compelled to cry out very loudly and weep very bitterly.[1]

And yet while Kempe certainly stands at the center of her book, other devotees often surround her, as in the example I used in the Introduction,

> Then the friars lifted up a cross and led the pilgrims from one place to another where our Lord had suffered his pains and his Passion, every man and woman carrying a wax candle in one hand. And the friars always, as they went about, told them what our Lord suffered in every place.[2]

The laypeople around Kempe also actively use visual devotional aids, if not with the same sensational results. Texts such as this remind us that the religious images surrounding the medieval laity did not simply reflect dominant themes, but that they also functioned as tools within lay piety. As James Marrow argues, late medieval artistic invention and consciousness in northern Europe "were focused above all upon problems of *how art works*," and specifically upon the issue of how art "structures experience and interpretation."[3] Most medieval works of art were created to be used, not simply admired, and performance was no exception, both influenced by and influencing modes of devotional seeing.[4] Accordingly, Beth Williamson suggests that scholars should devote more attention to the different ways that people respond to images, and, specifically, to how certain images may offer viewers "cues and encouragements to different types of devotional activity."[5] Such cues or encouragements were not prompted exclusively by an image's iconography, but also by its material presence.

Late medieval visual piety was, in many ways, a material piety. As Eamon Duffy notes, lay devotion was "rooted in the concrete, nourished by the sight of images and the touch of relics and of 'sacramentals' (sacred objects and ceremonies) like holy water."[6] The devotional gestures that laypeople integrated into their liturgical encounters, which often involved objects such as Books of Hours or rosaries, embodied this concreteness.[7] Images and objects, such as the candles from Candlemas services that laypeople brought into their homes, gave sanctity a degree of mobility. Even when laypeople constructed mental images as part of their devotional activities, especially those images involving Christ's life and death, they tried to replicate specific material elements or details. Laypeople responded to how an image could make an aspect of their faith physically present.

While many people examine a theatrical performance as a kind of text intended to represent an absent fictional world, David Saltz reminds us that audiences in fact go to the theater to experience a real event, to see real, flesh-and-blood actors performing real actions.[8] Medieval religious performance, a significant element of late medieval York's devotional culture, not only gave faith a material presence by constructing live, sacred images, but it also offered spectators acutely real experiences of and with those enlivened images. According to phenomenology and cognitive theory, understanding is not merely an after-the-fact reflection on experience; rather, it is more fundamentally the way we actually have experiences in the first place.[9] In this chapter, I examine medieval performance using a phenomenological approach informed by cognitive science in order to suggest how the spectator's bodily engagement with the moment-to-moment performance experience generated devotional meaning.

After outlining my theoretical framework, I turn to medieval theories of vision in order to demonstrate how medieval visual models share fundamental themes and principles with phenomenology and cognitive theory, in particular an emphasis on the physical body's role in perception. I then examine how this preoccupation with the body influenced medieval theories of performance and art. It is well understood that the medieval laity approached a religious performance expecting to derive devotional meaning from various aspects of the live theatrical event itself. Evidence from cognitive science enables me to suggest how people in the Middle Ages may have conceptualized and experienced such performance encounters. But cognitive theory also indicates that performance experiences could have an ongoing impact on future modes of understanding and interpretation; therefore, I will argue that laypeople may also have approached and "used" other elements of visual culture as if they, too, were "performances."

Theorizing Performance: Phenomenology and Cognitive Theory

Although laypeople may have read certain medieval plays in manuscript form,[10] most people encountered massive religious dramas such as the York Corpus Christi Cycle as live performance events. This does not mean these events had no relation to texts—they achieved devotional status precisely because of their connection to familiar sacred texts—but the images they presented did not exist as naïve reflections of these.[11] A religious performance certainly offered laypeople a rich supply of images with which they might actively construct visual piety,[12] but it also cultivated a specific process of devotional understanding that operated through the physical actuality of, and likeness between, image and viewer. In other words, the spectator's body played a significant role in how he or she made religious meaning out of the theatrical event. As Simon Shepherd argues, "effects are produced in the spectator simply as a result of materially sharing the space with the performance. Many of these effects, bypassing the intellect, are felt in the body and work powerfully to shape a spectator's sense of the performance."[13] Phenomenological inquiry, which redirects attention from an allegedly objective conception of the world to an understanding of the world as perceived by subjects, offers us constructive ways to explore how these effects may have functioned as devotional cues for medieval spectators.

Phenomenology "is intended to reveal the perspectival aspect intrinsic to any act of perception conducted by an embodied subject, a variable invariably present in terms of which individual perceptual experience is conducted," as Stanton Garner, Jr. explains.[14] Understandably, scholars in a variety of fields find the work of early phenomenologists such as Edmund Husserl troubling because in trying to isolate a "phenomenological attitude" from which an observer can apprehend lived reality and return to "the things themselves,"[15] these theorists seemed to ground their claims in concepts of fixity, determinism, universality, origins, and naturalness; in effect, their work appears to limit the definition of experience.[16] Valid criticisms of these early approaches prompted many subsequent phenomenologists, in particular Maurice Merleau-Ponty, to explore modes of inquiry into various subjective lived encounters.

Merleau-Ponty's work theorizes the role that corporeality plays in perception. He argues that "there is no inner man, man is in the world, and only in the world does he know himself."[17] According to Merleau-Ponty, our being of existence is a "being-in-the-world" (être au monde) and our body is the basis by which we perceive and differentiate ourselves from that world, thereby deriving meaning from it; the body is both open to the world and reflective of it.[18] Many theatre scholars have found Merleau-Ponty's ideas valuable for exploring audience reception. For example, Garner uses phenomenology to suggest how the spectator's visual encounter with a performance image can function as a lived, bodily experience:

> theatrical space is "bodied" in the sense of being comprised of bodies positioned within a perceptual field, but it is also "bodied" in the more fundamental sense of being "bodied forth," oriented in terms of a body that exists not just as the object of perception, but as its originating site.[19]

Garner defines the body as the "agent of theatrical experience,"[20] an assertion that has special implications for medieval religious performances, which simultaneously situated the body as the agent of devotional viewing through which the spectator generated sacred meaning.

Merleau-Ponty's work attends to *Leiblichkeit*, or "lived bodiliness." Although unstructured and difficult to recapture, as Paul Stoller notes, *Leiblichkeit* "is always historically, socially, and politically situated."[21] When applied by scholars such as Garner, phenomenological inquiry does not ignore or remove issues of agency from theory, but instead it challenges the strictly representational body by returning both experience and subjectivity to the forefront. This perspective is particularly valuable for theatre studies because live performances are sensual encounters. The environment and circumstances that surround the audience, as well as the physical ways in which spectators respond to the live event, all contribute to a performance's aesthetic of actuality.

According to Shepherd, this aesthetic functions rhythmically and a performance's rhythmic potential derives from various elements, with the actors' bodies generating some of the most powerful rhythms. He explains,

> A play's rhythm works on an audience. It does so through the agency of the performer body rhythm which stimulates response in audience bodies. The audience bodies are not, however, without their own rhythm, which is derived from their everyday lives. In watching, the rhythm of their bodies may be confirmed or drawn into a new rhythm by the play... Thus body rhythm is the agency whereby a play may negotiate with its audience an affirmation of or deviation from the rhythmic experience of their everyday lives.[22]

Body rhythms then are one of the sensual means by which plays communicate ideas; they function as "strategies for attending to and making sense of phenomena."[23] Every aspect of the performer's physical and vocal presence generates rhythms, with even slight gestures, looks, or utterances made rhythmically available to the audience. Manipulating a prop, entering or exiting the stage, and altering one's pace or tone all constitute changes in bodily rhythm. As Shepherd notes, although the text may prescribe certain bodily rhythms, performers' bodies also create the text's dramatic rhythm.[24] Moreover, as I will suggest in subsequent chapters, the stage space, material props and set pieces, the environment surrounding spectators, as well as the audience itself also generate rhythms that enter the performance frame and give the experience texture and meaning. Consequently, most spectators approach performances in a heightened state of openness to a play's rhythmic possibilities, arriving in bodies that expect to be confronted by, and take pleasure in, the play's rhythms.[25] Phenomenology acknowledges that each body arrives with its own needs, desires, and rhythms; therefore, this theoretical approach helps us understand how medieval spectators attending the "same" religious performance could derive very different devotional meanings from their own moment-to-moment rhythmic confrontations with the event.

Although this kind of nuanced phenomenological approach proves valuable, it does not entirely escape the complicated issue of assumed objectivity that has plagued phenomenology. For this reason, like many theatre scholars, I am drawn to recent work in cognitive theory, the goal of which is to better understand how humans perceive and, specifically, how our material, biological bodies contribute to perceptual experience. In the last two decades, evidence from cognitive science has profoundly influenced conceptualizations of embodiment and perception, in some cases substantiating phenomenological claims about *Leiblichkeit*. For instance, drawing upon cognitive psychology, Nelson Goodman argues that "having an [mental] image amounts not to possessing some immaterial picture in something called a mind but to having and exercizing certain skills."[26] Mental pictures are neither metaphors nor patterns of cerebral activity; instead, they are a combination of these, the result of both philosophical and physiological processes. This research complements David Morgan's assertion that mentally constructing a coherent devotional image depends upon the devotee's ability to reflect upon her experiences with images and then do things with those images—choose, ignore, combine, revise. Cognitive theory proposes that the mental activities of visual piety develop out of our bodily structure and experiences, and therefore from our conscious and unconscious *Leiblichkeit*. Like Merleau-Ponty, cognitive science challenges the Cartesian mind/body separation—a postmedieval rupture—by replacing the dualistic person with an inherently embodied mind whose reasoning processes are shaped by the body.

Despite this overlap, questions remain as to whether or not these approaches can really work together productively, especially since, as Shaun Gallagher and Dan Zahavi note, early phenomenologists, and Husserl in particular, "emphasized the limitations of a naturalistic account of consciousness."[27] Recent studies have helped clarify the value of using these approaches in tandem, coining such terms as "naturalized phenomenology" and "neurophenomenology" to describe this theoretical framework. According to Gallagher and Zahavi, naturalized phenomenology recognizes that the phenomena under consideration "are part of nature and are therefore also open to empirical investigation."[28] Related to this is neurophenomenology, which proposes "that biology and phenomenology can stand in a mutually enlightening, explanatory relation."[29] In short, both approaches maintain that "phenomenology needs to be able to understand and interpret its investigations in relation to those of biology and mind science."[30] Such work demonstrates the value—and necessity—of supplementing a philosophical approach with empirical research into the biological body. Significantly, as Evan Thompson explains, it also revisits many of Merleau-Ponty's central concerns and aims.[31]

A central goal of cognitive science is to find new models of understanding that acknowledge the body's role in forming conceptual knowledge. However, rather than universalizing claims about perception or meaning formation in the past, employing empirical evidence instead helps us to complicate our conclusions about interpretive processes. A naturalized phenomenology frames understanding as each individual's unique way of "being in a world."[32]

Medieval Visual Theories

The models of embodied perception offered by phenomenology and cognitive theory in many respects reproduce medieval visual theory. Long before the medieval period, ancient writers such as Euclid, Aristotle, and Plato proposed models of vision. Such theorizing continued throughout the Middle Ages, engaging many of the period's major writers and thinkers. As Suzannah Biernoff notes, vision and understanding are metaphorically and etymologically linked in Indo-European cultures, making the study of vision effectively the study of knowledge itself.[33]

But prior to Descartes' *camera obscura*, which effectively separated the mind and soul from the eye and body, the study of vision also constituted an exploration of the body.[34] Most ancient and medieval theories of vision rest on the principle of species, a substance believed to travel between object and viewer, thereby producing visual effects. Species was a concept "developed in order to bridge the physical gap between object and sense organ," according to Michael Camille.[35] Both of the most prevalent medieval visual models—extramission (by which vision results from species leaving the eye, making contact with the object, and returning to the eye) and intromission (by which vision occurs when rays travel from the object to the eye)—assumed the existence of species. A number of ancient theorists, including Euclid and Plato, championed extramission, but early fragmented ideas about intromission can be found in Aristotle's *De sensu* and *De anima*. The tenth-century Arab writer Ibn al-Haytham wrote the first systematic arguments for intromission, which were translated into Latin during the twelfth and early thirteenth centuries. The thirteenth century witnessed a general, though not universal, theoretical shift that privileged intromission. Writers such as Roger Bacon and John Pecham had modified al-Haytham's work in their own treatises and thus popularized intromission as a perceptual model.[36] But despite their differences, both extramission and intromission present seeing as a moment of physical contact between object and viewer.

It is difficult to propose a single medieval model of vision, since a variety of coexistent theories circulated throughout medieval culture and influenced thought. The work of English theorist

Roger Bacon (c. 1214–92) represents a synthesis of intromission and extramission—a merging of Greek, Islamic, and Christian visual theories up to the thirteenth century—that was later disseminated by John Pecham and Witelo. Bacon's theory reflects the influence of ancient writers, including Aristotle, as well as near contemporaries, such as the twelfth-century Robert Grosseteste; however, as David C. Lindberg contends, Bacon owed his greatest debt to al-Haytham.[37] Bacon's conceptualization of vision proved fundamental to late medieval thought and remained prevalent until Descartes. It therefore serves as a useful example for comparing medieval and contemporary theories of perception.

Bacon conceptualized vision as a mutual process requiring the agency of both object and eye. His *Opus majus* illustrates this point:

> The species of the things of the world are not suited to act immediately and fully on sight because of the nobility of the latter. Therefore these species must be aided and excited by the species of the eye, which proceeds through the locale of the visual pyramid, altering and ennobling the medium and rendering it commensurate with sight; and thus it prepares for the approach of the species of the visible object.[38]

The object's species impress themselves upon the eye, as Aristotle proposed, but the visual rays from the eye "alter" and "ennoble" the object's species in order to make this process possible. Although species are neither body nor matter, Bacon defines them as having "corporeal form that does not have dimensions of itself but is produced according to the dimensions of the air."[39] As Biernoff explains, Bacon's species prove "paradoxical" since they have material existence without being objects:

> *Bodied forth* in the matter of air, light, water or the transparent humours of the eye, species have corporeal being… One could say that species colonise matter: the corporeal nature of a species is identical to that of its recipient because the latter is merely a "host," transformed into the likeness of its colonizer.[40]

Perception is, to some degree, assimilation. In the medieval Christian context, this model required Bacon to bridge the polarity between matter and intellect, specifically in respect to how the body influenced knowledge of God.[41]

Although Bacon's ideas were dominant and continued to influence Western thought, a number of commentaries on Aristotle emerged during the later Middle Ages. Many of these outlined more sophisticated intromission models that, without contradicting Bacon, emphasized certain aspects of his theory over others, in particular the prominence of the body in seeing.[42] Biernoff points out that these theoretical developments coincided with a new devotional emphasis on the bodily experience of an increasingly human God and, consequently, helped promote the kinds of affective, body-oriented pieties associated with the late medieval period.[43]

Although no single visual theory dominated the later Middle Ages, discursive trends revolved around issues of touch and agency, themes that resurface in phenomenology. Both phenomenology and medieval models of perception situate the body as a "hinge between self and world,"[44] and vision as an experience during which the body inserts the self into the world. When Merleau-Ponty writes, "My eye for me is a certain power of making contact with things, and not a screen on which they are projected,"[45] he sounds remarkably medieval. Moreover, if we employ a naturalized phenomenology, supplementing this line of philosophical inquiry with empirical research, the evidence from cognitive psychology validates these medieval constructs by demonstrating that theories of sight as touch indeed have a basis in sensorimotor fact. In particular, experiments with mirror neurons suggest that medieval visual models may, at least in part, accurately represent what physically occurs during our perceptual encounters. Consequently, research into the mirror neuron system not only demonstrates the value of a naturalized phenomenological inquiry into perception and understanding,[46] but it also returns us to a medieval theory of seeing.

Medieval Cognition and Mirror Neurons

Scientists originally discovered mirror neurons, a specific class of visuomotor neurons, in the brains of monkeys. Subsequent experiments not only identified these cells in humans, but also suggested that the mirror neuron system may perhaps be more widespread in humans than in monkeys.[47] Mirror neurons are cells in the brain that fire both when we observe an action and when we execute that same action. Mirror neurons also fire when we just imagine the action. This neural process occurs in response to sound as well: when we hear someone else performing an action with a distinctive sound, we simulate that same action neurally.[48] As Vittorio Gallese and George Lakoff explain, "when we engage in imagining the performance of a given action, several body parameters behave similarly to when we actually carry out the same action."[49] In addition, mirror neurons also operate with respect to emotion.[50] This evidence suggests that we understand another person's actions and emotions—in part—because our own sensorimotor system reconstructs those same actions and emotions.[51]

Seeing, imagining, and doing are undoubtedly distinct activities that differ on many levels, including the neurological. However, the mirror neuron system reveals that, to some degree, these activities also share a neural structure. Although evidence of the mirror neuron system's role in higher cognitive functions is far from conclusive,[52] the preliminary, research suggests that vision ultimately involves a degree of physical engagement between subject and object analogous, in some respects, to what medieval discourse proposes. Gallese explains how at some level our bodies respond to what we observe *as if* we were executing the action ourselves—perceiving certain actions or emotions triggers us to simulate them internally.[53] He argues that this "as if" response, or equivalence, "enables the observer to use her/his own resources to penetrate the world of the other by means of a direct, automatic, and unconscious process of motor simulation."[54] Consequently, during a performance an actor's actions and reactions onstage are perhaps, to some degree, literally reenacted within the spectator. In a sense, mirror neurons allow spectators to experience "being-in-the-body" of the performer.[55]

Studies of mirror neurons reveal ways in which conceptual knowledge is mapped within our sensorimotor system, a system that provides structure to conceptual content and characterizes semantic content in terms of "the way that we function with our bodies in the world."[56] George Lakoff and Mark Johnson argue that our cognitive unconscious—a term used to describe all unconscious mental operations concerned with conceptual systems, meaning, inference, and language—functions "like a 'hidden hand' that shapes how we conceptualize all aspects of our experience."[57] Because this unconscious grows out of and employs our body, the ways in which we construct meaning are shaped by the "peculiar nature" of that body.[58] Cognitive theorists therefore consider embodied experience through the physiological body itself, a perspective that shifts the focus from *what* we think as embodied subjects to *how* we think as a result of living in our bodies.[59]

The discovery of the mirror neuron system has been used to support different models within "theory of mind" research. The theory of mind concept refers to how we attribute mental states to others. It constitutes the "mind reading" required in order to perform many of our social interactions and communication practices successfully.

The "standard simulation" theory proposes that this occurs through the following process: "the observer adopts the other's perspective, imaginatively generates 'pretend' mental states (desires, preferences, beliefs), and then infers the other's mental states."[60] The major rival model is "theory theory," according to which "subjects performing theory of mind (TOM) use a specific body of knowledge to predict or explain the behavior or mental states of others, that is independent from own [sic] mental states."[61] Some scholars involved in mirror neuron research have proposed a third model—"embodied simulation"—that challenges the "hypothesized intervening inferential processes" suggested by standard simulation theory.[62] Alternatively, embodied simulation

> constitutes a fundamental basis for an automatic, unconscious, and noninferential understanding of another's actions, intentions, emotions, sensations, and perhaps even linguistic expressions…[S]uch body-related experiential knowledge enables a direct grasping of the sense of the actions performed by others, and of the emotions and sensations they experience.[63]

In this model, when we "confront the intentional behavior of others, embodied simulation, a specific mechanism by means of which our brain/body system models its interactions with the world, generates a specific phenomenal state of 'intentional attunement.'"[64] Gallese, Morris Eagle, and Paolo Migone argue that intentional attunement provides the basis for empathy: "a person's observation of another's behavior elicits automatic simulation of that behavior, and it is this mechanism that enables empathic understanding, which can eventually lead to complementary or modulating responses."[65] Consequently, empathy is not an emotion, but is instead a precondition that leads to other emotional engagements. As Evan Thompson explains, the mirror neuron system is one of the "coupling mechanisms linking self and other at sensorimotor and affective levels" that helps to establish empathy.[66]

Bruce McConachie has used this research to explore how empathy operates in the theatrical encounter, maintaining that "empathy is a proactive search engine that is always ready to engage intentional onstage action and mirror it for meaning."[67] McConachie, like Thompson, is careful to distinguish between empathy and other responses such as identification, sympathy, or understanding. He argues that our mirror neuron system must "engage with other emotional and cognitive processes" in order for empathy to lead to these other results.[68] Cognitive theory suggests that our sensorimotor system prepares us to engage with—to remain open to—the lived experiences of the characters/actors we watch onstage.[69]

I interpret this research as, in many ways, revisiting medieval notions of perception's material interactivity. According to medieval theories of vision, meaning constitutes a part of the object that is transmitted during visual encounters.[70] Thus, many medieval theorists argued that a quality inherent in the object of perception entered and altered the perceiving subject's body both physically and emotionally; for these writers, psychological states "are not subjective responses to a thing or situation, but originate in the objects themselves."[71] As Suzannah Biernoff explains, according to writers like Bacon,

> when we perceive something, that thing in a very real way becomes *part* of us: the essence of the thing is drawn forth from the object...and impregnates the receptive matter of our sense organs and mind. So our perceptions are neither entirely our own, nor independent of, or indifferent to us. They are born of our intercourse between self and world.[72]

Consequently, many medieval theories maintained that sensation also engaged the soul, and therefore had ethical and spiritual consequences. For instance, the prolific and influential French theologian Jean Gerson (1363–1429) wrote, "for chastity, good reputation, *one's vision*, and one's faith are not toys. They are things that are all too easily harmed and corrupted."[73] Saint Augustine (354–430) argued that his ears, which could not be blocked as conveniently as the eyes, left him vulnerable to music that was not pleasing to God because that music might cause pleasure when it entered his body and "in these matters I sin unawares, and only afterwards become aware of it."[74] Perception did not end with the live encounter; rather, the experience remained within the perceiver's body and continued to alter that individual's way of being in the world.

Cognitive theories of embodied experience similarly propose that perception alters the body. In an effort to move away from a purely linguistic understanding of meaning construction, Mark Johnson uses the term "embodied schema" to analyze "embodied patterns of meaningfully organized experience (such as structures of bodily movements and perceptual interactions)." An embodied schema is an unconscious map that emerges as part of our meaningful interactions with things outside of us.[75] It is defined as "that portion of the entire perceptual cycle which is internal to the perceiver, modifiable by experience, and somehow specific to what is being perceived."[76] Embodied schemata are therefore internal and flexible, both specific to situations and altered by them. As Johnson notes, "they are not just templates for conceptualizing past experience" and constructing meaning from that experience, they also constitute "*plans* for interacting with objects and persons. They give expectations and anticipations that influence our interactions with our environment."[77] In short, an embodied schema is both a pattern of past action as well as a pattern for future action. I would therefore define embodied schemata as internal, physical memories that influence future activity and meaning.

Every society uses and deploys modes of communication in ways that serve its specific needs and goals. Tobin Nellhaus argues that these communication practices have fundamental cognitive effects because they generate embodied schemata that establish epistemological and ontological assumptions.[78] In other words, those embodied practices most closely connected to how we obtain knowledge of the world play an important, reflexive role in how we develop additional knowledge.[79] I have argued that medieval discourse about vision regularly portrayed the encounter between object and perceiver as a physical, material exchange or assimilation. We find this notion of assimilation echoed by Gallese's theory of equivalence. Neither cognitive theory nor medieval theory describe visual interactions as fleeting; yet, in the Middle Ages these encounters were also appreciated as having moral and spiritual consequences. Given this context, we can better understand why medieval religious performances, especially those performed by and for laypeople, sometimes provoked anti-theatrical anxiety.[80]

Embodied Vision and Anti-Theatrical Prejudice

Although we can glean medieval theories of theatre from play texts and performance records, some of the most comprehensive pieces of extant theatrical theory are anti-theatrical texts. The authors of these texts provide us with opinions concerning theatre's value, its impact on audiences, and its efficacy with respect to a variety of goals. Such documents are therefore useful places to look for medieval theories about how performance functioned as a religious, visual medium—whether appropriately or inappropriately, depending upon the author's viewpoint.[81]

One of the more widely studied English texts of this kind is *A Tretise of Miraclis Pleyinge* (*ca.* 1380–1425).[82] This treatise has prompted much debate among scholars as to what kinds of performance events the author(s) specifically condemns.[83] While early scholars such as Jonas Barish interpreted this text as a purely anti-theatrical tract, later scholars have demonstrated how indeterminate its vocabulary truly is; words such as "ludus," "pleyinge," and "miracula" had a range of meanings during the later Middle Ages.[84] For example, Lawrence Clopper argues that the author of this text is not attacking liturgical drama or vernacular religious performances, like York's cycle, but rather irreverent festivities.[85] My conclusions about the *Tretise* are less concerned with what content its author finds disagreeable, and more dependent upon how the author describes the nature of performance itself and to what aspects of that nature he specifically objects. Therefore, while the views of the *Tretise*'s author might be, as Glending Olson claims, "much more severe than the dominant tradition," it is the particular theatrical elements and relationships he chooses to discuss when building these arguments that interest me here.[86]

The *Tretise*'s author is more concerned with responses to dramatic content than with the content itself. Although this exemplifies a medieval preoccupation with the performance encounter, rather than the dramatic text, the *Tretise*'s repeated emphasis on "pleyinge's" bodiedness is striking. Like Claire Sponsler, I am interested in how this treatise, by reciting the many ways in which dramatic activity "caters to the bodily at the expense of the spiritual," links "miraclis pleyinge" with the body.[87] In the first half of the *Tretise*, the author worries that "pleyinge" will lead men to serve "desires [lustis] of the flesh [fleyssh] and pleasure [mirthe] of the body" and entice people away from proper activities, such as "works [werkis] of mercy to his neighbor."[88] He summarizes and then refutes a number of prevalent arguments used to support drama's devotional efficacy, and his responses suggest contradictions within medieval religious drama inherent because it is a medium comprised of bodies. For example, he counters the claim that these plays are performed in the worship of God by asserting that, on the contrary, such plays "are presented more to be seen by the world and to please [plesyn] the world than to be seen by God or please Him." Furthermore, he contends that these plays are "only signs, love without deeds" [onely singnis, love withoute dedis] and therefore "contrary to the honor [worschipe] of God."[89] Although plays may present religious, ritual actions, the author argues that these actions should not be confused with true worship because they are only empty gestures, not pious deeds. The author appears troubled that because "miraclis pleyinge" portrays bodies engaged in sacred activities, spectators might interpret these plays as religious worship, thus implying that religious drama created a degree of confusion between play and worship. I surmise that this confusion occurred primarily because theatre, like worship, was "bodied forth."

The author is not only concerned with the mental confusion that "pleyinge" might cause, but he also seems to perceive the event itself as a physical threat to the body. The author refutes the belief that by visualizing the effectiveness of the devil "such miracle playing makes men committed to moral living [gode livinge]" by arguing that these plays may convert some individuals, but only as they pervert the community as a whole.[90] This perversion seems to be an issue of bodily virtue, since as evidence the author cites the Old Testament story of Sarah:

> a young woman of the Old Testament, in order to keep her bodily virtue of chastity [hir bodily virtue of chastite] and to worthily take the sacrament of marriage when her time came, abstained from all manner of idle playing [idil pleying] and from the company of idle players.[91]

The author asserts that priests should likewise abstain from taking part in or attending plays. Thus, the author shifts from discussing the spectator's visual experience at the plays to discussing his presence at or around "pleyinge." These examples begin to expose the author's fixation on how live "pleyinge" impacts bodies.

The author next argues that "miraclis pleyinge" makes men "weep for the play of Christ's passion, failing to weep for their own sins and those of their children."[92] This troubles him thus:

> Therefore, hence as the weeping that men commonly weep at such play is false witnessing that they love more the pleasures of their bodies and of worldly prosperity [the liking of theire body and of prosperite of the world] than the pleasures in God and prosperity of virtue in the soul, and, therefore, having more compassion for pain than for sin, they falsely weep for their lack of bodily prosperity more than they do for their lack of holy prosperity, just as do the damned in hell.[93]

The author expresses concern that by focusing spectators on their own bodies, playing draws them away from meditation on Christ. Later, he maintains that "miraclis pleyinge" should be avoided because it "is intended to delight men bodily" [ben made more to deliten men bodily].[94] His central objection to "pleyinge" seems to be its intrinsic ability to access and influence the spectator's body.

The second part of the *Tretise*, which may or may not have been written by the same author, reflects a similar attention to the bodily effects of "pleyinge." One argument from this section maintains that "since Ismael was born of the flesh, and Isaac of the spirit, as the apostle says, to make an example of playing of the flesh [pley of the fleysh] is neither appropriate nor helpful to the spirit, but takes away from the spirit's heritage."[95] Thus, play of the flesh cannot aid the spirit, but ultimately harms it. Similarly, the author articulates the Christian assertion that the Old Testament is the testament of the flesh, whereas the New Testament is of the spirit, and therefore "fleshy play [fleysly pley] is not allowable alongside the spiritual works [gostly werkis] of Christ and of his saints" but, instead, in "pleyinge" "the flesh is most maintained and the spirit less" [the fleysh is most meintenyd and the spirite lasse].[96] As in the first section of the *Tretise*, here the author specifically opposes "pleyinge" because it represents "going backward from deeds of the spirit to only signs made after desires of the flesh [lustis of the fleysh]."[97] "Pleyinge" is spiritually detrimental not only because of its associations with the flesh, but also because it provides an experience of God founded in the body's undesirable fleshy instincts.

The *Tretise* contends that performance emphasizes the flesh in ways that draw the spectator's attention to her own body and bodily experience, and the danger resides in how the act of looking upon dramatic images may effect changes within spectators. This fear is prompted not by dramatic iconography, but by how the actual performance encounter "bodies forth." Saint Augustine's much earlier account of theatre spectatorship expresses a similar concern about the ancient Roman theatrics he attended.[98] Augustine proposed a tripartite model of the senses. When applied to vision, this model located corporeal vision at the lowest level of the hierarchy, with spiritual vision in the middle and intellectual vision as the highest form. Corporeal vision is perceived through the body and presented to the senses. Spiritual vision is what we imagine in our thoughts when the objects themselves are not before us. Intellectual vision is pure and imageless, involving no sensory referent.[99] Augustine's discourse places corporeal vision in an inferior position, thereby promoting a general suspicion of all experience or knowledge attained through physical seeing. As Biernoff notes, "The point being made is invariably that in this mortal, sinful, fleshly body we cannot know, or see, the truth with clarity."[100] In his *Confessions*, Augustine writes that the soul is tempted both by pleasures of the flesh and by curiosity for knowledge, and he locates both temptations in the senses:

> Beside the lust of the flesh which inheres in the delight given by all pleasures of the senses (those who are enslaved to it perish by putting

themselves far from you [God]), there exists in the soul, through the medium of the same bodily senses [sensus corporis], a cupidity which does not take delight in carnal pleasures but in perceptions acquired through the flesh [experiendi per carnem vana]. It is a vain inquisitiveness dignified with the title of knowledge and science.[101]

He identifies the eyes as playing "a leading role in acquiring knowledge" and argues that the eyes, like the ears, are often abused for such non-spiritual ends:

To entrap the eyes [inlecebras oculorum] men have made innumerable additions to the various arts and crafts [artibus et opificiis],...things which go far beyond necessary and moderate requirements and pious symbols. Outwardly they follow what they make. Inwardly they abandon God by whom they were made, destroying what they were created to be (10.34).

These "arts and crafts" keep the soul trapped in corporeal vision, which ultimately prevents it from seeking a more elevated knowledge of God. Augustine's interpretation of theatre is informed by his belief in this hierarchy of vision. He considers theatre a particularly dangerous instance of people seeking out and experiencing pleasure through corporeal sight.

Augustine begins Book Three of his *Confessions* by discussing his own physicality. He describes his soul as "rotten in health. In an ulcerous condition it thrust itself to outward things, miserably avid to be scratched by contact with the world of the senses" [et ideo non bene valebat anima mea et ulcerosa proiciebat se foras, miserabiliter scalpi avida contactu sensibilium]. He recounts his desire to love and be loved, and describes "being flogged with the red-hot irons of jealousy, suspicion, fear, anger, and contention" [ut caederer virgis ferreis ardentibus zeli et suspicionum et timorum et irarum atque rixarum].[102] He then turns his attention to the theatre in Carthage and describes how it captivated him as a young man. Augustine's responses to Roman theatrics are all sensual in nature; theatre worked on his body. Objecting to the encounter with performance and the way a spectator "wants to suffer the pain given by being a spectator of these sufferings, and the pain itself is his pleasure" [et tamen pati vult ex eis dolorem spectator et dolor ipse est voluptas eius], he argues that performance diverts feelings, leading friendly feelings to "run down into the torrent of boiling pitch, the monstrous heats of black desires" [decurrit in torrentem picis bullientis, aestus immanes taetrarum libidinum].[103] Theatre creates opportunities to shed tears and wring the heart, to find delight in sorrow. Augustine's descriptions concentrate on the immediate, often pleasurable, reactions that performance prompts.

Yet, by placing this section on theatre immediately after very visceral descriptions of his own physical yearnings, Augustine implies that theatre's crime is not simply moving the emotions, but indulging the body, something that begins with the sensual viewing experience. The spectator's body is engaged by and in performance, and it is this bodily experience that Augustine condemns.[104] As Donnalee Dox notes, in Augustine's *Confessions*

> [t]he attraction of theater and the emotional affect it produced were as powerful and dangerous as his sexual appetites. Augustine condemns theater because his desire of it in his youth had clouded his spiritual sight. The emotional intensity of the theater played out in ways that, in Augustine's retrospective, seemed only to simulate true feelings.[105]

The way these feelings work on the body—this simulation—is theatre's challenge to reason; "[p]rior to his conversion, Augustine claims he could not distinguish between what he saw on the stage and his own experience."[106] Like the author(s) of the *Tretise*, Augustine fears the uncontrollable responses provoked by theatre's physical engagement with spectators, as well as how these emotions might remain in, and subsequently influence, the spectator's body.[107]

Cognitive science demonstrates that theatre does indeed, as these authors suggest, work on the body. It is precisely because medieval anti-theatrical prejudice describes reactions similar to what neural mapping reveals—spectators simulating in their own flesh the actions and emotions they see others enacting—that cognitive science provides us with a means of locating and analyzing the crux of this prejudice. Cognitive theory reminds us that issues of spectatorship are not concerned strictly with representation, or even necessarily with conscious reactions, but instead that anxiety about performance often stems from fears about how performance unconsciously works on and in the body.[108] Our bodies arrive at plays open to a performance's rhythms, and these rhythms trace into our embodied schema patterns through which we understand that performance's ideas and concepts. Seeing a performance does indeed leave a lasting physical mark.

Troubling Images Richly Arrayed

Medieval writers recognized what neurobiology has now shown to be fundamental—that we understand our world, in great part, from our body's experience of and in it. And, more significantly still, that the body has never been divorced from our acts of interpretation. In the Middle Ages this attention to material actuality was not exclusively applied to religious performance. Like performance, devotional art was a contested site and the discourse surrounding it suggests that art's material presence was one source of concern.

The pedagogical efficacy of religious images was debated throughout the Middle Ages. In 600, a letter attributed to Pope Gregory the Great declared, "For what writing offers to those who read it, a picture offers to the ignorant who look at it, since in it the ignorant see what they ought to follow, in it they read who do not know letters; whence especially for gentiles a picture stands in place of reading."[109] Although scholars do not agree on the exact interpretation of this passage, as Celia Chazelle notes, variations on Gregory's words "appear in a multitude of Latin writings throughout the rest of the Middle Ages, including in the decrees of the sixteenth-century Council of Trent which responded to the Protestant Reformation."[110]

In describing religious imagery's value or threat, medieval authors often use language that sounds similar to what we find in texts about drama.[111] Theodore K. Lerud argues that medieval discourse about images and image veneration is applicable to the study of drama, specifically because, like art, drama functioned as a "thesaurus" of key Christian images for the laity, and people conceptualized them as similar genres.[112] In particular, Lerud analyzes Reginald Pecock's *The Repressor of Over Much Blaming of the Clergy*, an anti-Lollard tract written around 1450, which defends the use of images by the clergy and the laity. Pecock argues that Christ ordained images because they act as memorable signifiers, and his central claims rest in great measure on the premise that images are easier to remember, require less labor to understand, and touch the mind more deeply than words.[113] Pecock asserts that laypeople are able to register the difference between the images themselves and what they signify, and that the laity employ devotional images because it is customary, not because "they believe and feel that this image is the Trinity, or that such an image is truly Jesus, and so forth for other images."[114] Pecock expresses confidence in the layperson's ability to negotiate the relationship between sign and signifier.

As Lerud points out, in one case Pecock actually uses a performance image as evidence. To counter the Lollard argument that people themselves serve as more appropriate images of God than stone or wooden objects, Pecock argues that a crucifix is a better image of God than any living man because it meets three conditions necessary for any image to be a perfect representation: it resembles the thing it claims to represent, it was originally designed for the purpose of representation, and it is intended to represent only a single thing. He writes of this last condition that if any image tries to represent too many things at once, our minds become distracted by the multiplicity and fail to remember the image's original representational purpose.[115] The only exception Pecock makes is "when a living man is placed in a play hanging naked on a cross and seemingly wounded and scourged."[116] Lerud argues that this passage "places plays firmly in the same phenomenological realm as images."[117]

Although I agree that this phenomenological similarity pertains to vision, I see another phenomenological continuum implied by Pecock's validation of the performance image. In this passage, Pecock endorses the representational efficacy of the human body. Although the average person cannot serve as a model of God because s/he does not meet Pecock's three conditions, the body in performance—reenacting the crucifixion—functions as the most effective representation of God. A performance image is more effective than stone or wood because of its material similarity to the lay devotee; it is an image made of flesh. By privileging the performance image above all other examples, Pecock acknowledges materiality's contribution to the encounter between devotional image and lay viewer. In the case of the performing body, rather than causing confusion in respect to representation, design, or signification, material affinity clarifies and heightens the image's devotional efficacy. The bodily state shared by viewer and image helps to ensure a clear devotional interpretation.

Medieval discourse about devotional images often addresses the ways that materiality influences reception, employing body-oriented words to do so. *Tretyse of Ymagis*, a text that appears in the same manuscript as *A Tretise of Miraclis Pleyinge*, offers particularly good evidence of this preoccupation. Although their pairing does not mean that the same person wrote both treatises, it may suggest that these texts functioned as part of a coherent manuscript program, or were at least interpreted by the manuscript's compiler as somehow related.[118]

At the beginning of *Ymagis*, the author initially takes a rather conservative approach to images. He argues that men err when they make religious images, such as those of the Trinity that show God and Christ in human form, because such activity is prohibited by the Old Testament commandment.[119] But, quickly thereafter, the author points out that "since Christ was made man, it is acceptable for unlearned men to have a simple crucifix, to serve as memory of the difficult passion and bitter death that Christ suffered willingly for the sins of man."[120] The author then clarifies his reservations regarding certain images: "And yet men err greatly in this crucifix making, for they paint it with great cost, and hang much silver and gold and precious clothes and stones thereon and about it."[121] Rather than their representational features, it is instead the expensive material additions to these images that rouse the author's ire.

Throughout the treatise, the author repeatedly condemns richly arrayed images as contrary to God's law. One of his arguments against elaborate images is that the money spent on such decoration would be better spent on helping the needy[122]; the author of *A Tretise of Miraclis Pleyinge* raises a similar objection. But most of the arguments articulated in *Ymagis* stem from the great power elaborate images seemingly exert over laypeople, especially over their bodies. He describes how "simple people" [symple puple] are overwhelmingly drawn to such ornate images, rather than to properly modest ones,

> For to the gayest and most richly arrayed image will people make offerings most quickly, and not to the poor image [pore ymage] standing in a simple church or chapel, but if it stands royally enshrined and with carving and painted with gold and precious jewels [stoned ryaly tabernaclid wiþ keruyng and peyntid wiþ gold and precious iewelis] as I said before, and within a minster or a great abbey where there is little or no need for such offerings.[123]

The author implies that people are drawn to the rich materiality of these images, rather than to the devotional reflection that they should prompt. He maintains that the laity "should be more spiritual and take less heed of such sensible signs" [shulden be more gostly and take lesse hede to siche sensible signes], again sounding remarkably like the author of *A Tretise of Miraclis Pleyinge* ("fleshy play is not allowable alongside the spiritual works of Christ and of his saints" and represents "going backward from deeds of the spirit to only signs done after pleasures of the flesh").[124] Both authors believe lay devotees should employ sensible means only if it directs them toward (preferred) spiritual contemplation.

Although these arguments obviously reiterate the privileging of spiritual and intellectual sight over corporeal sight found in Augustine's hierarchy of vision, and then repeated throughout the Middle Ages, they also imply a concern beyond differences in meditative vision. The authors of both treatises insinuate that a critical problem with these images relates to the ways they manifest themselves in the bodies of laypeople. The author of *Ymagis* writes that "since these images serve as books for unlearned men to stir them on to memory of Christ's passion [sture þem on þe mynde of Cristis passion], and to teach by their portrayal, vain glory that hangs upon them [veyn glorie þat is hangid on hem] is a public error against Christ's gospel."¹²⁵ While such images should turn the mind toward Christ, their rich material details instead orient the mind to an inaccurate understanding of the Passion. He argues that people

> conceal their own sinful lives using these false paintings; and therefore they misrepresent the saints, turning their lives to the contrary to comfort men in worldly pride, vanity, and pleasures of their bellies and other lusts [to counfort men in worldly pride and vanyte and lykyng of her wombe and eʒen and oþer lustus].¹²⁶

By representing the saints or Christ in rich array, these images inadvertently validate a worldly, corrupt lifestyle. Consequently, they not only give laypeople erroneous ideas about Christ's life, but they also encourage laypeople themselves toward sinful ways of living.¹²⁷ The image's materiality overwhelms its iconography with the result that it conveys (incorrect) theology and thus moves the devotee to vain contemplation and action, rather than to proper devotion.

Concerns about devotional images did not focus solely on lay misinterpretation of representational features. The material presence of certain images, and the effects of this materiality on lay bodies, also provoked anxiety. As a countermeasure, sometimes clerics wrote texts that were designed to help control the effects of these images and objects. For instance, Sara Lipton examines the trajectory of the phrase "the sweet lean of his head," versions of which recur fourteen times in medieval texts dating from 1127 to the fifteenth century.¹²⁸ This phrase refers to the crucifix and, in some cases, may have been used by preachers to direct attention to a physically present crucifix. Lipton concludes that this survey of "writing about looking" reveals "a rich and complex dialogical relationship among text, reader/viewer, and object," and that "writing was a means by which some clerics sought to balance the promise and the dangers of vision, to resolve the paradoxes inherent in the devotional image, to assemble isolated impressions into a significant whole, and to create meaning out of tension and contradiction."¹²⁹ In other words, texts could function to control material devotional images, which, on their own, contained the potential for misreading. Furthermore, Lipton asserts that these texts acknowledge that "the objectness of the crucifix was an integral aspect of its meaning" and she identifies how different authors are affected by an image's distance, height, or material accessibility.¹³⁰

Ymagis reflects a similar preoccupation with the "objectness" of devotional images.

Ultimately, the author of *Ymagis* argues that laypeople see elaborately decorated images differently than they see simple images. Inherent qualities of an image bring their own history to the perceptual encounter; medieval artisans and patrons recognized this fact and chose materials accordingly.[131] The author of *Ymagis* argues that richly decorated images of holy people convey the erroneous idea that these holy people "lived in wealth of this world and desires of the flesh" [lyued in welþe of þis world and lustus of þeire fleyshe].[132] It is not the image's iconography, but instead the fleshy meanings communicated by its rich material qualities that validate pride, vanity, and lust. The image no longer connotes humility; instead, additions of gold and jewels redirect its meaning toward worldly desires. Overt (attractive) materiality moves the viewer from interpreting the sign to interacting with the material image itself. While some people recognized that this material interaction could orient the mind toward spiritual associations, such as when gemstones and gold connoted the glorification of the heavenly realm,[133] others, like the author of *Ymagis*, believed it more often kept laypeople mired in their fleshy and earthly concerns.

Performing Literacy:
Seeing Time and Mortality through the Body

Materiality not only impacts the viewer's moment-to-moment encounter with religious images, it also influences the way those images generate long-term spiritual meaning and devotional memory. In a 1989 article, J. Giles Milhaven describes his viewing experience before a three-dimensional pietà:

> Before the Pieta I rested in pain. In every line of stone or wood, I felt Christ, God and man, dead for love of me. I felt the mother grieving him dead. That was all I felt. I felt nothing else at the moment, nor wanted to... The art itself pinned me down within the Passion of Christ and Mary. It held me fast in their pain and sorrow.[134]

Milhaven not only suggests that sculpture's materiality may "convey more powerfully than painting a tactile experience," but he also contends that the traces of this viewing experience will continue to influence subsequent devotional encounters: "After the devout person's experience of the Pieta, she cannot go back in memory and distinguish in the original experience a nonbodily union with Mary from a bodily one."[135] The distinctive material encounter traces a physical memory in spectators, an embodied schema, that functions as both a pattern of and a pattern for devotional action.[136]

This is the problem with which the *Ymagis*'s author struggles. The objects he describes not only provoke what he finds to be inaccurate theological ideas, but they might also move the viewer's body to enact improper devotional acts; a similar possibility disturbs the author(s) of *A Tretise of the Miraclis Pleyinge*. In *Ymagis*, the author claims that people are drawn to these images and give them offerings rather than visiting and helping their neighbors.[137] The anticlerical author argues that in this respect images are yet another of the clergy's many (according to him, very effective) ways of obtaining the alms needed to fund their richly endowed lives.[138] But other claims made in the text suggest that another fault of excessively material images is that, like performance, they prompt people to behave in excessive ways. The author blames images for leading men on pilgrimage, a practice he associates with promoting lechery, gluttony, drunkenness, extortion, and other worldly wrongs and vanities.[139] He contends that laypeople, deceived by their "vain trust" [veyn trist] in these images, perform inappropriate devotional acts, such as stroking, kissing, and clinging to the images.[140] And, significantly, when the author criticizes priests who when appointed to hear confession and assign penance also instruct the laity to give alms to images, he pointedly disparages these same priests' "long cursed prayers and trilling of curious song in men's ears [grete cnakkyng of curious song in menes eeris]," almost as if the material excess of the images has insinuated itself into the priests' bodies and caused them to worship with similar excess.[141]

Like bodies and objects staged in religious performance, the actuality of devotional images, and the material spaces in which people encounter them, reach out to viewers and engender devotional patterns in their bodies. Material characteristics may therefore draw the viewer toward the object's "thingness." As Alice Rayner writes, the thingness of an object

> gathers matter and time together with whatever is beyond human power to know within the context of mortality, namely that unity of being projected by the unity of perceptual experience [...] Thingness is thus not an attribute of an object but something more like an event or a moment when a material object is recognized as belonging to more

than its representation, to more than is knowable, but also belonging to time and to mortality.[142]

For example, although we might see the sides and bottom of a water jug, the "holding nature" of the jug—its thingness—is not these elements, but instead the jug's empty space, the void that does the holding, and this thingness is only apparent in the event of filling the jug.[143] An object's thingness houses its past and present use, offering access to those alternative spaces that cannot be designated by representational modes of signification.[144]

Evidence from cognitive science can help us connect this notion of thingness to our perceptual experiences with performance and visual art, and perhaps suggest how thingness impacts our ways of making meaning from these encounters. Bruce McConachie discusses how puppets and other performing objects stretch our mirror neuron system, and specifically how the moment of manipulation that links a prop "to an actor/character's intentionality...is a crucial transition for spectatorial vision."[145] However, while manipulation may be necessary for the viewer's perceptual system to generate visuomotor representations, manipulation is not necessarily required in order for spectators to see this same rhythmic potential and intentionality brought to bear in the visual perception of the object. Work by Vittorio Gallese and David Freedberg suggests that embodied simulation and the empathy it generates play a crucial role in our aesthetic contemplation of visual art. As they explain, the fact that mirror neurons respond not only to actual actions, but also to implied intentional actions, has ramifications for how we see works of art:

> Research on the human MNS [mirror neuron system] has shown that the observation even of static images of actions leads to action simulation in the brain of the observer. The observation of pictures of a hand reaching to grasp an object or firmly grasping it activates the motor representation of grasping in the observer's brain...On the basis of these results, it stands to reason that a similar motor simulation process can be induced by the observation of still images of actions in works of art.[146]

Gallese and Freedberg use this evidence to examine viewers' responses to the form of art work. Brain imaging experiments with humans have shown that observing manipulable objects at rest activates the motor areas of our brain normally involved in our interactions with those objects.[147] As Gallese and Freedberg argue, "even a still-life can be 'animated' by the embodied simulation it evokes in the observer's brain."[148]

Particularly relevant to medieval devotional art is Gallese and Freedberg's contention that embodied simulation also occurs in response to traces of the artist:

> We propose that even the artist's gestures in producing the art work induce the empathetic engagement of the observer, by activating simulation of the motor program that corresponds to the gesture implied by the trace. The marks on the painting or sculpture are the visible traces of goal-directed movements; hence, they are capable of activating the relevant motor areas in the observer's brain. Despite the absence of published experiments on this issue, the mirror-neuron research offers sufficient empirical evidence to suggest that this is indeed the case.[149]

Their conclusion suggests that human brains do, indeed, respond to at least some aspects of an object's thingness.[150]

I would argue that in medieval pre-print culture the thingness of communication practices was always in the foreground; people received information either through oral presentation (such as sermons, public announcements, trials, performances, gossip, conversation, and storytelling) or through handwritten documents and handmade objects. Traces of creation and use were evident within the media/practices themselves. The fact that medieval communication practices belonged "to time and to mortality" was self-evident and often fundamental to how they established claims to authority and truth.

Moreover, I would contend that medieval visual theorists, as well as certain authors of anti-theatrical and anti-image texts, were grappling with viewers' overt responses to the thingness of devotional imagery. These authors repeatedly articulate how art communicates meaning through its nonrepresentational aspects that belong to time and to mortality. The medieval concept of species—unseen aspects of an object that not only convey meaning but also physically alter both the body and the soul of the perceiver—supported this theoretical preoccupation.[151] Furthermore, the traces of human presence—the links between objects and human intentionality—inherent in medieval media may also have turned attention toward thingness by encouraging people to see devotional objects as mortal things with their own life processes[152]; brain imaging suggests an empirical basis for this kind of intentional attunement. Consequently, cognitive science has the potential to enhance our ability to understand the culture of the Middle Ages because it offers us a productive means of integrating the ideas expressed in medieval visual discourse with current research into the human brain's processes.

With prevalent theories of perception proposing that "objects and their species have the power to captivate and seduce us because they are agents and we are recipients,"[153] people in the later Middle Ages may have recognized all objects as dense with intentionality. This way of seeing devotional media in the Middle Ages would have influenced what David Saltz calls the "infiction." Saltz argues that while we usually only consider the fictional meanings we *extract from* artworks, there is also a level of fiction that we *bring to* an artwork. Infiction is the set of conventions or assumptions we take into an art encounter that help us make sense of that work's specific kind of "make believe."[154] In the theatre, infiction informs how we perceive the reality on stage by "structuring and giving meaning to the actual events that transpire" during a performance.[155] Infiction is therefore a "cognitive template," an embodied schema, that exerts a powerful influence over how we understand and make meaning from art encounters.

I am arguing that the medieval attention to thingness encouraged laypeople to approach all devotional media as spectators typically approach live performances—with bodies prepared for and expecting rhythmic encounters with nonrepresentational elements that belong to time and to mortality.[156] This expectation was not merely a theoretical belief, but the infiction—the cognitive template—inscribed into the layperson's body through his/her repeated physical and cultural interactions in the world. Religious performances function as one particularly powerful example of such interaction that embedded within laypeople patterns for understanding religious meaning through live presence at and with the rhythmic actuality of these live events. I therefore call this specific cognitive template "performance literacy."

Explaining her theory of "liturgical literacy," Katherine Zieman asserts that the medieval layperson understood liturgical texts through a "visceral" relationship that was "grounded in the body."[157] For the person who is not connected to the Mass in a grammatical relationship, one that is subsumed by linguistic knowledge conveyed through grammatical instruction, Zieman argues that "meaning is perceived in the body, not in the mind."[158] I am suggesting that medieval laypeople expected to understand a devotional image, object, book, or space, in part, through their bodies, and that this way of translating devotional meaning through the body's rhythmic experience of a medium was most powerfully and persistently learned and reinforced through religious performance events.[159] Performance literacy then is a flexible cognitive structure comprised of both the infiction that laypeople brought to religious performances, as well as the embodied schema that experiencing these performances through that infiction embedded into their bodies and that they then brought to subsequent encounters with other devotional media.

Defined in this way, performance literacy allows for a high degree of agency. Stanton Garner, Jr. argues that an essential element of "lived" experience is the invariable variability of perception, an assertion supported by research within cognitive science. As Vittorio Gallese explains, experimental evidence indicates that our simulation mechanisms "are highly plastic and are highly influenced by the personal history of the person bearing them, which also implies that a naïve eye or an expert eye, an artist's eye or a naïve eye, when looking at the same artwork, will probably display different responses."[160] Although influenced by neural reactions that appear to operate in all humans, the infiction that informs a devotional encounter, as well as the experience that coalesces into an embodied schema, is unique to each audience member.[161] Cognitive theory therefore not only helps us expand how we identify and define agency within medieval devotional seeing, but it also reminds us that understanding can never be completely controlled or circumscribed because meaning is generated through each body's individual experiential history.

The inherent agency within performance literacy also reveals its potential function as a tactic of lay visual piety. According to Michel de Certeau's theory of consumption, the marginalized "other" uses tactics to seize and manipulate events temporarily in order to transform them into opportunities, thus turning the order of things to his/her advantage. Consumptive agency is socially determined and develops in response to social forces.[162] The acknowledgment of thingness that I am arguing pervaded medieval discourse may have encouraged people to employ performance literacy as a tactic of visual piety when they encountered objects and images.[163] Thus, performance literacy may have supplied laypeople with avenues for constructing religious meaning that were not entirely constrained by religious rhetoric, discourse, or physical rituals, but were instead based upon each individual's unique physical encounters and interactions with the thingness of medieval devotional media.[164]

By using the term performance literacy I am also suggesting that aspects of medieval devotional culture can be understood more clearly if examined through the rubric of performance, in particular because, as I have tried to demonstrate, during the Middle Ages people perceived objects and spaces as active entities.[165] Rather than offering a performative reading of these media and contexts, I am instead arguing for a somewhat revised application of the term performance itself. In doing so, I am echoing recent work in media studies that has challenged conventional notions of what constitutes a performance. For instance, Oliver Gerland notes that according to U.S. copyright law, regardless of the medium

> "to perform" means to operate an instrument that converts an arrangement of expressive elements into a stream of patterned energies that might or might not be perceptible, and to convey those streaming energies to another performer or perceiver who might or might not be physically present...Within this system, performance is an event during which a composition is converted into streaming energies that are conveyed to other performers or to perceivers.[166]

Like medieval discourse about artistic media, Gerland's expanded definition of performance focuses attention on *how* the medium works, and therefore fits comfortably with my arguments about performance literacy in the Middle Ages. Furthermore, the term "streaming energies" acknowledges a level of physical interaction within the performance event that is not necessarily visible, a notion echoed throughout the different medieval and modern theories of perception that I have analyzed in this chapter.

Here I return to Aleksandra Wolska's notion of "theatre as a mode of becoming."[167] Wolska's idea of "becoming" is very similar to the medieval (and cognitive theory) model of perception as assimilation: seeing a performance does not end after the show, but, instead, continues within us.[168] Likewise, performance literacy lingers in the body after the live encounter as a cognitive pattern for devotional seeing and understanding to be applied in other contexts. In the next five chapters, I examine York's late medieval devotional culture—its spaces, objects, rituals, as well as its dramatic performances—through performance literacy. York's public performances not only entertained spectators, but they also constituted an important means by which the city created, maintained, and proclaimed its identity, interests, and values.[169] Although we can never hope to recreate the original medieval theatrical experience, the numerous civic documents and dramatic texts that survive from York offer an entry point into the medieval performance encounter, providing evidence of performance practices, as well as of views laypeople held regarding drama's function within the community. In particular, religious performance was a process of devotional image-making and image-viewing, and York's laity, recognizing the power of dramatic images, repeatedly manipulated them to serve secular, as well as sacred, ends. But, as I explained in the introduction, York is also a city for which many devotional texts, images, and spaces from the late Middle Ages survive. This rich body of evidence supplies us with opportunities to think directly and immediately about the medieval layperson's rhythmic experiences of material piety.

Chapter Two

Material Devotion: Objects as Performance Events

The medieval laity approached religious media with bodies prepared to construct devotional meaning from their live, physical encounters with these works. I have called this devotional tactic performance literacy because it involves seeing and relating to images and objects as if they are live performance events. Performance literacy constitutes an embodied schema; therefore, it is comprised of both the infiction that a person brings to the art work, as well as the patterns for understanding that this encounter with the work traces within the viewer. Like other embodied schemata, performance literacy is not only the means by which spectators may generate meaning through their experiences with devotional art, but it also functions as a plan for future bodily interactions with devotional media. By employing the concept of performance literacy, I aim to foreground the body's role in visual piety.

Images contain within them strategies of interpretation and intention.[1] Sometimes these strategies prompt viewers to see and derive meaning from an image via an atypical cognitive system, as when optical illusions cause us to "see" action or motion where there is none. As research by V. S. Ramachandran and Sandra Blakeslee suggests, "the mechanisms of perception are mainly involved in extracting statistical correlations from the world to create a model that is temporarily useful."[2] Dominant theories of vision and devotion in the Middle Ages may have required people to extract different kinds of correlations from the material world than we might now. The visual models and theories circulating during the later Middle Ages conceptualized art objects and images as "active" entities, and thus recognized the viewer's body and the object of perception as physically interacting with one another; seeing was understood to be kinesthetic, a form of movement.³ As I suggested near the end of chapter one, the infiction—the conventional assumptions of medieval visual theory and visual devotion—that medieval laypeople brought to their nonperformance devotional encounters may have prompted them to attribute degrees of intentionality and liveness to "static" objects and images; York's laity may have "seen" images and objects as conveying the same kinds of rhythmic energy as do performances. In this chapter, I use performance literacy to suggest how this tendency may have impacted the devotional meaning that laypeople derived from these media.

Material Memory and Funeral Practices

In general, the later Middle Ages witnessed an increased emphasis on seeing and on identification through vision. Sumptuary laws, spectacles of punishment, and livery are all evidence that late medieval laypeople understood and ordered many aspects of their world through visual signifiers. Visuality also figured prominently in attempts to create and perpetuate memory, especially in those rituals surrounding death. The possibility of being forgotten after you died was a central concern in the Middle Ages, and people developed tactics that would, as Eamon Duffy notes, keep their memory alive and "make it impossible for the living to forget or ignore" them after death.⁴ Chantries, memorial statuary, monumental inscriptions, donor images, candles, funeral processions, and other posthumous rituals were all visual means for accomplishing this goal. But medieval wills suggest that the materiality of these visual media also played an important role in how they functioned memorially. In particular, the medieval funeral ritual was a communication practice designed to memorialize the deceased by constructing a synesthetic experience for those who attended it. In their wills, testators outlined the activities and displays they wanted at their funerals, often specifying what clothing, movements, lighting, texts, music, and participants to include. These rituals functioned like performance events and therefore provide an especially fruitful devotional medium to explore through performance literacy.⁵

I draw my examples of funeral practices from York wills dated between 1390 and 1550.⁶ Although wills offer us a great deal of information related to medieval funeral practices and devotional materiality, they are somewhat problematic sources. Because wills often emphasize the individual testator without also relaying the importance that other people and corporate activities had in this person's spiritual life, these documents, as Clive Burgess explains, offer only a "key-hole" vision.[7] Moreover, because wills disclose only one force in a complex system of lay piety and convention—the testator's own giving patterns—they do not "illustrate reciprocation and so fail to represent one of the period's most crucial pious characteristics."[8] More troubling, and yet obvious, is that wills only tell us about those individuals for whom such documents exist, and therefore supply demographically limited evidence. Although by the fifteenth century more wills of ordinary townsmen and villagers in England tend to survive,[9] especially in the diocese of York, Jeremy Goldberg reminds us that these wills represent only a small percentage of all laypeople.[10] When using this evidence we effectively eliminate from our studies those who did not make wills or for whom none survive.

Interpreting the evidence that wills do provide is also complicated. Individuals who held large estates were more apt to create wills, and the length of a will may signify an individual's wealth and social standing; however, this is not always the case. Established parish practices dictated many posthumous arrangements and many of these plans may have remained undocumented. A short will might reflect good management or foresight, rather than meager funds.[11] Furthermore, these documents follow strict conventions in form and content, and therefore constitute a very specific and standardized public genre. Scribes may have excluded practices, items, or objects they thought inappropriate, or added unstated bequests based on custom. It is therefore necessary to draw any conclusions based upon testamentary evidence with a degree of caution. But even given these limitations, wills offer us a unique perspective on the ways that laypeople attempted to control the communal memory of their lives and legacy.

The reciprocation that wills do not explicitly document may, in fact, be implied by the material choices that testators do expressly prescribe. The wills of York's most affluent citizens, particularly former mayors, provide the most detailed evidence of the great degree of control that laypeople could exercise over their funeral's visual and material arrangements.[12] For example, Thomas Bracebrig's 1436 will exemplifies the specificity that laypeople of great means could choose to include in their postmortem instructions.[13] Bracebrig, a York merchant, served as mayor of the city in 1424. As in most wills, Bracebrig begins by offering his soul to God almighty, the blessed Virgin, and all saints, and his first directive refers to burial; he asks that his body be buried in his parish church of St. Saviour in York before the image of the crucifix, and beside the bodies of his wives and children. By the late medieval period, access to burial within the church was a symbol of status in England.[14] Most of the wills that I reviewed request burial in a church, and many of them, like Bracebrig's, use a particular image or object within the church as a reference point. For instance, in his 1459 will John Dautre, a lawyer, requests burial in his parish church before the altar of the Holy Trinity and "before the image of St. John the Baptist whom, since I was a child, I have loved more than all other saints."[15] John Mirk, an English canon and preacher (*ca.* 1382–1414), expressed frustration at this practice, arguing that only those who have served as ministers and defenders of the holy church should be afforded this privilege.[16] Although such requests may not always have been granted, they reveal one way that laypeople used material images to mark their lives as sacred.

In his will, Bracebrig stipulates a number of rituals common for the period. He bequeaths two candles made of thirty pounds of wax to burn at his funeral procession and ten torches, each containing fourteen pounds of pure wax, to burn around his body on the day of his burial. Wax was the layperson's most common pious gift and therefore testators often specify the amount, and sometimes the type, of wax to be used in their funeral candles and torches.[17] Bracebrig also stipulates where each of the ten torches should be placed after his burial: two should remain at the high altar for reverence at the elevation of the Host, while five others should be installed at the altar of the Virgin Mary, the altar of St. John the Evangelist, St. Anne's altar, St. Nicholas's altar, and the altar of St. James. The remaining three should be placed individually in a mortice of stone—made specifically for this purpose—to burn at the elevation of the Host.[18] He also bequeaths specific amounts of wax over the course of fifteen successive years to maintain candles standing before a variety of images and objects in his parish church.[19] These candles contribute to the overall synesthetic memory that Bracebrig is attempting to construct.

Like other wealthy testators, Bracebrig specifies particular funeral participants, such as ten poor men to carry the ten torches at his funeral rites. Bracebrig leaves money to dress these men in gowns of black cloth lined with white wool. He bequeaths money to pay chaplains to pray for his soul and the souls of his family and benefactors, as well as money for a number of masses to be sung immediately following his death. He gives money to various religious institutions in York—the Friars Carmelites, Friars Preachers, Friars Minors, and Augustinians[20]—as well as to numerous chaplains and to every rector of the parish churches in the city and suburbs of York to sing and pray for his soul. He also leaves money to guilds, anchoresses, hospitals, chapels, hermits, nuns, and prioresses, as well as alms to the poor and needy in various parishes and hospitals, all for the purpose of remembering his soul.

Wills only document "moveables," since the distribution of land and real estate was typically already arranged. However, not all moveables were divisible by the will. The standard practice in England at this time was to divide a man's moveable estate into three equal parts. One part was distributed to his wife, one divided among his children, and the final third went toward his soul's salvation. This last third is what wills typically document,[21] and, as Burgess suggests, these bequests still represent only one half of a devotional dialogue. Bracebrig stipulates specific rituals—prayer recitation, his Placebo and Dirige,[22] masses, bell ringing, requiem music—as spiritual reciprocation for his monetary gifts. This reciprocal system uses "performing" bodies to create a longer-lasting memory of Bracebrig's life. When individuals repeat liturgical words in honor of a specific individual, that person's memory and the ritual action fuse; the speaker "bodies forth" the deceased.

Ultimately, Bracebrig choreographs specific physical activities in order to generate mnemonic value. Anne Bagnall Yardley suggests that the act of singing and walking simultaneously in liturgical processions creates bodily memory by "embedding the music very deeply in the body of the participant." In this way, those who participate physically in a procession "absorb the events of salvation history kinesthetically and emotionally as well as intellectually."[23] Wills suggest that laypeople used similar physical activities to embed a memory of themselves within the bodies of the living—a memory likewise intellectual, emotional, and kinetic. For instance, in a number of late medieval wills testators request that someone make a pilgrimage on their behalf. This act operates on two levels.[24] As Eamon Duffy notes, surrogate pilgrimage allowed individuals to receive vicariously the blessings and indulgences related to that pilgrimage location.[25] But there may also be a second intention behind such bequests. Pilgrimage was extraordinary in nature and therefore quite likely a very memorable experience in the pilgrim's life. When testators request pilgrimage by proxy, they embed a powerful memorial within the pilgrim's body. When the pilgrim later recalled the experience, saw an image of the same saint, or undertook future pilgrimage journeys, this reactivated a bodily memory of the testator. Furthermore, if others knew about this request, then seeing the pilgrim would also activate memories of the deceased for those individuals. Medieval laypeople recognized the body as a unique time capsule for devotional memory and took advantage of this fact in their last requests. Performance literacy can help us recognize how the material characteristics of funerals could similarly embed memories within the bodies of spectators.

Candles are some of the most common items mentioned in funeral arrangements. While the light from candles set around the body served to ward off evil spirits,[26] donating candles to altars or images in the church reinforced the testator's memory by linking it to the physical rituals that laypeople performed at those places, such as kneeling and reciting prayers. But a candle also functioned as a powerful physical presence. As Drew Leder notes, "the materiality of a perceptual object correlatively implies that of the perceiver."[27] Torches and candles are material objects with acutely sensual qualities. They emit sound, smells, warmth, and varying degrees of light, all of which foreground the viewer's presence before them. Like staged bodies, candles project rhythms that synesthetically engage the viewer in the memory that they signify. A candle can effectively reach out to the viewer's body and draw it into a mnemonic experience.

When dictating how objects like candles were to be used in their funeral rituals, York's laypeople may have taken cues from other public events staged in the city. Authorities and organizations in York harnessed the power offered by devotional materiality when they designed public rituals. This was particularly the case with the city's Corpus Christi procession, an intricately choreographed, but repeatedly contested, public event. Attempts to control the public meaning of this event often involved manipulating its material components.

The feast of Corpus Christi was officially established by Pope Urban IV in 1264, but its celebration was not widespread in Europe until the fourteenth century. By 1318, the feast had been established in England. Although originally commemorated with a mass and an office, by the early fourteenth century a public procession was the common way that communities celebrated this feast day.[28] York's procession followed common practice: the clergy carried the host in a decorated vessel that was covered by an elaborate canopy held aloft by prominent laypeople.[29] By the fifteenth century, the feast had prompted the formation of a Corpus Christi guild in York.[30] The guild's register, which begins in 1408, prescribes:

> We ordain that on the feast of Corpus Christi all chaplains walk in the procession in surplices in a decent manner, processionally in the age-old order [ordine], unless they can reasonably be excused. And in order that the worship of God may be increased more reverently [venerabilius augeatur], in order that the priesthood may be thought of more worthily, and that the people may more suitably be incited to devotion [ad devocionem excitetur] by these things, we ordain that the six masters, or at least two of them, who must manage others in processions of this kind, shall carry white rods, during their terms in

every general procession to distinguish them from others, considering that such a firm and devout pace may be due, ordered and proper to the praise of God, the respectability of the priesthood, the edification and good example [edificacionem ac bonum exemplum] of all Christian people, but most of all for the honour of God and of the city of York.[31]

This description invests the procession's visual design and decorum with a great deal of significance. The white rods distinguish certain men from others, while the proper manner of the procession itself is meant to increase devotion, elevate the priesthood, and bring honor to God and the city. Similar tactics are outlined in the seventh ordinance of the guild, which specifies "that ten great torches be borne before the sacrament in the procession of Corpus Christi, and that only six processionally before the body of a deceased brother."[32] The guild recognized that visual and material components could convey hierarchical social meaning and therefore it regulated these elements in an effort to control that meaning. Likewise, the description of the procession emphasizes the need for physical decorum; the chaplains are instructed to walk in a "decent manner" [modo honesto], while the masters maintain a pace that is "firm and devout" [solidus et deuotus], "ordered and proper" [ordinatus & maturus]. The procession achieves its goals—reverence, respectability, edification—through proper material and bodily rhythms.

Other city and guild documents include similar language. A 1476 entry in the House Books, which contain the minutes of the city council's meetings, orders all participants in the procession "to present themselves and go peaceably in their order, manner, and places" according to the instructions of the Common Clerk or otherwise pay a penalty of forty shillings.[33] A 1477 entry in the Corpus Christi guild register instructs those in the procession to walk "decently and reverently" [honeste & reuerenter], and indicates that clothing was used "to distinguish" [ad distinccionem] certain people from others.[34] By the middle of the sixteenth century, descriptions of the procession become more elaborate, suggesting that views on acceptable decorum may have changed. In 1544, the House Books specify that the Corpus Christi guild master and the priests in the procession should be dressed "in the best cloaks that can be obtained within the said city" and that every house on the processional route "shall hang before their doors and facades the best bedding and bed coverings that they can get. And place before their doors branches and other such flowers and strewing as they think right and proper [honeste & clenly] for the honor of God and honor of the city."[35] It is unclear whether these accoutrements were included, just not prescribed, in earlier processions, or if they were a sixteenth-century development.

City authorities monitored material objects—clothing, torches, and particularly the Corpus Christi shrine—as closely as they did the bodies of participants. A 1432 agreement between the guild and the city reports that the men and women of the Corpus Christi guild presented the city with

> a certain shrine of sumptuous work, lately both carved and moreover painted with gold, which henceforth (is) to be enriched and ornamented more preciously with the purest silver and gold with the Lord's help...with sacrament of the body of Christ enclosed in it and in crystal or beryl or some other thing open to the sight of men more suitably for the sacrament.[36]

The agreement also clearly stipulates that the shrine is to remain locked in St. William's chapel on Ouse bridge with free access granted only to the fraternity's wardens and the mayor. The mayor is given his own key to prevent any delay should he wish to show the shrine "to any honourable persons, lords or ladies, or others of noble birth wishing to see the same uncovered."[37] These terms essentially control access to the sight of, and presence before, the shrine.

The stated purpose of using this elaborate object is "so that from this, faith and devotion may be increased among the present people."[38] But the language used in civic documents also links this devotional goal to the bolstering of civic prestige. The 1432 agreement between the city and the Corpus Christi guild explains that when "any honourable persons" see the shrine uncovered, "their devotion may grow from this and the honour of the said city increase, and most especially that the praise or honour of the beholders may redound to the Lord."[39] The shrine's lavish decoration enhances the city's reputation, just as public religious events like the Eucharistic procession reflect the city's power and prestige; a city with such elaborate pious exhibitions truly must be blessed by God. The visual program aligns devotional aims with community honor.

Throughout York's history, city officials monitored the bodies and material items included in the city's public processional events in order to ensure that they conveyed appropriate visual and rhythmic meaning.[40] I identify a similar preoccupation reflected in wills. Most wills, including Bracebrig's, leave out many formal details about the order and timing of events because these would have been considered standard practice in York.[41] Therefore, when a testator did include specific material guidelines it may suggest that the individual recognized these elements as particularly significant in constructing memory. Bracebrig, a former mayor and therefore likely attuned to the power of the visual event, uses tactics in his will that recall those used by the Corpus Christi guild during his lifetime. Bracebrig requests that his wife, children with their husbands, his brothers, and his executors and their wives be present at his burial, clad in black cloth if they wish, "as the manner and dignity of the City require" [modus et honestas civitate exposunt].[42] By specifying clothing and decorum, Bracebrig is perhaps reminding these attendees that their presence communicates significant visual meaning, while also taking measures to guarantee a decorous visual event; he does not want his family and friends to spoil the impact by dressing or acting inappropriately. That Bracebrig knowingly creates a visual spectacle is further suggested by a note in the will that specifies that his body should be carried to church "by daylight" [lucem dies].[43] Bracebrig's relatives and executors were components of his burial's spectacle, with their dress and behavior constituting important visual cues.[44]

But Bracebrig may also specify clothing and behavior in an effort to ensure that his funeral's sensuality is similarly appropriate. Not only does Bracebrig want others to see his funeral in certain terms, he may also want them to experience it in specific ways. In addition to visual meaning, dress and manner communicate rhythmic meaning that is translated through the bodies of viewers. Evidence suggests that mirror neurons triggered viewers to simulate the actions and emotions of a funeral's participants within their own bodies, a process of assimilation similar to the interactions described in medieval visual theory. By specifying certain material elements, a testator exerted control over the texture of this assimilation and, therefore, over the quality of the memory that a funeral embedded within spectators.

I am suggesting that materiality, rather than being incidental, was in fact crucial to how funeral events constructed lasting memories. Those who had great financial means used materiality to create highly sensual mnemonic experiences for those who attended their funerals. This same approach to materiality was also employed in York's cycle performance. The York Mercers, the guild responsible for the cycle's spectacular final pageant depicting the Last Judgment, exemplifies this attention to the material performance.[45] By the 1430s, the Mercers' organization was the wealthiest of the city's trade and craft guilds,[46] and a 1433 indenture detailing the guild's pageant, which offers us the most extensive description of any York pageant set, reflects this affluence.⁴⁷ The following are only excerpts from the lengthy description,

> A pageant with four wheels, Hell mouth, three garments of three devils, six devil faces in three masks. Array for two evil souls, that is to say two shirts, two pair of hose, two masks, and two wigs. Array for two good souls, that is to say two shirts, two pair of hose, two masks, and two wigs, two pair of angel wings with iron on the ends. Two...A cloud and two pieces of rainbow made of timber. Array for god, that is to say a wounded garment, a crown with a gilded mask. A large curtain of red damask painted for the back side of the pageant...Four squared to hang at the back of god, four irons to support heaven, four fastening bolts and an iron bolt. A swing of iron that god shall sit upon when he shall ascend up to heaven, with four ropes at four corners.⁴⁸

The Last Judgment performance and funerals both attempted to materialize the immaterial. The pageant materializes the end of time, while funerals and other posthumous rituals aim to materialize a testator's identity and religious devotion. These goals are not accomplished solely by the visual nature of these events, but also by their material texture, which conveyed rhythms that impacted how spectators experienced and, therefore, understood these events.

Giving Sense to History: Staged Objects in the York Cycle

Stage props help illustrate how Shepherd's notion of performance "rhythms" extends to inanimate objects and therefore how we might apply performance literacy to a devotional event like a funeral. Stage props establish phenomenological links with both the actors and the audience. Garner argues that "props constitute privileged nodal points in the scenic field, asserting a powerful materiality and a density both semiotic and phenomenal." These objects not only signify, they also offer the actor/character a way to "operate intentionally in the material sphere."⁴⁹ In medieval religious plays, these phenomenal links often conveyed theological meaning. For example, certain props that appear in the York pageants situate the actor/character in the material world, which draws attention to the bodied similarity between actor/character and spectator, and consequently reinforces the humanity of the cycle's sacred characters. Joseph's complaint about the broken stable roof in *The Nativity* pageant characterizes him as human, while the real ropes and boards used in *The Crucifixion* pageant underscore Christ's humanness. Interactions with objects are not simply representations;

instead, these constitute bodily interactions that help establish the world onstage, and its corresponding theology, as relevant to the spectator's own world and experiences in it.

In one York pageant, a prop's real presence onstage helps validate the lay spectator's own material practices with devotional objects. *The Assumption of the Virgin* begins with a lengthy monologue from Thomas, the same character that appeared in the earlier pageant, *The Incredulity of Thomas*.[50] *Incredulity* presents Thomas as the absent, doubting disciple, but in *The Assumption* he becomes the sole eyewitness to a miraculous event. In the pageant's opening monologue, Thomas reiterates the story of Christ's life and Passion before explaining his own struggle to find direction now that Christ has ascended to heaven. An angel chorus then appears and sings a nine-line "Rise" series (beginning with "Rise Mary, thou maiden and mother so mild," 45.105) followed by a four-line "Come" series (opening with "Come chosen childe," 45.114), both addressed to the Virgin. The angels command Mary to rise and "Come up to the king to be crowned" (45.117).[51] The words "rise" and "come" reinforce Mary's physical assumption and thus her fleshy reality. After Mary appears, she instructs Thomas to go and tell the other disciples that he has seen her ascend. When Thomas doubts that they will believe him ("For they do not pay attention to the tales that I tell," 45.164), Mary replies,

> I shall show you
> A token true [token trewe]
> Very brightly colored,
> My girdle, lo, take them this sign.
> (45.166–9)[52]

The girdles used in the Middle Ages might be better understood as belts and were worn on the body as an outer garment. After Thomas thankfully accepts the girdle, or belt, Mary reminds him (and the audience) that all who find themselves in despair or peril should pray to her for intercession on their behalf. A 1415 list of the pageants, the Ordo paginarum, describes *The Assumption* as "Mary ascending with a crowd of angels, eight apostles, and Thomas, the apostle of India, preaching in the desert."[53] Therefore, it is likely that Mary physically ascended as part of the stage action.

Constituting part of the preexisting Assumption tradition, the Virgin's girdle was layered with theological significance.[54] Andrew Sofer reminds us that when props appear onstage they "bring their own historical, cultural, and ideological baggage with them,"[55] and this was certainly true of the girdle. More than a sign, the Virgin's girdle, a "token trewe," functioned as an object within a longstanding tradition. But Sofer also reminds us not to let the material presence of the onstage object cause us to forget how it also works "as part of a discrete theatrical event." The girdle's appearance in the pageant amounts to a "material stage event" that accomplishes important devotional work.[56] Even more than words such as "rise" or "come," phenomenologically this prop places Mary and Thomas firmly in the same bodied, material realm that the audience inhabits. Furthermore, during the play, the girdle's "objectness" becomes tightly linked to the Virgin's body. This relationship grows especially pronounced when the disciples wax poetic about the girdle's material use:

> Peter: It is welcome, indeed, from that worthy person,
>   For it was customarily used to encircle that worthy virgin.
> James: It is welcome, indeed, from that lady so radiant,
>   For her womb was wrapped with it and wore it to good effect.
> Andrew: It is welcome, indeed, from that healer of sin,
>   For she wrapped it around her as blossom so bright.
> John: It is welcome, indeed, from the key of our people,
>   For about that holy one it went very well.
>   (45.274–81)[57]

These lines give the object a physical history, situating it as something that existed and functioned within the material world. Alice Rayner explains how objects are able to give material, tactile presence to what has been lost, as well as to loss itself.[58] *The Assumption* pageant substitutes a material object for Mary's absent, lost body. Mary's previous bodily use of the girdle enables this material object to obtain the status of human flesh.

The disciples' physical responses to the girdle attest to its holy "fleshiness." Immediately after the lines cited earlier, Peter says, "Now kneel we each / Upon our knees," to which Jacobus adds "To that gracious lady" (45.282–4).[59] We obviously do not know how this moment was staged; however, because these lines appear immediately after the disciples welcome and describe the girdle, it seems likely that the actors directed their (most likely, devotional) gestures toward the object. If so, then the girdle prompts the same pious responses that the Virgin's body would provoke if present. In addition, since Thomas receives the girdle from the Virgin (who perhaps removes it from her body at that point) and then presents it to the disciples, the prop was almost certainly handled by the characters/actors. As

Rayner suggests in respect to staged objects, "In touching the object, one touches time in the register of the senses, time that is not separate from the object (as in the effects of time) but incorporated *as* the object in its present."[60] In *The Assumption* pageant, the Virgin is incorporated as part of the object's material state. The girdle does not replace the Virgin, but functions instead as an extension of her material, bodily presence into the present.[61] The Virgin is integrated within the girdle's "thingness."

The Virgin's girdle offers the disciples—and, by extension, lay audience members—devotional agency through objects. The object reinforces the fleshy materiality of which the actors/characters are composed and therefore reminds spectators of the human relevance of these pageants. The human element is further underscored by the fact that lay spectators would have recognized the girdle, an object frequently mentioned in medieval wills and inventories, as a familiar object, and perceived the prop in relation to their own personal experiences with girdles.[62] When staged, this kind of personal object does not merely signify its owner/user; rather, its physical presence constitutes a visible and material extension of that person into the sensual world. The stage prop's material presence "gives sense to history," in this case, to a sacred history.[63] Allowing this kind of familiar object/prop to invade, and perhaps even dominate, the pageant's dramatic space may have encouraged spectators to derive meaning through performance literacy when they encountered similar objects outside the performance frame. In addition, as cognitive theory reveals, an audience member understands an actor's/character's physical interactions with objects, in part, by the way the sensorimotor system simulates those actions within the spectator's body; even just the object's material form might trigger simulations of the actions that form implies. In many ways, then, the devotional practices and objects presented onstage insinuated themselves into the medieval viewer's embodied schema, and, consequently, may have validated that spectator's own practices with devotional objects.

During performances spectators are open to these kinds of rhythmic possibilities; theatrical infiction prepares audience members to derive meaning from the phenomenal links between the stage event and their lived reality. But because medieval culture framed sacred objects as functioning like stage props, carrying with them traces of a devotional past that belonged to time and to mortality, I would argue that York's medieval laity approached and understood many devotional materialities as behaving in ways that were similar to what I have identified in *The Assumption* pageant. Funeral arrangements represent one such case. By giving sense to the deceased individual's history, funerals perpetuated that person's memory by embedding rhythmic patterns into the embodied schema of attendees. Medieval notions about visual interactivity and embodiment in perception may have encouraged a funeral's viewers to be more open to such an experience. Funerals, like performances, achieved their goals by functioning as "modes of becoming."

Devotional Props

In addition to outlining funeral arrangements, most wills from York also contain rich evidence regarding the religious images and objects that laypeople owned. Throughout the Middle Ages, artisans in England and on the continent produced a range of devotional images for the laity. But, by the early sixteenth century, England was importing devotional art and objects in unprecedented numbers.[64] These images were used by laypeople in many different environments and for many different purposes. Some made their way into churches through testamentary bequests. Others passed through different hands while remaining in the domestic or private sphere. No longer exclusively designed for wealthy patrons, the images available for laypeople to purchase constituted a wide range that varied greatly in cost and quality. Although some laypeople still personally commissioned images, others bought devotional objects like alabaster sculptures or small painted images off the shelf. Some scholars have interpreted this late medieval proliferation of devotional objects as a response to—and thus evidence of—the laity's desire for more control over and access to their own spiritual development.[65] Objects certainly offered the laity a variety of ways to influence piety—both for themselves and others. I conclude this chapter by examining cases in which I believe laypeople used specific material objects to create rhythmic encounters that, like funerals, gave sense to aspects of their devotional histories.

York's laity owned many different kinds of religious images and objects, including rosaries, rings, tapestries, sculptures, books, painted images, decorated silver plate, and crucifixes. Terminology is inconsistent among late medieval wills and inventories, in which the simple, but not particularly specific, term "ymaginem" is regularly employed; therefore, scholars must often resort to guesswork when attempting to determine the specific material characteristics of the private art in circulation.[66] The entries that prove most useful are those that indicate the subjects represented in the images, but laypeople who owned few religious objects did not need to use such specificity in their bequests, nor did those who appraised their estates need to include these details in their inventories. Only in instances when an individual owned a large collection was specificity required and often only for the practical purpose of differentiation. In some cases, a layperson might use location to differentiate among objects or images. In her 1546 will, Annas Thomson, a York widow, gives a "painted cloth hanging in my hall with one pieta upon it," "one painted cloth hanging at my bedside having upon it one Image of our Lady," and "one of the little painted cloths that hang in my bed."[67] But, in most cases, we derive our evidence about the location of images within homes from inventories.

Almost all English inventories begin with a standard preface followed by a note about the amount of cash the deceased had on hand. They then work their way through the deceased's house, room by room, listing what possessions were found in each.[68] The standard terminology for rooms includes: "aula," interpreted as a large general purpose room used by family and employees; "camera," which roughly corresponds to a living space for the master and mistress of the house and thus usually includes the bedding, but sometimes also includes dining furniture; and, "coquina," or kitchen. Following these rooms, the shop or work rooms, chapel, and other spaces appear, when applicable.[69] Although we might wish to associate certain kinds of images with specific rooms in a house—such as painted tapestries with the aula or camera—medieval inventories suggest that laypeople kept images in all of their rooms.[70]

As with wills, the level of detail used in inventories to describe images varies. For instance, in addition to painted papers, decorated pillows, rings, and rosaries, the 1446 inventory for Thomas Gryssop, a York chapman, includes fourteen images valued at 7d.[71] Painted "hallings," or wall hangings, are particularly common in York inventories, and many of these entries include descriptions of their subjects. The 1440 inventory for John Collan, a York goldsmith, includes "an old halling with the Trinity three yards long 3d. Another with an image of Saint George and of the blessed Mary 4d...A tester [bed canopy] with an image of the blessed Mary 6d.," all found in the parlor. This inventory also lists "a hanging cloth with an image of the blessed Mary of mercy 8d." in the great camera.[72] Laypeople wealthy enough to have private chapels usually owned extensive collections of religious images, and their inventories and wills often contain a large amount of descriptive detail. On the other hand, the 1485 inventory of John Carter, a York tailor, includes discouragingly vague entries under the aula: "A striped halling 1s. 8d. Another painted cloth 6d. Another painted cloth 6d.

Another painted cloth 8d. Another painted cloth 6d. Another painted cloth 1s. 4d. Another small painted cloth 3d."[73]

Owning religious images and objects was not specific to the laity. Many inventories made by York's clergymen contain detailed lists of domestic religious art. The 1449 inventory of Thomas Morton, a canon in York, includes a long list of religious images and objects, among them: a tapestry with arms of the Archbishop Bowet of York; another tapestry showing the arms of St. Peter in the middle; an ornamented chasuble made of gold cloth; a frontal and a reredos of stained work for the altar, red and blue in color with an image of the blessed Mary and Saint John; a small table lined with ivory carved with various images; a silver bowl with a base and a lid with an image of Michael; and a bowl with a lid and an image of the blessed Mary.[74] The 1452 inventory of another canon from York, William Duffield, includes: a cross of gold with bones of the saints on the back (an object that may have been a reliquary); a number of pieces decorated with roses; ewers (pitchers with wide spouts) with a Catherine wheel, weighing fifteen-and-a-half ounces; a number of chalices and patens that have inscriptions and images noted; various badges, rings, and belts; a pendant; and different religious books, including an illuminated Psalter.[75] Such items may have helped to ensure that the spaces these clergymen inhabited conveyed rhythms of sanctity.

Testamentary evidence suggests that at least some members of York's clergy conceptualized both performance and personal religious imagery as supporting a lay devotional program. The 1446 will of William Revetour, a chaplain in York, is standard in many respects: he requests burial in his parish church of St. John the Evangelist at the end of Ousebridge in York, and leaves money to the fabric of this church, as well as to various religious and charitable institutions in the city, to the four orders of mendicant friars, the poor in York's monastic hospitals, the lepers in the suburbs, different recluses, various canons and chaplains, the nuns in the house of St. Clement, and the guild of St. Christopher.[76]

Theatre scholars have found Revetour's will particularly compelling because he bequeaths play texts as well as props for a Corpus Christi pageant.[77] Near the end of his will Revetour leaves the guild of Corpus Christi "a certain book called the Creed Play with the books and banners belonging to it."[78] The next bequest is a play about Saint James the Apostle in six "paginis"—either pages or pageants, according to Alexandra F. Johnston—which he gives to the guild of St. Christopher ("Et gilde sancti christofori quemdam ludum de sancto Iacobo Apostolo in sex paginis compilatum").[79] In the codicil,

Revetour leaves a gilded crown and a girdle with gilded and enameled bosses to the girdlers of York for their play on Corpus Christi ("Item lego zonariis Ciuitatis Ebor ad ludum suum in festo corporis Christi vnam coronam auricallcatam deauratam & vnam zonam cum Boses deauratis & enameld").[80] We can infer from these entries that chaplain Revetour not only believed religious drama functioned as a useful tool for devotion or instruction (or both), but that he also found its *performance* efficacious; he not only donates dramatic texts, but also performance props—banners, a crown, a girdle. This suggests a keen interest in the material presentation and performance of religious plays.

An emphasis on materiality pervades Revetour's will. Like many priests and clerics, Revetour bequeaths a large collection of religious imagery, objects, and books. He gives Alice Bolton "one book treating the Lord's Prayer and the Prick of Conscience in English." Other books include one on the gospels and lives of the saints, a small Bible with "interpretation" [interpretione], and a glossed Psalter.[81] Like other testators, he donates vestments to altars, money to the lights before religious images, and candles to churches. He also bequeaths different personal devotional images. He leaves "an alabaster crucifix" [crucifixum de alabastre] to Katerine Tutbag, "a large primer with seven pictures" to his god-daughter [vnum Primarium largum cum ymaginibus intus septem], and to John Bolton "a large Bible roll with images on one side and a Latin table of the Lord's prayer on the reverse" [magnum Rotulum tractatum de Biblia in Latina cum ymaginibus ex vna parte et de Tabula oracionis dominice in latina ex altera parte].[82] Revetour's will suggests that he promoted both public religious performance and private lay devotional practices involving images and objects. He may even have considered these as two elements within the same program of religious instruction.

In *The Assumption of the Virgin* pageant, the girdle not only triggers the memory of the Virgin, but in her absence it also functions as her material embodiment in the present. Medieval York's residents—both lay and clerical—deployed devotional objects in a similar fashion for analogous memorializing reasons. As was sometimes the case with funeral arrangements, testators might try to ensure the success of this mnemonic process by stipulating how a bequeathed object should be used. For instance, Thomas Wod gives some of his best bedding of Arras work to Trinity church of Kingston upon Hull, the parish church where he is buried, under the condition that it be laid yearly over his grave at his Dirige and Mass, and hung annually in the church on the feast of St. George.[83] Sometimes testators plainly state that a bequest is intended for remembrance. Katheryne the Countes of Northumberlande left her daughter "a gold ring to remember and pray for me."[84]

Many possessions mentioned in York wills are, like the Virgin's girdle, objects that had previous contact with the testator's body (rings, pendants, necklaces, girdles, or beads—most likely rosaries) and therefore functioned in a similar way as does the stage prop. Particularly in the case of distinctive objects that laypeople wore or handled on a regular basis—decorative crucifixes, religious jewelry, ornate rosaries, Books of Hours—other people in the parish community may have come to associate these devotional objects with the people who used them. This legacy of ownership and use—part of its "thingness"—was passed down along with the object itself, thereby perpetuating these associations across generations.

But in handling an object, the owner also traced her/himself into its material presence. As Vittorio Gallese and David Freedberg contend, research indicates that our mirror neuron system responds to the actions and activities we have come to associate with objects, and perhaps also to the noticeable traces made by people who have materially altered these objects.[85] Given this evidence, objects like rosaries would have proved especially effective at sustaining a person's memory. However, so too would any devotional object that retained evidence of the user's meaningful actions—a devotional book's torn cover or marked pages; a silver ring rubbed smooth and shiny; a pilgrimage badge worn thin. Such "fleshy" objects—devotional props—would subsequently function as extensions of their (absent) owners, thereby establishing not only visual, associative memorials, but material, bodily ones as well. As with the Virgin's girdle, touching such an object constitutes a sensual encounter with its previous owner(s) in the material present. But evidence reveals that simply looking at these objects, and at the traces left by the owner's sensual encounters with them, triggers embodied simulations of that departed person's actions. This, too, might continue across generations. The mnemonic value of these bequests is found in how they give sense to the deceased person's history while functioning as portable, easily shared modes of becoming.

As these practices reveal, York's dramatic traditions operated within a devotional culture in which memory could be generated and controlled rhythmically. It would not be surprising then if some of the same tactics used by individuals to promote their own memories were also employed on the larger civic scale to advance various social agenda. A community performance event like the Corpus

Christi cycle, which annually drew spectators to the city from across the region, represented an exceptional tool for imparting powerful social and political statements. Much of this power was located in and manipulated through the play's visual images, and, as I will demonstrate, the extant civic records related to York's various public performances, particularly its cycle, emphasize the importance of seeing and spectatorship at these events. But, as with funeral practices, any effort to influence the cycle's visual program impacted the performance's rhythmic program, and, consequently, affected how spectators understood the cycle's meaning by means of their bodies.

Rhythmic Performance and Civic Memory

The first extant description of York's Corpus Christi cycle is the 1415 entry in the *A/Y* entitled "Ordo paginarum ludi Corporis Christi" (The Order of the pageants of the play of Corpus Christi), which contains two lists of the pageants.[86] The Ordo paginarum frames the cycle not as a text, but as a visual medium whose full meaning only became apparent during the performance event. The first list records the guild names on the left side of the manuscript folio and their corresponding episodes in the cycle on the right. This list does not refer to the episodes by name or title, such as "The creation of heaven and earth"; only the second list includes those titles. Instead, the first list identifies each pageant by summarizing the play's major action using descriptions that seem to be based on what was seen in the plays. For example, the Coopers' play is recorded as "Adam and Eve and the tree between them, the serpent deceiving them with fruits, God speaking to them and cursing the serpent, the angel with a sword casting them from Paradise."[87] The Pinners, Latteners (brass workers), and Painters produced a play described as: "The cross, Jesus stretched out on it on the ground, four Jews beating (him) and dragging him with cords, and afterwards raising the cross and the body of Jesus nailed to the cross upon the mount of Calvary."[88] These sketches sometimes provide more production details than can be gleaned from the extant play texts. For example, the text for *The Ascension* pageant does not specify how Christ physically ascended during performances, but the Ordo paginarum's tableau summary offers some clues about the staging: "Mary, John the evangelist, eleven apostles, two angels, Jesus ascending above them, and four angels bearing a cloud."[89] Although the pageants were assigned titles in the second list, this first list records them as visual tableaux, initially memorializing them as performance events engaged through the eye.

The decision as to whether a pageant would be included in the annual event was also based upon live performance. A 1476 entry in the city's House Books stipulates,

> that yearly in the time of Lent there shall be called before the current Mayor four of the most expert, discrete, and able players [Connyng discrete and able playeres] within this city to examine in accordance with guild regulations, to hear and to examine all the players and plays and pageants throughout all the craft guilds belonging to the Corpus Christi play. And to admit and make ready all such that they shall find sufficient enough in person and competence [sufficiant in personne and Connyng] to honor the city and honor the said crafts, and to discharge, remove from position, and avoid all other persons insufficient either in voice or person.[90]

Acceptance was contingent upon an "audition" before four players whom the Mayor believed would be best able to determine if a pageant was sufficient enough "in voice or person" to bring honor to the city. This way of adjudicating the plays acknowledged that their meaning, as well as their ability to honor the city and its guilds, was not confined to the text, but was largely communicated through visual and oral spectacle.

A similar principle guided subsequent regulation of the cycle. By 1501, the Common Clerk was stationed near the first cycle stop, where he checked the pageant performances against the textual register.[91] Although this act inevitably attributes a degree of authority to the official text, it simultaneously defines live production as a space in which visual and verbal cues may change that text. These efforts suggest that the guilds did not always stick to the "approved" versions of their plays. They also imply that some of the incendiary or potentially problematic elements in the pageants were only perceptible during live performance. Civic authorities recognized the text as only one component of a dramatic event and therefore developed performance-oriented mechanisms for regulating the cycle.

Certain concerns raised about the cycle's devotional impact also reflected a performance-centric perspective. For example, on January 31, 1432, representatives from the Painters, Stainers, Pinners, and Latteners craft guilds requested that their two plays—"one on the stretching out and nailing of Christ on the cross, and the other, indeed, on the raising up of the Crucified upon the Mount"—be combined into a single pageant because the cycle had grown too long and unwieldy.[92] According to the *A/Y* entry, the guilds argued that the cycle,

the institution of which was made of old for the important cause of
devotion and for the extirpation of vice and the reformation of customs, alas, is impeded more than usual because of the multitude of
pageants, and unless a better and more speedy device be provided,
it is to be feared that it will be impeded much further in a very brief
passage of time.[93]

The guild representatives suggest that a new, combined pageant, performed by the Pinners and Latteners, will result "rather profitably for
the people hearing the holy words of the players."[94] This proposal
reveals some concern over whether or not the audience was able to
hear the holy words spoken in the pageants, thereby insinuating that
the verbal message could potentially be confused or misunderstood
during performances. The verbal is thus framed as a fragile mode
of communication easily distorted by an imperfect or overly long
performance.[95]

In other cases, performance circumstances became an issue. In
1432 the Goldsmiths, who were then performing two pageants,
requested that one of these be reassigned to the Masons. According
to the *A/Y* entry, the Masons were unhappy with their current pageant, in which Fergus was beaten, "because the subject of this pageant
is not contained in the sacred scripture and used to produce more
noise and laughter than devotion."[96] But it was not only the devotional or biblical aspect that left the Masons unsatisfied. They were
also upset because "they have rarely or never been able to produce
their pageant and to play in daylight as the preceding pageants do"
and are therefore relieved to be assigned a play "which is in harmony
with sacred scripture, and which they will be able to produce and
play in daylight [clara die]."[97] As with Bracebrig's 1436 will, which
also contains a note about daylight [lucem die], this entry reflects an
awareness among York's lay population that the circumstances of a
performance event could promote or inhibit its impact, particularly
when so much of its potential was contained within and conveyed
through visual elements. The record also specifies that the Masons
will produce the new pageant "in the more lavish manner which is
seemly for the praise of the city."[98] Not only will the guild include
spectacle in its play, but this spectacle is designed to convey meaning
beyond the dramatic premise, in this case, to bolster civic identity
and pride. Although the verbal aspects of the cycle performance are
important, and records often describe spectators paying to "hear" the
pageants, the Masons' concerns call attention to the importance of
a performance's visual and material presentation.[99] These examples

suggest that at least some laypeople in York thought holistically about how the pageants communicated meaning to spectators.

Images play an important role in constructing communal religious memory. David Morgan asserts that "as a collective or social act of memory, the image connects devout viewer to fellow believers, that is, to those who see in it the same likeness. Visual piety, therefore, exerts a strong communal influence."[100] As I noted at the end of chapter one, medieval devotional theatre was a process of religious image-making and image-viewing. In both its dialogue and spectacle, medieval drama, not only in York but throughout late medieval Europe, emphasized spectatorship.[101] Civic records from York repeatedly describe performance events like the Corpus Christi cycle in terms of their visual impact. But the visual images presented in these religious performances also had a rhythmic dimension; set pieces, costumes, props, and bodies supplied these events with rhythmic texture. In doing so, these material elements helped a play generate sensual memories of sacred events, and, in this way, supported the play's devotional goals. In this chapter, I have argued that other elements within lay devotional culture, specifically funerals and personal devotional objects, also functioned in this way, giving sense to an individual's memory.

Chapter Three

Claiming Devotional Space

The most prominent architectural feature of medieval—and twenty-first-century—York is its Minster.¹ The cathedral's overall length is 518 feet, the breadth of its transepts measures 249 feet, and its central tower rises 197 feet high. Although the Minster stands on the site of a seventh-century church begun by King Edwin, construction of the current Minster began in 1220. Its design reflects three architectural periods of the Middle Ages: Early English Gothic (1220–1260) mainly constituted by the north and south transepts; Decorated Gothic (1280–1350) represented by the nave and chapter house; and Perpendicular (1361–1472) corresponding to the choir, most of the Minster's eastern arm, and its central tower.² The Minster project consumed the diocese of medieval York, with its wealthy citizens donating money for, and its craftsmen producing, the windows, sculpture, carving, and stonework. The Minster also figured as the location of the tomb of Richard Scrope, archbishop of York from 1398 to 1405 and locally celebrated for his martyrdom after being executed for leading an insurrection against Henry IV.³ As Barrie Dobson reminds us, "The 'concourse of people' who came to worship at Scrope's tomb serves as a reminder that the most formally hierarchical church in northern England was at the same time the centre of the most striking manifestations of popular religion and piety."⁴ The numerous bequests to the fabric of the Minster from men and women of all economic levels are evidence of the laity's pride in and commitment to the cathedral.⁵ The cathedral stood as a central character in the lives of York's medieval laity, as they both interacted with and helped sustain its material space of devotion. It therefore provides a logical place to begin analyzing performance literacy and devotional space.

Rhythmic Worship Spaces

The Minster, a massive space, impresses itself onto the bodies of those who enter it. Particularly during Mass or other ceremonies, the sounds of bells, singing, and chanting reverberate through the bodies of those who stand in the nave. In the Middle Ages, the Minster would have been painted top to bottom and filled with altars, commemorative plaques, and statues, only a small fraction of which appear there today. It also housed a variety of donor images, some of these in the form of painted glass windows. One window in particular, the Bellfounder's window (*ca.* 1330), commemorates its donor (a goldsmith and bellmaker) through various depictions of bells and their casting and tuning. This window is the second window west of the transept arm in the north aisle of the nave. Although visible, the lowest lights are located far above any viewer's head and the rest of the window extends upward from there. The window does not remain fixed to the nave—the lay space—but reaches away from that space toward God; thus, the window does not situate its donor in the nave among other lay worshippers, but instead, extending toward heaven, it places him closer to God. The material window maintains a physical distance between image and viewer that creates a strong visual and material relationship between the donor and heaven, and, accordingly, between the donor and heavenly peace in the afterlife. The material disassociation of viewer from image imparts a central element of the window's devotional and mnemonic meanings.

Other images in the Minster generate meaning by creating a specific physical relationship with the lay viewer's body. For instance, a roof boss in the cathedral's nave depicts Christ's Ascension in a way that attempts to choreograph the spectator into a very specific devotional posture. The boss reflects iconographic choices typical for this period, and, even within the Minster's large space, most people standing in the nave and looking up can see the representation—the soles of Christ's feet centered in the boss, with the faces of the apostles and the Virgin arranged around them and gazing up at Christ's disappearing body.[6] The object's placement prompts the layperson to replicate physically the postures of these original witnesses at the biblical event, and, perhaps also, the postures of some of the actors and spectators at the performance of York's *Ascension* pageant. The roof boss situates viewers as participants in the biblical event, and while this choice may deepen the devotee's visual experience, it also very explicitly tries to circumscribe the way the devotee's body figures into the mode of visual piety that he or she practices with the image.

Like clerical texts that endeavor to limit "the multiplicity of possible approaches to the crucifix" by pointedly directing the way laypeople looked upon the object,[7] the Minster's roof boss attempts to control the viewer's gaze and posture, and therefore the individual's devotional experience of/with the image. The image tries to dictate *how* it is seen; the viewer witnesses the Ascension, but in a very specific way physically.

As with my examples in the previous chapter, here again we find strategies of interpretation and intention contained within the image itself. In this case, it is the image's placement coupled with its iconography that provokes the desired physical reaction. Alternatively, performance literacy emerges out of an experience with an image's rhythmic materiality; while an image's iconography, textual and cultural references, and artistic style all convey meaning, so too does its very objectness. As texts like *Tretyse of Ymagis* suggest, this aspect of an image is difficult to regulate. In the large space of the Minster, the ability to access and derive meaning through objectness is severely reduced—though not eliminated entirely—when images like the Bellfounder's window or the Ascension roof boss are placed so far physically from the bodies that gaze upon them. It is not the Minster, then, but the more intimate medieval parish church that engendered materially oriented visual encounters and, consequently, fostered performance literacy.

The medieval parish church constituted a powerful force in the lives of York's inhabitants and fulfilled a number of the laity's social and devotional needs. In particular, the parish church represents a striking instance of lay-oriented and lay-controlled material religion. As Katherine French explains, "The laity's involvement in their parishes went well beyond attending the liturgy and paying tithes. Episcopal mandate also required them to maintain the nave and churchyard and to supply various liturgical items such as mass books, candlesticks, and chalices, while the clergy took care of the chancel."[8] The church's physical interior constituted a space over which laypeople exercised a large degree of control, and therefore its appearance and overall aesthetic helped to define the parish community.[9] In this respect, the parish church, like a funeral or community performance event, constituted a place where laypeople could assert identity and priorities publicly by orienting communal visual piety through material means.

A number of medieval texts attest to the importance of images in the devotional rhythms of the parish church, among them Robert

Parkyn's "Narrative of the Reformation" (*ca.* 1555), a lengthy diatribe against Reformation doctrine.[10] Parkyn devotes a large percentage of his text to recounting how Reformation proscriptions altered the visual culture of South Yorkshire churches. For instance, he writes that at Lent in 1547 "all images, pictures, tables, crucifixes, tabernacles, were utterly abolished and taken away from the churches within this realm of England, and all serges of wax (except two standing upon the high altar)."[11] In 1548 "the pixes hanging over the altars...were despitefully cast away as if very abominable," and on All Souls Day in 1548 "the pix with the blessed sacrament therein was taken down in the York Minster and set upon the high altar; likewise did all parish churches in York and diverse deaneries within the shire."[12] In December of 1550, he recounts how all stone altars were replaced by wooden altars, and, in the next year, that the playing of organs in churches was forbidden.[13]

By outlining these Reformation injunctions, Parkyn testifies to how fundamental physical interactions with material objects were to medieval piety: "no palms were sanctified nor carried in men's hands"; "no altars were washed"; "All other ceremonies, such as creeping to the cross...were utterly omitted"; "no fire or paschal candle was sanctified, no procession to the baptismal font performed, no candle present at the sanctification"; "neither bread nor water were sanctified or distributed among Christian people on Sundays, but clearly omitted as things tending toward idolatry"; "[there was] made no elevation at Mass after consecration"; "it was strictly forbidden that any adoration should be shown toward" the elements.[14] When Mary claims the throne, Parkyn heralds the return of these customs: "Holy bread and holy water were given, altars re-edified, pictures and images set up, the cross with the crucifix prepared to be carried in procession."[15] Parkyn describes religious reform largely by recounting changes in the presentation and use of material objects. These objects were the means by which medieval laypeople defined, structured, and understood their worship spaces.

In relation to art in the English parish church, Paul Binski contends that "the color, finish, expressivity, structuring, iconography, and even idiom of medieval images and installations...may be far more important than we have been inclined, or dared, to think." He argues that scholars should consider the parish church as "medium" and develop analytical tactics that, moving beyond liturgical reconstruction, offer "a richer sense of activity, of movement, of performativity within these buildings."[16] Like the Minster, the parish church interior offered the layperson many visualities—sculptures, hammerbeams, painted windows, carved bench ends, vestments and altar cloths, liturgical vessels, candles, and various other decorations. In these smaller spaces this materiality extended out toward the viewer and therefore implied accessibility to a degree that the spacious Minster, although it too was filled with these same materialities, could not achieve. In this chapter, I argue that for devout laypeople the various material devotional encounters supplied by the parish church triggered the same patterns of religious seeing that I associate with performance literacy.

A number of York's parish churches still stand today and many contain impressive collections of late medieval art. As the commission on historical monuments indicates, "the city of York contains the greatest concentration of medieval stained glass in England. Much of this is in the Minster but that in the parish churches is exceptional by the standards of other cities in the country."[17] Arguably, All Saints North Street, on the Mickelgate side of the River Ouse, holds the city's most notable parish collection of medieval painted glass and art, including a number of donor images. This church houses two particularly well-known medieval windows—The Corporal Acts of Mercy (*ca.* 1410) and The Pricke of Conscience (1410).

Although I recognize that the medieval parish church as it exists today is a vastly different space than it was in the Middle Ages, my analysis relies in part upon my own encounters with these spaces and their material features. As with studies of performance in which our own spectatorship constitutes evidence, I have tried to "use" these material spaces as a means of historical inquiry.[18] For instance, All Saints North Street, a relatively small parish church in York, still today offers visitors an exceptionally rich material devotional space.[19] Gazing upon its painted windows constitutes a more physically engaged act than is possible in the Minster. A viewer standing in the nave can see the facial expressions, details in clothing and gesture, and individual brush strokes in a window's lights; the traces of human effort enter the visual field. Other medieval features in this church similarly promote material immediacy. Fifteenth-century hammerbeams in the nave and chancel ceilings are carved in the form of large angels that extend out over the bodies of worshippers in the space below.[20] Medieval commemorative monuments, like a fourteenth-century engraved stone grave slab, also appear throughout the church. Moreover, the potential for material encounters within this space increases exponentially once we consider that in the Middle Ages All Saints' interior was brightly painted and contained at least four altars in addition to the high altar: an altar dedicated to the Virgin Mary in the north choir or chancel aisle; one to St. Thomas the martyr in the north nave aisle; one to St. Nicholas in the south chancel aisle; and an altar to St. James the Great in the south nave aisle. There were also at least eight chantries established in All Saints between 1324 and the English Reformation.[21]

Mass in a parish church like All Saints followed most of the same liturgical rituals as did a Mass performed in larger churches or the Minster. From the end of the twelfth century onward, the consecrating priest held the Host over his head after speaking the words of institution so that the laity could adore it,[22] and a bell sounded to warn worshippers to look up from their prayers at this moment. At Sunday Mass, the late medieval lay congregation was separated from this ritual by the rood screen, which divided the high altar from the nave. But, as Eamon Duffy contends, we should interpret the rood screen as "both a barrier and no barrier. It was not a wall but rather a set of windows, a frame...Even the screen's most solid section, the dado, might itself be pierced with elevation squints, to allow the laity to pass visually into the sanctuary at the sacring."[23] The rood screen physically separated laypeople from the Elevation, but it did not obliterate their visual access, and perhaps in some ways even served to heighten the liturgical moment sensually by giving it material texture. In addition, some churches developed lighting and special effects, such as a machine that caused sculpted angels to descend from the roof, in order to accentuate the encounter with the Host.[24] Accounts from the later Middle Ages of laypeople running from church to church to see the Elevation as many times as they could in a day indicate that, despite the presence of the rood screen, laypeople still gained visual access to this sacred moment.[25]

The smaller parish church offered most laypeople closer proximity to the Elevation during High Mass than did a cathedral. Furthermore, some parishioners also attended daily Masses, or "low" Masses, at side altars, which offered an intimate worship space that was not concealed behind screens.[26] These altars, adorned with fabrics, images, books, and, above all, candles, provided laypeople with rhythmically enriched encounters with the Host.[27]

Parish churches also supplied laypeople with more intimate, and therefore rhythmically based, experiences before devotional images. For instance, the Pricke of Conscience window in All Saints North Street represents the events of the final fifteen days of the world as recounted in an anonymous late fourteenth-century poem of the same name (see figure 3.1).[28] The lights in the window read from the bottom left to the top right. Each panel is devoted to a single day

Figure 3.1 *Pricke of Conscience* window, All Saints North Street, York (*ca.* 1410). Photograph by author.

and includes at the bottom a short text summarizing the part of the poem it illustrates. The first lights show the destruction of the earth, with scenes of the seas rising and falling, earthquakes, and fires. The second half of the window illustrates mankind's reaction to this devastation, as well as its inevitable fate. The fourteenth light represents the death of all humankind, and the final light depicts the stars falling and the world burning. Given the window's proximity to viewers, anyone standing before it can see all of these images quite clearly.

Like funeral rituals, the parish church provided laypeople with opportunities to memorialize themselves through visual means. For instance, the hammerbeams in the chancel of All Saints, as well as a misericord, were donated by the Gilliot family.[29] As in the Minster, individuals and families also donated a number of the windows in All Saints. In his 1429 will, Reginald Bawtre left 100s to the fabric of All Saints for a new window in the south part of the church,[30] and it seems his family split the cost of this window with the Blackburn family. The Blackburns also donated the All Saints window that depicts the Corporal Acts of Mercy.[31] Historians believe that the Pricke window may have been donated by the Henryson and Hessle families, who were among the urban elite of the period.[32] Members of the donor family appear in the bottom lights of the window.

The Pricke window and the Corporal Acts of Mercy window were originally installed in the north wall of the church.[33] Important urban families often sat near the high altar in the north and south side chapels, and these spaces consequently evolved into high status areas of the church.[34] As French notes, "Seating arrangements shaped the laity's experience of the liturgy and show that they did not consider themselves to be an undifferentiated or homogeneous group."[35] As wealthy York families, the donors may have sat in the north chapel or chancel aisle during Mass and therefore chose to install their window in this area of the church in order to mark with their images the space where they typically practiced public devotion. Duffy notes that donating torches to the high altar could function as "a sort of proxy for the adoring presence of the donor close by the Sacrament."[36] So, too, a window in the north chancel, by visually recalling the donor's physical presence at Mass, fulfills one of its primary functions—to remind the parish community of the donor family and its presence in, and contributions to, the parish church.[37] Those who gazed upon the Pricke window would not only remember the family members, but would also recall their physical attendance at services and, thus, their devotional commitment to the parish and to God. The image layers sacred connotations onto the family's identity through visual juxtaposition.

But when installed in a small parish church like All Saints, this window also acquires a remarkable material presence that contributed to its devotional function. The Pricke window and the Minster's Bellfounder's window both physically inhabit the lay space, but they relate to the viewer's body in very different ways. The Bellfounder's window hovers above the devout spectator, while the Pricke window dwells alongside the viewer. Standing before the Pricke window, I could look directly into the eyes of the donors pictured in the bottom lights; the rest of the window extended upward from this point of contact (see figure 3.2). Rather than reaching toward God and away from the viewer, the figures in the Pricke window inhabit the viewer's physical space, kneeling and praying alongside his or her body. This window does not stretch toward the heavens and beyond reach, but instead remains materially connected to the nave and the people in it, thus securing for the donor family a perpetual presence within All Saints' parish community that is simultaneously visible and beyond visible modes of representation. The window collapses the donors into the church's "thingness," thus incorporating them into the church's ongoing devotional rhythms.

Like staged actions and objects, windows installed in smaller parish churches not only marked space, but they also left a mark in the embodied schemata of spectators. Although gazing upon a window in the Minster generates a physical experience, the nature of that

Figure 3.2 Donor image in *Prick of Conscience* window, All Saints North Street, York (*ca.* 1410). Photograph by author.

experience directs the viewer away from the material earth toward contemplation of heaven. The encounter is somewhat similar to hearing music while standing within the cathedral. The sound fills the body, but one is conscious that it emerges from a space far removed from the listener; the music's manual production does not invade its reception. Viewers find relevance in the Bellfounder's window because they can relate to the individuals it depicts. But even though the figures in the lights are shown engaged in earthly work, they physically reside high above the viewer's body, seeming to have already left behind the earth and the fleshy, visceral concerns that may tend to distract the window's viewer.

On the other hand, the images at the bottom of the Pricke window situate the donors in their earthly bodies with their fleshy concerns—both visually and materially. Figure 3.2 shows the middle figure in the window's center donor panel. The brush work in the eyes and hands, the expressive facial features, the folds in the gown, and the window's thick leading all assert this object's material presence. This window retains a tactile quality that, especially when put "in process" or activated by light shining through the panels, may have engendered rhythms that functioned similarly to those generated by the actor's body.[38] By offering the viewer tactile, even enlivening, representations of emotions and actions, the window "bodied forth" the donors' responses to the end of time. The window's accentuated materiality and close physical proximity to the viewer might also promote embodied simulation of the donors' depicted actions and emotions, etching their fear and humility into the viewer's body and possibly impacting how that viewer subsequently remembered them. Viewers would therefore understand the window's spiritual meaning, in part, by means of performance literacy.

In small parish churches, the material objectness of donor images invades their reception. These images assert their "presentness" before viewers and, through material rhythms, offer spectators a being-in-the-world of the donor that inscribes a synesthetic memory of the deceased into the embodied schemata of those who look upon the window. For those who could not afford an image like the Pricke window, the parish church space provided many other opportunities to create memory sensually. Donations to churches could be as simple as torches before altars, particularly at the Elevation of the Host, or the sounds of liturgical rites and bells, but they might also include religious images, altar clothes, vestments, chalices, silver plate, and liturgical books. One common practice was to donate to religious images in the church personal objects associated with the body, such as clothing and jewelry. For example, in addition to giving rings to friends and family, Katherine de Craven, a York widow, bequeaths,

> To adorn the image of Our Lady in the Minster of St. Peter, York, my best girdle and one set of best beads with gold necklace, and to St. John of Bridlington another girdle of the next best. Also to the shrine of St. William of York, a girdle of black and gold, and to St. Richard Scrope a small striped gold girdle. Also I bequeath to adorn the image of Our Lady in the chapel of St. Mary's abbey, near York, one set of amber beads with a gold clasp.[39]

I have already analyzed how these kinds of objects could function like stage props when bequeathed to individuals, extending the deceased's presence into the material realm and thereby giving sense to his or her history and memory. When donated to statues installed in parish churches, such items placed the donor as another layer of that sacred statue's visual meaning.

This same kind of visual layering occurs in other medieval media, including York's dramatic cycle. During the cycle's performance, spectators not only saw the biblical story, but they also saw the contemporary allusions made throughout the pageants, as well as the actors, the characters they played in the pageants, the role/s these actors typically held in the community (guild and professional associations, civic offices), the set design on the carts, and the city backgrounds against which these were placed. Throughout each pageant, spectators navigated these multiple visual layers, while also engaging them all simultaneously as entertainment and devotion. Over the course of the cycle, or even a single pageant, viewers slipped into and out of various viewing positions (I am a witness at the crucifixion; I am before an image of the crucifixion; I am before a dramatic version of the crucifixion; I am a spectator at a play; I am standing on my street; I am a citizen of York; I am a member of the Christian community). A collage of social and sacred identities remained present within the spectator's visual and experiential fields.

As with object bequests to individuals, donating personal effects like clothes, rings, rosaries, and girdles to religious statues not only inserted an owner's identity visually, but also placed testators physically at devotional sites. Like a stained glass window, material donations exerted rhythmic influence over viewers. This may have been especially the case with donations of personal effects, since such objects were often placed on a statue in the same fashion as the donor would have worn them; the statue appears to "body forth" the donor quite literally. These donations effectively incorporated the individual into the church's sensual rhythms; when laypeople prayed to or before these statues, they engaged the donor as part of those devotional practices.

The reverse was also true. Sometimes laypeople temporarily brought images from the church into their homes for specific ritual purposes. For instance, Mary E. Fissell discusses the many different objects kept in churches or religious houses that women borrowed during childbirth, such as girdles, necklaces, relics, crosses, rings, and staffs.[40] Pilgrims' souvenirs offer another example of sanctity moving by material means. Pilgrims purchased badges and other souvenirs as proof and mementos of their journey, but also because they believed that these objects had therapeutic powers acquired through contact with the relic, shrine, or image they commemorated. The market for such objects grew and developed steadily from the twelfth century onward.[41] A related process occurred during the Palm Sunday liturgy. As Pamela King notes, "it was widely held that crosses made during the Gospel reading had apotropaic powers, and people carried sticks and string to church for the purpose of making them."[42] The rhythm of the Gospel reading transformed these objects from ordinary into the extraordinary; the encounter embedded the word of God within these crosses. In all of these cases, divine presence or power is a critical component of the object's thingness.[43]

The laity could control the parish church space by endowing chantries, establishing chapels, commissioning large images (windows and sculptures), or donating smaller objects (rings and rosaries); laypeople with fewer resources could use candles and torches to achieve a similar goal. Those who had great financial means exerted considerable influence over how their parish church's space looked and felt to those who entered and worshiped within it. In some cases, the material result of someone's death probably created a sudden sensual explosion within that space—a visual and visceral "pop" that reverberated through the bodies of fellow parishioners. We might liken this visceral pop to the one generated by the combination of props, costumes, and effects listed in *The Last Judgment* pageant's 1433 indenture. Although the laity are often described and analyzed as "passive" spectators at the liturgy, Katherine French argues that the lay congregation in fact influenced the liturgy by controlling the interior design of the church and, thus, its processional patterns.[44] Likewise, by influencing the parish church's material worship environment, the laity also controlled how this sensual space rhythmically engaged the parishioner's body, thereby affecting some of the ways that parishioners derived meaning from it.

The "Everyday Body" in the Medieval Home

The home constituted another environment in which York's laypeople used material objects to create devotional rhythms. Although John Schofield identifies three spheres of activity that developed within the medieval urban house—commercial, domestic, and service[45]—in actual practice the separation between these was subtle. There could be more than one industry associated with a household and wives sometimes managed businesses independently from their husbands. This was particularly the case when husbands were employed in building crafts performed on-site rather than in a home workshop.[46] The fluidity of the domestic space was critical to how it functioned for families. The home was a site of negotiation where multiple identities and associations coexisted.

Although the medieval household fulfilled various public functions, people in the Middle Ages did associate the home with particular forms of intimacy. Although many historians consider intimacy a modern phenomenon, Felicity Riddy explains that in the Middle Ages the meaning of the word "homly," the equivalent of domestic, suggests that people understood the medieval home as "an intimate sphere in which private identities were formed," even when this space also housed a place of work or business. She notes that "the meanings of 'homly' cluster round ideas of familiarity, closeness, affection, privacy, intimacy, and everydayness."[47] Riddy identifies different kinds of everyday familiarities associated with the home and argues that, according to late medieval English texts, tending to household concerns often meant dealing with the body's demands.[48] She concludes that "home understood the body as needy, vulnerable, hungry, cold, growing up and growing old, and endlessly leaky" and coins the term "the everyday body" to describe it.[49] Performance literacy engages exactly this kind of body—an everyday body of the flesh with its accompanying needs, vulnerabilities, and desires.

For the clergy, this everyday body was trapped in its fleshiness and thus needed experiences that would help it transcend its materiality. Augustine and the authors of *A Tretise of Miraclis Pleyinge* and *Tretyse of Ymagis* all seem to imply as much. But for the layperson, this everyday body connected her to a Joseph who complained about a broken roof, to a Virgin who wore a belt, to a savior who suffered and died on a cross. This body, and the mundane activities and spaces associated with it, could be made sacred by employing a religious object that incorporated traces of the everyday flesh into its material, devotional presence. When the thingness of these objects collapsed the everyday body into visual piety, these objects simultaneously validated that everyday body and its fleshy concerns.[50] Functioning like religious performances, these objects not only visualized their devotional content, they also actualized and rhythmically embedded that content into the viewer's body.

The domestic alabaster panel constitutes one such devotional object. Although alabaster was used for many different kinds of sculptures, including altarpieces and tombs, by the late medieval period a large market had developed in small mass-produced panels carved in high relief. These were usually stocked ready for sale, rather than made to order, and sold in private shops or at markets.[51] Evidence situates the production of alabaster carvings in England as simultaneous with performance of the York cycle, beginning as early as 1340 and ending around 1540.[52] Although Nottingham appears to have been the major center of alabaster production in England, there are references to carvers in a number of cities, including York, and evidence in the Register of Freemen of York specifies eight alabastermen and two "marblers," who may have worked alabaster as well, active in the city from 1456 to 1525.[53]

Alabasters were reasonably priced, attractive, and colorful, qualities that stimulated great demand for them throughout England and abroad. Richard Marks notes that alabaster carvers "produced work for the cheaper end of the market," and records from the borough of Nottingham, as well as York probate evidence, reveal that individual panels could cost as little as one or two shillings.[54] Inventories indicate that a significant number of these panels were kept as private devotional images in the home, especially during the late fifteenth and early sixteenth centuries.[55] Panels kept in the home were sometimes placed in wooden housings with two doors that could be opened and closed. Some of the citizens in York who purchased these alabasters almost certainly also produced, performed in, or, at the very least, attended the annual cycle. Among the wills I surveyed, twelve included specific alabaster bequests and the stated professions of these testators include: merchant, chapman, priest, mariner, chaplain, prebendary, baker, wool packer, widow, glover, and knight. York's artisans and merchants were among those who owned and bequeathed alabasters.

Carved alabasters operated under principles of visual composition similar to those of York's cycle of plays.[56] Although covering a range of sacred themes and subjects, both genres focus primarily on the Passion of Christ and the Joys of the Virgin, and both seem to follow visual conventions in style and iconography in order to present compressed images of these events in small, unrealistic spaces. Like many media, alabasters often construct a scene that offers viewers a position from which they can imagine themselves as visual witnesses.[57] This is the case with panels originally installed in churches, as well as those used in homes. For instance, alabasters depicting Christ's Ascension typically offer devotees an excellent position from which to view the sacred event—directly in front of the scene and thus able to see all characters clearly. In most of these panels, the Virgin and the apostles are shown clustered around a platform, looking up at the feet of Jesus, the only part of his ascending body still visible.[58] The Virgin and John the Evangelist stand on either side of the platform, facing one another, surrounded by the apostles. The figures are usually gazing up at the feet of Christ, thereby directing the viewer's gaze while also situating him or her as a member of the community present at the original event. As with the Minster roof boss that represents this same event, sacred witnessing is the alabaster's theme.

Visually, it is easy, and even enticing, to imagine these alabasters as duplicating the staging of York's *Ascension* pageant. In the majority of Ascension alabasters, all of the characters from the pageant also appear in the panel, with John and the Virgin placed centrally. In York's play these two characters speak to one another as Jesus is ascending, so it would be reasonable in performance to place them facing one other in a central spot on the pageant wagon. It would also make sense to have Jesus and the other speaking actors arranged in the center of the stage, with nonspeaking actors placed on the sides. After Jesus delivers his lengthy monologue, ropes around his shoulders or a platform might then raise him into the stage sky above.[59]

It is not my intention to argue that the staged image replicated the alabaster image, or vice versa; however, in order to understand how a layperson imagined this event, we must recognize which images were in popular circulation. For the layperson who saw an Ascension alabaster regularly, it might be easy during the cycle performance to ignore a platform or ropes lifting Christ and see instead the familiar sacred image, sans machinery. In the same way, a live and dynamic Ascension, dramatically enacted each year, might help impart a similar liveness and sense of intentionality to the familiar alabaster.

Most Ascension panels depict a moment of live action—Christ's feet are just leaving the frame as all the spectators look up. Many alabaster images portray similar moments of "activation." In a Harrowing of Hell carving, Jesus grasps the wrist of Adam and strides forward, leading the souls from the Hellmouth. Carvings of the Resurrection often show Christ stepping out of the tomb, his foot pressing down hard on the shoulder of a sleeping soldier.[60] Betrayal carvings compress many actions (holding, striking, stepping, and grabbing) into a single moment—a standard medieval visual technique. These panels distill, or collapse, a sacred story into one significant moment, often its narrative climax, and present it as a pause in the action. Like performances or the Pricke window in All Saints, these alabasters allow viewers to witness "enlivened" sacred moments.

Other alabaster images grant the viewer a position as visual witness, but the depictions themselves appear more static and less like pauses in action. The head of John the Baptist was the most popular alabaster image kept in the home, as is clear from the number of wills in which it is mentioned.[61] According to Francis Cheetham, most of the ninety-seven extant examples follow the general pattern illustrated by figure 3.3: a large image of John's head appears in the center, usually on a platter, with his soul in human form pictured above it.[62] The soul is sometimes held in a cloth by two angels, as in this example, while in other cases it simply appears as a naked figure kneeling in a mandorla. An image of Christ appears below John's head; in early alabasters Christ is represented by the Agnus Dei emblem, while in later examples he appears as the Man of Sorrows. Almost every John the Baptist alabaster shows St. Peter standing to John's left holding keys and St. Thomas Becket to his right. St. Peter was the patron saint of York's Minster, so his inclusion in these alabasters strengthens the local connection for owners from York. In addition, Cheetham notes that although the figure to the right is often identified as Thomas Becket, he could also be St. William of York, archbishop of York from 1143 to 1154 and the city's patron saint.[63]

Miri Rubin explains that a

> widespread and peculiarly English development was the drawing of St John the Baptist into the eucharistic sphere, not only as a precursor of Christ, but as a sacrifice in his own right...The severed head of the Baptist on a platter was an offering like a host on a paten, and for some could evoke imagery of the grail as the platter of the Last Supper sacrifice.[64]

Rubin specifically mentions that York's breviary, which contains a passage explaining the association between John's head on a tray and the Eucharist, helped to reinforce these connotations, and also that

Figure 3.3 Head of John the Baptist, alabaster panel (*ca*. 1470–85). Cultural and Sport Glasgow (Museums).

this image was "adopted as a badge by such bodies as the Corpus Christi fraternity of York."[65] The alabaster panel would offer devotees in York an ideal position for contemplation of John's head and, when installed in the home, a private opportunity to meditate on its various theological associations and significations.

John's decollation is not enacted in York's cycle. John's major appearance comes in York's baptism play, a pageant that includes only four speaking characters: John, Jesus, and two angels. The play opens with John addressing God, but as the action continues, John begins preaching to the play's audience. He announces that the Savior who comes will bring baptism by fire and spirit, and reminds his listeners that God will dwell in them if they live a clean and sinless life. The play thus conflates the medieval audience with the crowd that first heard John's words. An angel then appears to tell John that Jesus will soon arrive and that when he does John must baptize him. John expresses doubt and fear that he will not be "able to fulfill this deed certainly" (21.60–1). The angel instructs him to be obedient, but also warns him that when he baptizes Christ the heavens will open and the "holy ghost shall be sent down" (21.67).[66] John continues to struggle with his role in this extraordinary event, even after Jesus enters the scene. He asks Jesus to baptize him instead, explaining that since a rich man would not beg at the door of a poor man, it is not right for Jesus to come to him for a blessing. Jesus replies that righteousness is not only "fulfilled in word but also in deed" (21.130).[67] Although John finally agrees, he is still timorous about physically touching the divine—whether Christ or the Holy Spirit. He says that he trembles and asks for God's help in this "werk" (21.147). After baptizing Jesus, who then announces that all who are baptized and believe will "come to blisse" (21.163), a newly confident John promises to spread Christ's message of baptism and salvation for the rest of his life. The pageant enacts Christ's baptism, but this act seems to constitute a relatively small part of the play. As in *The Ascension* pageant, issues of human witnessing dominate the action. John expresses confusion, struggles to understand what he hears, and shows fear when initially called by God. But in the end, John proves himself to be an exemplum of proper Christian witness and service.

Art of devotion does not convey theological ideas or didactic intention, but instead, as Henk Van Os argues, it reveals "what the pious patron had learned to regard as the most important moments of God's redemptive relationship with him."[68] Although the alabaster and play imagine very different moments from John's life, they may impart a similar message through their material rhythms. Both genres foreground John's human qualities, suggesting that the laity found these characteristics particularly relevant to their own personal devotional needs. The pageant not only represents John's efforts to control very human (fleshy) emotions, but, like the other plays, it places spectators in a bodily relationship with John that allows them to generate devotional meaning from this physical affinity and consequent embodied simulation. John's emotions and his spiritual struggle become the spectator's own, reenacted in the spectator's body and incorporated into his or her embodied schema. By emphasizing human aspects of the Baptism story, the pageant encourages spectators to develop a strong empathetic relationship with John that will embed within spectators the knowledge that they too can resist fear and doubt through faith.

The alabaster not only foregrounds John's humanity representationally, but also materially. Alabaster sculptures combine color and dimensionality in a strikingly "live" way. The materiality of these images—even when they depict relatively static scenes—may generate rhythms similar to those Simon Shepherd ascribes to performance; as David Freedberg and Vittorio Gallese argue, the form of an art piece can provoke viewer simulation.[69] Rather than suggesting depth through receding planes, alabaster panels present an extreme form of high relief sculpture that pushes forward into the spectator's space. In the John panel, the angels at the top do not simply look at the viewer, but they extend toward the viewer, necks thrust out and tense, holding John's spirit nearly two inches out from the frame. Almost their entire bodies are visible as they reach out to the viewer, meaning that these figures appear to exist virtually separate from the background; the wooden box frame accentuates this dynamic. At the bottom, Christ the Man of Sorrows also leans out and toward the viewer. Carved in high relief, the panel's three-quarter image not only creates a perceptual quality of live movement, as the figures emerge from the background and move toward the viewer, but this material quality also allows the figures to enter and claim the viewer's space. The paint, still evident in some examples, created mimetic brightness that enhanced this effect.

The dimensional materiality of the sculpture fixes the viewer as a bodied witness and thus draws a phenomenological connection between the spectator and the sacred moment it depicts. In this way, the alabaster space constitutes "bodied" space that not only foregrounds the viewer's physical presence before it, but also invites the viewer to understand the panel's devotional meaning by means of his or her own material body. In the case of John's head, this bodied space may have prompted spectators to meditate on John's human traits—including his struggles with "fleshy" emotions.

The material aspects of the alabaster panel may have also sacralized the everyday body of the home. Like York's cycle performances or personal effects donated to statues, alabasters participated in a medieval tradition of visual layering.[70] This layering could be used to associate the domestic space and its inhabitants with piety. A craftsman may have chosen to place in his home an alabaster image that depicted his guild's pageant episode in order to perpetuate on a daily basis the sacred associations generated during the annual cycle performance. In this case, the panel might also serve to remind other members of the household that the craftsman's everyday body possessed sacred value. As I have noted, York's parish churches and Minster overflowed with medieval images. Herbert Kessler explains how "[t]he ordered narratives and rich material inside churches stood in dramatic contrast to the chaotic urban life or untamed landscapes outside, in themselves conveying the sense of a more elevated world."[71] When the laity encountered alabaster altarpieces in cathedrals and parish churches their bright color and rich texture would have been just a part of the larger sensual kaleidoscope. Alternatively, when the lay user opened an alabaster panel's wooden housing in his home, the object's color and texture activated the image, perhaps taming and spiritually elevating the everyday body and its chaotic urban life outside the church.

Just as an alabaster's materiality will claim the viewer's space and thus validate the everyday body, so too could these images physically claim the domestic space and thereby validate the home as a devotional site. Alabasters were different from smaller pieces of devotional art purchased by the wealthy, such as ivory diptychs, that could easily travel with their owners.[72] Too unwieldy to move frequently, alabasters would likely have found a more permanent location in the home. Private ritual or prayer before these objects may have marked the home as holy, but the materiality of these sculptures also generated the visual effect of moving into and taking up residence within the domestic space. By penetrating the home with the pious events they portrayed, these images rhythmically engaged that "homly" space and the bodies that inhabited it during both work and leisure, thereby sacralizing the many different aspects of domestic life. The cognitive theory of conceptual blending can help us better understand how that everyday body might "live in" the sacred spaces that these sculptures created. Conceptual blending's role in the material culture of medieval lay devotion is the subject of my next chapter.

Chapter Four

Devotion and Conceptual Blending

Laypeople used funerals, objects, and images to extend themselves physically into the devotional lives of those who survived them. By tracing themselves into the bodies of friends and family members, thereby promoting embodied remembrance, laypeople were able to retain a posthumous presence in York that operated well beyond visual representation. The cognitive theory of conceptual blending can enable us to better understand how elements of material culture helped laypeople achieve this goal. Conceptual blending is the cognitive process by which we transform various inputs into coherent structures of meaning. As we navigate in and interact with the world, we reconstruct it into "mental spaces," what Gilles Fauconnier and Mark Turner describe as "small conceptual packets constructed as we think and talk, for purposes of local understanding and action."[1] Mental spaces are connected to schematic knowledge since they "become entrenched in long-term memory."[2] We build mental spaces from immediate experiences, as well as from what people tell us about the world, and once we organize a mental space's elements and the relations between those elements into a "known" package, we have "framed" it.[3] As Fauconnier and Turner explain, a space can have minimal abstract framing that offers little specification, but its organizing frame "specifies the nature of the relevant activity, events, and participants"; therefore, learning a mental space often involves learning its organizing frame.[4] We create complex meaning by connecting or selectively blending mental spaces into integration networks. Which mental space's organizing frame we choose to project into that network will impact how we derive meaning from the blend.

Objects and physical places can function as material anchors for conceptual blends that are otherwise extremely abstract. For example, Fauconnier and Turner examine how material culture plays a role with respect to honoring and remembering the dead, suggesting that posthumous rituals and monuments effectively anchor our notions of personal identity; while the conceptual blend of identity finds a material, physical anchor in "the active living biological body that we can see and with which we can interact...When the person dies, the conceptual network with the unique person persists...[b]ut the material anchor is gone."[5] The significance of tombstones and cemeteries is "the role they play as material anchors for the blend of 'living with the dead,'" a very abstract concept.[6] Similarly, sacred spaces, such as churches and cathedrals, supply material anchors for "spiritual and personal integration networks."[7]

But while Fauconnier and Turner suggest that tombstones, grave plots, and cathedrals "attract the sacred and focus it in a particular location,"[8] in this way creating isolated blends associated with extraordinary spaces or places, most of the elements of medieval material culture I have explored in the preceding chapters do not function in such isolation. Instead, while they may be employed in extraordinary circumstances, they are actually intended to trace a sacred identity into the everyday body. Objects like alabaster sculptures could sacralize domestic space and identity because the sacred frame prevailed over the domestic, everyday input. A ring bequeathed to a daughter might prompt a more perpetual blend of living with the dead if it were worn daily. Although installed in All Saints, the Pricke window was seen regularly by parishioners and consequently integrated the donors into the routine rhythms of the parish church. Even funeral rituals may have traced patterns into the everyday civic spaces in which those activities were performed; funerals that involved a range of sensual inputs, such as Bracebrig's, might create such powerful experiences that they prompted living with the dead to continue into daily life. I have argued that the sensuality of these media traced meaning into the spectator's embodied schema, thus enabling them to function, like performances, as modes of becoming. In some cases, the physical reality of these objects and spaces may also have encouraged spectators to construct certain ongoing conceptual blends.

Performance spectatorship compels a very sophisticated process of blending; spectators at a play do not merely construct and navigate through blends, but they also "live in" those blends. Living in the blend is crucial to how theatre works. As Fauconnier and Turner explain, "[theatre's] power comes from the integration in the blend. The spectator is able to live in the blend, looking directly on its reality."[9] When watching a play spectators make sense of the action by blending the living actors with the identities of their characters.

If a play is based on a real event, another degree of blending occurs. Within these blends, the spectator selectively navigates multiple frames. Although audience members might "decompress the blend" if they notice something amiss on stage, such as a wobbly set or a flubbed line, typically a performance's actuality is powerful enough to overcome these distractions. Fauconnier and Turner suggest that while a blend that results from using material objects "is a product of cultural evolution, and the inputs and their outer-space relations are much more accessible," alternatively, in theatre "the ability to live in the blend provides the motive for the entire activity."[10] Therefore, while the medieval laity used material objects and architectural environments to generate specific devotional blends, such as "living with the dead," medieval performance events offered them sensually enhanced blending opportunities that could generate extremely powerful devotional encounters. It was precisely theatre's ability to create such "living in the blend" experiences so effectively that made it a valuable tool for generating, manipulating, and perpetuating devotional meaning in the Middle Ages.

Mending Discord through Blends

Civic authorities and groups in York regularly used performances to reimagine the city's physical space precisely because these events could encourage spectators to live in blends that served their various agenda. Royal entries into York represent particularly calculated instances of this process. York hosted six kings between 1377 and 1569, and entries in the city's House Books for the months leading up to each royal visit document the city's detailed planning process. For example, in 1483 York officials decided on September 2 that the city would perform its Creed Play for Edward V, who was set to arrive on September 7.[11]

Particularly rich are the records for Henry VII's 1486 visit to the city.[12] These not only provide extremely detailed accounts of the preparations for and execution of this event, but also expose the anxiety that surrounded this visit. As Lorraine Attreed writes, the dynastic struggles of fifteenth-century England "presented unique problems for towns and the welcomes they were expected to extend."[13] York had supported Richard III's claim to the throne during the Lancastrian-Yorkist conflict, and, by receiving Richard into its city walls and Minster in August of 1483, had publicly endorsed him as the rightful king. Henry VII's August 1486 visit to York occurred not long after Richard's defeat at the Battle of Bosworth, and the lavish, intricately designed reception that city officials prepared for Henry functioned as a visible public apology for its "mistaken" loyalties. Civic authorities monitored the entry's various elements quite closely in order to ensure that they conveyed appropriate symbolic meaning. The House Book entries document the close attention paid to the event's visual signs:

> The Mayor and aldermen in similar clothing of scarlet, the common council and clerk in violet, chamberlains in blood-red, and many of the inhabitants in red on horse-back shall wait for the king at Bilburgh cross, about five miles from the city, and the other inhabitants, who may not ride or be in the position to have red gowns, to give their attendance on foot between Dringhouses and the city beside a certain number of children that shall be gathered together around Saint James chapel calling joyfully "King Henry," in the manner of children.[14]

Once Henry entered the city itself, the royal entry then integrated him into a sequence of scenes staged in York's streets along a route that closely mirrored that of the cycle. The area at the first gate was "craftily designed" to look like a glorious and joyful heaven, with an array of trees and flowers beneath it. In the midst of this tableau, a red rose and then a white one suddenly "spring up," and "all other flowers shall bow [shall lowte] and evidently give sovereignty [yeue suffrantie], showing the Rose to be principal among all flowers."[15] All flowers bow down to the red rose, representing the Lancastrians, and the white rose, associated with both York and Henry's new wife, Elizabeth of York. This scene continues with a crown descending from the clouds to cover the Roses and with Ebrauk, York's legendary founder, addressing Henry. Ebrauk gives Henry the keys to the city, his title, and his crown, saying,

> To you Henry I submit my city key and crown
> To rule and correct your right to defense
> Never to this city to presume nor pretense
> But wholly I grant it to your governance
> as a principal piece of your inheritance.
> Please, I beseech you for my memory
> Since I am of your family line
> Show your grace to this City with great Abundance
> So the realm may recover into prosperity.[16]

Ebrauk continues for ten more lines and then concludes by reminding Henry that the city not only welcomed his visit, but that its inhabitants also uniformly recognized him as their sovereign and king.[17]

Such staged submission pervades the entire eight-scene event, which also included a device that rained rose water on the crowd when Henry appeared; a royal throne of six kings symbolizing the six Henries; King Solomon offering Henry his royal scepter; a greeting from King David, who surrenders his sword of victory and castle to Henry; and a final scene in which the Virgin descends to welcome the king before returning to heaven with "angel song" [angell sang] as "it snows by means of wafers made in the manner of snow" [it snaw by craft tobe made of waffrons in maner of Snaw].[18] Like Ebrauk, the other figures who address Henry—Solomon, David, and the Virgin—verbally reinforce the city's affection for the King, as well as its contrition, obedience, and loyalty. Gordon Kipling notes that because York symbolized Henry's adversary, the city's civic leaders designed a program that allowed the king to demand allegiance and "perform" various miraculous deeds, such as the spectacle with the flowers.[19]

The four main speaking characters in the entry, all of whom show Henry deference and loyalty, help reshape York's identity by positioning it within a longer English and Christian history. These authoritative figures not only address Henry, but also interact with him through gestures and gift-giving, thereby incorporating him physically into the local, national, and biblical histories they embody. As the King moves through York, he is in some sense enacting a role in the history of rightful kingship and, concomitantly, performing his own ascent to the throne—an ascent with local, historic, and divine qualities. This royal entry is not simply a tableaux series with monologues; it is instead an enactment containing visual and material cues that blend the fifteenth-century King Henry into a longer history of good sovereignty, which is then blended with the physical reality of a historically significant and seemingly obedient York. Henry "lives in" a blend of sovereign identity that is aligned with, enhanced by, and, since all of the speaking characters make specific reference to York, perhaps in some way dependent upon York.

Fauconnier and Turner note that "one of the central benefits of conceptual blending is its ability to provide compressions to human scale of diffuse arrays of events."[20] The royal entry took the diffuse, and somewhat un-imageable, events of Henry's ascent to the throne (with its associated notions of the divine right to rule) and York's obedience and contrition, and compressed these into a single, physically realized blend. The scenes allow Henry to embody and enact the role of powerful monarch by means of material signs (causing flowers to appear and bow; producing rose rain or a "snow" shower), while also compressing the entire event into material anchors (the keys, crown, and scepter).[21]

The larger goal of this performance of contrition is to unite Henry and York within a new mutually beneficial relationship. Cognitive research into actor training suggests that physically placing Henry into specific relationships during the entry was significant to the cultural work of mending wounds between city and crown. Rhonda Blair explains that there is "measurable neurological evidence that emotion and feeling sometimes follow 'doing.'" In respect to the actor, this suggests that physical behaviors can prompt or impact emotions. Based upon this research, Blair has proposed a reoriented approach to using emotion or sense memory in rehearsal, where the goal "is ultimately not to retrieve the memory but to support *the life lived in the moment of performance*. The point, in other words, is about a present, not the past."[22] Blair sees cognitive theory as offering strategies to help "*act*ivate" actors in sensory, affective, and kinesthetic ways, thereby providing us with ways of recognizing acting "as an evolution of a single organism in a very specific, very material way."[23] I identify a similar philosophy guiding the 1486 royal entry. Henry's bodily participation in the event was designed to prompt certain emotions or feelings within the king that would serve York's interest in mending its relationship with the crown. The goal of those emotions was to support the "life lived" during the entry, to create powerful sense memories "in the moment of performance." I would argue that those designing the event imagined Henry in the way that Blair describes, as evolving and accumulating meaning with each physical, material scene he encountered along York's streets. In this way, the royal entry traced into the king's body schema emotion-based mnemonic blends that were designed to fuse Henry's identity and feelings as a rightful sovereign with the city of York itself.

Living in Sacred Blends

Those mounting the Corpus Christi cycle also promoted certain connotations and associations by constructing various "identity" blends. The guilds appear to have funded their own pageants in the Corpus Christi cycle through general collections, as well as fines paid to the guild throughout the year.[24] Usually half of all fines were applied to the pageants. Entries such as this 1398 note about the Saddlers are typical: "henceforth a half of all said fines of their guild and ordinance . . . be paid to the searchers and governors of their said guild to support their pageant of Corpus Christi."²⁵ Most guilds seem to have followed this model.

Guilds penalized their members for an assortment of reasons, and fined nonmembers who threatened their monopolies by practicing a craft within the city without belonging to the associated guild. For example, in 1401 the Saddlers and Lorimers fined nonmembers who practiced their trade 13s. 4d., half of which went toward their pageant. A guild's searchers were not only responsible for identifying those craftsmen who were practicing illegally, but also for disciplining members who broke guild rules regarding the keeping of apprentices, quality control, or selling goods. Guild members were also charged for preventing searchers from inspecting their craftsmanship.²⁶ Virtually any crime that threatened the integrity of the craft was punished monetarily, and the accumulated funds were almost always used, at least in part, to finance the guild's pageant.

In this system then, misbehavior and consequent discipline essentially funded York's pageants. The cycle's performance might therefore be interpreted as a public act of penance offered to and witnessed by the entire community, with the staged images signifying the guild members' confession and subsequent reintegration into the craft community. An exceptionally lavish or spectacular pageant may have—in part—reflected both the unruliness of that guild's members, as well as the guild structure's disciplinary response to such misbehavior. The pageants constitute material anchors that actualize the process by which worldly acts of penance lead to forgiveness.

But, as with the 1486 royal entry, performance's ability to materially anchor the abstract may also have served to trigger blends that would ease social anxieties. According to Jeremy Goldberg, by the late fourteenth century York's craftsmen were undertaking a project of self-fashioning in which the cycle played a significant role. He posits that

> It was the desire of collectivities of craftworkers to give religious meaning to their labours and to participate in this collective manifestation of civic pride, this act of devotion, and this work of mercy that in many instances gave rise to the gilds...With the exception of the weavers and the girdlers, we have little evidence for the existence of craft gilds before the ordinances are first recorded in the city Memorandum Book from the end of the fourteenth century. Equally we have no notice of the Corpus Christi play before 1376...What this chronology suggests, however, is that a multi-pageant Play cycle had already evolved by 1376 and that large numbers of craft gilds had come into existence within a decade or so of that date.²⁷

Disputing arguments that the cycle was imposed upon the craft guilds,[28] Goldberg argues that the plays enacted the very notion of a "gild ethos" that craftsmen were trying to promote—that "gild values and godly values are inextricably combined."[29] Sarah Beckwith similarly posits that the York pageants offered an "artisanal ideology" that linked the cycle's sacred moments to craft labor.[30] In addition, the craftsmen were equally committed to integrating themselves into York's social fabric in the form of acceptable self-governing guild units. One way to accomplish this was to convince those outside the artisanal classes that the guild system contributed positively to the city as a whole; the cycle performance may have promoted this message by enacting and thus giving material form to these new social relationships and structures.

The 1399 *A/Y* entry that first lists the cycle stations indicates that it was the Commons who asked civic leaders ("the honourable men, the mayor and aldermen of the city of York") to regulate the cycle more formally, in particular by limiting all playing except at those stations "assigned by you and by the aforesaid commons previously."[31] Until 1517, "les Comunes," the largest of the three civic councils in York, was composed of forty-eight members drawn from the crafts, and appears to have represented the interests of the craft guilds.[32] The guilds may have believed that a codified route would help demonstrate that the guild structure provided social order and promoted decorum, functions that benefited the mayor, the senior councils, and the city as a whole. As with funeral rituals, a well-ordered processional cycle would embody the very stability and control that the craft members argued a self-governing guild structure supplied, conveying those benefits to spectators rhythmically as well as visually. At this moment in York's history, when the guild system was relatively new, it was to the crafts' advantage to present pageants that were embodiments of order, decorum, and self-discipline. Both their content and their well-executed presentation generated a sacred blend of guild and godly values, which the cycle's spectators could consequently experience and live in.

In the 1486 royal entry, Henry's status as king is essential to how the event functions. The same is true of the guild members; for the guild/godly blend to work successfully, the craftsmen's "real life" identities must remain active even as they enact the sacred characters. The goals of most of York's performance events required spectators to keep aspects of the present medieval frame activated within the blend. There are many kinds of integration networks that humans create through conceptual blending, but the most sophisticated and generative are double-scope networks; theatre requires spectators to develop advanced double-scope blends. According to Fauconnier and Turner, in double-scope networks "both organizing frames make central contributions to the blend, and their sharp differences offer the possibility of rich clashes. Far from blocking the construction of the network, such clashes offer challenges to the imagination; indeed, the resulting blends can be highly creative."[33] For example, the metaphor "digging your own grave" is a double-scope blend of the "digging the grave" and "unwitting failure" inputs. In order to make sense of and use this network, we must translate information back and forth between the two inputs, and also from the blend back into the inputs: "[The blend] inherits the concrete structure of graves, digging, and burial, from the 'digging the grave' input. But it inherits causal, intentional, and internal event structure from the 'unwitting failure' input. The two inputs are not simply juxtaposed. Rather, emergent structure specific to the blend is created."[34] What initially might seem like a fragile relationship between two widely unrelated inputs can, according to Fauconnier and Turner, result in double-scope networks that generate "extraordinarily rich emergent meaning."[35]

When watching a play, spectators do not necessarily lose their frame in the real world entirely, but instead oscillate between that frame and the performance event's frame. Which of these frames spectators choose to project—consciously or unconsciously—into the moment-to-moment blend will transform how they understand that performance's meaning. During many theatrical events, the real physical-world frame is oftentimes suppressed. For example, Fauconnier and Turner describe how spectators do not project many aspects of their existence at a play into the blend, such as the physical reality of sitting in a seat in a darkened theatre surrounded by other people. Furthermore, they note that during a play spectators usually must inhibit certain typical physical responses, including their motor and speech powers, and the desire to respond to what they see.[36] But most of York's public performance events, in particular its Corpus Christi cycle, did not require this same level of inhibition or suppression. In fact, the York cycle was an outdoor event that placed spectators in city streets standing or sitting alongside other bodies in crowds, often exposed to the elements, and perhaps responding verbally to the characters' actions, all physical realities that—at particular moments—worked to heighten and reinforce the blend. In addition, while the wagons created some distinction between playing space and audience space, the extant pageant texts suggest that there were degrees of fluidity between these zones, with actors sometimes moving through the audience.[37] Fauconnier and Turner indicate that "As long as our perceptual and sensory systems are working properly, it is almost impossible for consciousness to see outside the blend of cause and effect."[38] In various ways, the York cycle's dramatic structure, staging conventions, and surrounding performance conditions, all directly engaged a large range of the spectator's perceptual and sensual inputs, and consequently may have more powerfully situated spectators inside blends than do other kinds of performance events.

Moreover, these characteristics also helped keep the medieval frame active during the spectator's moment-to-moment performance encounter. Notably, Bruce McConachie points out that conceptual blending challenges our romantic notion of the "willing suspension of disbelief" by emphasizing the agency of theatrical spectatorship; rather than ignoring or eliminating inputs, conceptual blending requires the spectator to engage in "imaginative addition."[39] The anachronistic design choices and dialogue frequently used in York's public performances, as well as the rhythmic actuality of these events, encouraged spectators to add themselves into the past without losing their medieval reference point or frame. Spectators derived devotional meaning by situating their medieval present *inside* the blend.

Communities or individuals in York could manipulate the cycle's theatrical conventions and performance conditions in order to prompt blends that supported their personal interests. In particular, the cycle's dramatic structure offered multiple opportunities to reconfigure the spectator's rhythmic relationship with city space. In his work on memory and English medieval drama, Theodore K. Lerud demonstrates that the images in the York pageants were the kinds of "quick images" prescribed in medieval treatises on memory.[40] While ancient texts describe memory images as active, three-dimensional constructions or scenic tableaux,[41] medieval writers tended to infuse these mnemonic tableaux with even more activity. In his treatise *On Acquiring a Trained Memory*, Thomas Bradwardine, a fourteenth-century academic and cleric, maintains that a mental image "should have some other quality such as movement, that thus it may be commended to memory more effectively than through tranquility or repose."[42] One of his examples for memorizing the signs of the zodiac is quite violent:

> a woman may be placed before the bull as though laboring in birth, and in her uterus as if ripped open from her breast may be figured coming forth two most beautiful twins, playing with a horrible, intensely red crab, which holds captive the hand of one of the little ones and thus

compels him to weeping and such outward signs, the remaining child wondering yet nonetheless touching the crab in a childish way.[43]

This striking image moves through the zodiac as if it were a performed dramatic sequence. Laypeople learned to use these kinds of techniques for devotional purposes from preachers, who included instruction on mnemonic theory in their sermons.[44]

Like these mnemonic images, the York pageants, although staged on wagons narrow enough to navigate medieval streets, presented "activated" images of Biblical stories. For instance, *The Crucifixion* pageant creates vivid mental images as the soldiers describe pulling Christ's arms and nailing them to the cross. But it also provides a memorable living image when the soldiers finally raise the cross with Christ upon it. Likewise, *The Ascension* play seems highly static except for the moment when Christ physically ascends. Like images described in mnemonic texts or some of the devotional objects that laypeople used, such as alabaster sculptures, the pageants enlivened the pivotal or climactic moment in a play's episode in order to fulfill similar memorializing goals. But these live images also generated rhythms. Staging choices or elements such as direct address could be used to adjust or provoke the lived associations those rhythms embedded within spectators' bodies and, thus, how spectators derived devotional meaning from inside the blend.

For example, various lines spoken during the cycle assimilate the city of York into the historical or biblical places staged in the pageants. In the opening pageant, *The Fall of the Angels*, Deus pronounces how he will mould "A place full of abundance [plenté] to my liking [plesyng]" (1.12), and the medieval actor playing Deus may have gestured to the city during this line in order to strengthen this geographic association. During *The Creation*, as he is making the earth, Deus says,

> The firmament shall not move,
> But be an intermediate place, thus will I intend,
> Over all the world to stay in one place and remain suspended,
> And be there *two waters between*.
> (2.41–4; Emphasis mine)[45]

Much of York is geographically located between two waters—the rivers Ouse and Fosse. Thus, even as Deus describes his creation to the York audience using an allusion to the seas of Genesis, he simultaneously references this familiar topographic characteristic of the city itself. Again, the actor's gestures and gaze may have reinforced this association. The early plays in the cycle situate York at the very center of the action and, perhaps, propose a world created in its image.

Later pageants, especially those that cover the life and Passion of Christ, maintain this geographic assimilation, but with more emphasis placed upon the spectator's presence within it. As Amy Cook explains, linguistic choices are not isolated from perceptual experience. Rather, "The fact that the brain exploits sensory-motor neurons to understand abstract concepts or poetic language suggests that language makes us feel, not by communicating a final feeling-state, but by activating our own experience of that state."[46] Therefore, the dialogue used in these pageants may have activated the spatial blend on a neuronal level. In *The Temptation*, Diabolus says to Christ,

> For I have all this world to command,
> Tower and town, forest and field:
> If you will yield thine heart to me
> With words polite,
> Yet will I obediently be thy help
> And faithful friend.
> Behold now sir, and you shall see
> Various kingdoms and diverse country;
> All this will I give to thee
> For evermore,
> If you will fall and honor me
> As I said before.
> (22.145–56)[47]

As he offers Christ the world—both town and countryside—Diabolus instructs him to "behold" it. He tempts Christ with the world directly before them: the city and diocese of York. Many scholars have identified a similar conflation in *The Entry into Jerusalem* pageant; staging the Palm Sunday events in York's streets effectively transformed the city into another Jerusalem.[48] As in *The Temptation*, characters in *The Entry* pageant likely gazed out at York as they remarked upon the biblical setting, thereby verbally and gesturally fusing the two worlds into a single entity. Lines such as Christ's lament "I grieve, I sigh, I weep also / Jerusalem to look on thee" (25.470–1) reinforced this blend.[49]

These geographic assimilations operate effectively because stage space is constructed and experienced through bodies. Spectators not only mentally register the spatial associations made in the pageants, but, as a result of various cognitive responses, they also experience being-in-the-biblical-world. Many of the audience members understood the cycle as a living story that began in the past and continued through their own lives and into their futures; the worlds of the play and York are ultimately the same. This merging is critical to the cycle's salvation message: York *is* creation; York *is* the world that Diabolus offers Christ; York *is* the community that Christ mourns and saves. Therefore, the spectators must exist within the theatrical space. Stanton Garner, Jr. identifies the actual "as the currency of ludic exchange."[50] One of the most basic actualities of the York cycle was the spectator's physical presence at sacred events—in the stable at Christ's birth, in the crowds on Palm Sunday, at Christ's trial, at the foot of the cross—experiences triggered especially by the actors' presence. The plays allowed laypeople to live in a blend that merged the biblical past with the medieval present.[51] Living in this blend prompted spectators to construct meaning by means of their live, material bodies, bodies that arrived prepared for and open to the devotional possibilities offered by this kind of spatial fusion.

Manipulating Sacred Blends

Religious performances did not create sacred space simply by presenting religious imagery in front of homes and businesses; instead, these performance images penetrated the city rhythmically. As Simon Shepherd asserts, "senses of rhythm and space have bodily impact on audiences, and...such impact is part of the mechanism whereby theatre, through the theatricalised body, engages with its cultural context."[52] The cycle performance did more than represent civic space as a devotional site; the cycle's overall structure, which is predicated on notions of selection, grouping, and sequencing, used the city space to create a mnemonic landscape.[53] As a result, the cycle's rhythmic sense embedded within the spectator's embodied schema ways to "live in" a sacred blend of York that would continue to operate long after the moment-to-moment performance encounter ended.

Medieval mnemonic texts often recommended that people create a "locational memory system." As Mary Carruthers explains, this kind of system is "any scheme that establishes a set of ordered, clearly articulated, and readily recoverable background locations into which memory 'images' are consciously placed."[54] In his treatise on memory, Francesc Eiximenis, a fifteenth-century Catalan Franciscan, tells preachers to arrange their material in an orderly fashion and suggests different structures into which they might mentally place their images, including "in major roads and paths known to us, in anything that is straight and situated in an orderly way, in large and ornate homes, in the human body and its ordered members."[55] Eiximenis recommends using a familiar, existing order. By separating the Christian narrative into smaller, individually packaged units and processing these before the spectator's eyes, the York cycle operates under this same principle and ultimately creates a locational memory system.

Medieval writers conceptualized these memory systems as physical journeys. For example, Carruthers describes early monastic meditation as "initiated, oriented, and marked out especially by the schemes and tropes of Scripture. Like sites plotted on a map, these functioned cognitively as the 'stations' of the way, to be stopped at and stayed in mentally before continuing."[56] These journeys encouraged directed movement through a text, what Carruthers identifies as the ductus. She writes, "ductus is what we sometimes now call the flow of a composition...[I]t is the movement within and through a work's various parts."[57] As Eiximenis suggests, the cycle borrowed an existing order—York's street design—and impressed sacred stories onto it, with the pageants, rather than the spectator, journeying through the streets.[58] This structure visually fused images of Christian history with the stations themselves. But standing in a designated place to watch the cycle also generated powerful visceral links between that physical location and the performance's religious message. It is not altogether surprising then that, like the pageants themselves, the cycle's processional route was also aggressively regulated and contested.

Throughout its life, the York cycle followed the same basic route described in the first extant record of the pageant stations from 1399.[59] The pageant wagons assembled at Toft Green, an open public space next to the city's Dominican Friary located to the west of the River Ouse. The cycle began near Mickelgate bar at the gates of Holy Trinity Priory before progressing down Mickelgate, crossing the Ouse Bridge, and entering the city center. Here it continued through the most affluent areas of the city, along Coney Street, Stonegate, and Petergate, before concluding at the open market space called the Pavement, flanked by the churches of St. Crux and All Saints Pavement. Records, some dated prior to the 1399 list, suggest repeated efforts made by civic officials to prevent any deviation from the approved route. A 1394 *A/Y* entry reads, "it was agreed that all the pageants of Corpus Christi shall play in the places appointed from ancient times and not elsewhere, but just as they shall be prearranged by the mayor, the bailiffs, and their officers."[60] The punishment for failure to follow this instruction was payment of 6s. 8d. by the craft to the common purse.

In 1399, and throughout most of its fifteenth-century life, the cycle route consisted of twelve stations. During the sixteenth century, the number of stations grew to as many as seventeen, but the route followed the same streets through the city. Until it reached the Minster Gates, the cycle followed the same route as the Corpus Christi procession of the Eucharist. But while the Eucharistic procession then wrapped its way west to conclude at St. Leonard's Hospital, an ecclesiastical institution, the pageant cycle continued east toward the Pavement, a public, civic space. One characteristic of this path, still apparent today, is the number of stations situated in close proximity to parish churches. As table 4.1 demonstrates, the 1399 list suggests that as many as nine of the twelve stops were located near a parish church. I indicate in this table whether or not the church building is still extant or if its location is only suggested by records and

Table 4.1   Station locations of the Corpus Christi Cycle in York

	Station location as specified in 1399 A/Y Memorandum list	Parish church	Extant or suggested
1	Gates of Holy Trinity Priory	Holy Trinity Church	Extant
2	Robert Harpham's house	St. Gregory	Suggested
3	John de Gyseburn's door	St. Martin, Mickelgate	Extant
4	Skeldergate and North Street	St. John	Extant
5	End of Coney Street opposite Castlegate	St. Michael	Extant
6	End of Jubbergate in Coney Street	—	
7	Henry Wyman's door in Coney Street	St. Martin, Coney Street	Extant
8	End of Coney Street next to the Common Hall	St. Helen	Extant
9	Adam del Brigg's door	—	
10	Gates of the Minster of blessed Peter	Minster*	Extant
11	End of Girdlergate in Petergate	Holy Trinity, Colliergate	Suggested
12	On the Pavement	St. Crux and All Saints Pavement	Both extant

*I include the Minster in this list because cycle spectators would certainly have been conscious of the Minster towering in the background even though pageants were not performed directly before it. I would in fact argue that the cycle purposefully did not construct the same visual association with the Minster as it did with the parish churches.

archaeological evidence; most of these churches still stand today.⁶¹ The cycle's mnemonic possibilities are unmistakable.

As I have explained, the parish church played an important role in the life of the medieval laity since it formed the basis of one of the many communities of which each layperson counted himself or herself a member. Parish limits were geographic, which, as Gervase Rosser notes, did not usually lead to exclusivity within that community, although some parishes developed professional associations.⁶² For instance, many laypeople whose crafts contributed to the Minster's construction or upkeep lived in districts around the cathedral; the parishes of St. Helen and St. Michael-le-Belfry included a number of glaziers and masons. Therefore, degrees of professional association within a parish's identity might develop.

As a geographic force and place of worship, parish churches may have functioned as convenient locations for communities to gather and watch the Eucharistic procession on Corpus Christi day. The cycle may have initially used a similar route because it provided convenient audience clusters throughout the city; both events originally occurred on the same day.⁶³ However, the 1399 list suggests that, at least by this date, more was at stake with respect to where spectators gathered to watch the performance. This list specifies that four of the twelve stations were located before a particular person's door. As I noted in the introduction, I agree with Sarah Beckwith's suggestion that prominent citizens used the cycle's visual arrangement to inscribe themselves onto the pageant.⁶⁴ But these station designations may also reveal how one particular civic community employed the processional structure to promote its own agenda.

During the cycle performance, medieval spectators could "live in" the sacred world while physically standing at and gazing upon a specific city site. Such blending effectively "sacralized" that station and, perhaps also, sacralized those individuals associated with it. Julia A. Walker contends that theatre is devoted to oscillation because it offers us "a glimpse of the world as it can be imagined from an objective analytical viewpoint and an experience of the world as registered within our body's viscera in the form of an affective engagement that is very much in the moment and real."⁶⁵ The York cycle's tendency to conflate dramatic space and audience space may have privileged visceral experience and affective engagement over objective analysis. Furthermore, this privileging may have been tactically employed to encourage spectators to live in sacred blends that served certain interests.

The four individuals named in the 1399 list are Robert Harpham (second station, in Mickelgate), John de Gyseburn (third station, in

Mickelgate), Henry Wyman (seventh station, in Coney Street), and Adam del Brigg (ninth station, in Stonegate). All four men were members of the city's merchant elite with familial or social ties to the Mickelgate community. Although Mickelgate was the main street of southwestern York, its surrounding neighborhood was separated from the commercial center of the city by the river Ouse. Not until the fourteenth century did this area grow prosperous and become an affluent quarter of mercantile importance, due in large part to the wealthy noble and gentry families that moved there from the country.[66] Exemplifying this change, during the late fourteenth and fifteenth centuries a large collection of civic officials, including a number of mayors, lived in Mickelgate, among them Gyseburn (mayor from 1371 to 1373 and from 1379 to 1381) and Del Brigg (sheriff 1403). As Sarah Rees Jones and Felicity Riddy explain, the Mickelgate community, and particularly the late-fourteenth- and early-fifteenth-century mayors from that neighborhood, "took the lead in developing new forms of civic religion, such as the major city fraternities, and the civic regulation of public ritual in the city, including, most notably, the increasing civic control of the York mystery plays."[67] The cycle route, as recorded in 1399, may be evidence of this community's emergent authority when it came to civic enterprises.

This first extant station list emerges from an historical moment when people began interpreting wealth as a "reward for piety and hard work."[68] As Pamela King notes, the wealthy mercantile elite of this period had to negotiate "the spectre of usury" associated with their profession, and often used money "to smooth over the anomalous relationship between commercial activity and their spiritual aspirations."[69] This changing interpretation of wealth is reflected in the late medieval "semantic shift in the word charity from the Latin sense, *caritas*, altruistic love, to the modern vernacular, essentially post-capitalist, sense of altruistic expenditure of cash."[70] I interpret affixing the identities of prominent citizens from, or associated with, Mickelgate to the cycle stations as an effort by the "new" merchant elite living in Mickelgate to associate themselves—and their wealth—with pious practices visually, and thereby to incorporate Mickelgate more completely into the devotional landscape of York. Performance transformed these visual associations into experiential ones; "living in" the world of Mickelgate and living in the sacred world merge (consciously or not) into a single pattern within the spectator's embodied schema.

The cycle's design encouraged religious experience and city space to unite within the seeing body. Simon Shepherd argues that "bodily effects in theatre presumably flow from the placing of performance attendance in relation to the rest of daily life."[71] Performing religious plays in the midst of houses, businesses, and the people of everyday life produced bodily effects that traced certain spiritual feelings and religious associations into the spectator's embodied schema. In the months between cycle performances, these feelings and associations—both patterns *of* seeing and patterns *for* seeing—may have influenced how that spectator subsequently understood or interacted with certain areas of the city, such as Mickelgate, and with those who lived and worked in them.

The cycle was a powerful tool for generating such patterns because it interacted with the spectator on many different perceptual fronts; performances encourage and then sustain blends sensually. In the previous chapter, I suggested that other spaces that York's laity inhabited and used may have functioned similarly. When filled with devotional ornamentations, parish churches and homes also generated rhythmic patterns of piety and, like a performance, may have sensually triggered those who entered them to "live in" sacred blends. As with the cycle, these blends may have fused secular and sacred interests—if those are ever distinguishable in York's late medieval community. For example, by claiming the domestic space, an alabaster allowed its inhabitants to live in a sacralized home and, if the sculpture depicted a scene in the York cycle that corresponded to that family's craft association, perhaps also to live in a blend of guild and godly values. Likewise, when in the days after an individual's death that person's parish church was filled with memorial images, objects, candles, torches, prayers, bell-ringing, and other rituals, those who worshipped in the space may have lived in a double-scope blend. As the deceased individual's "presence"—like a performance—engaged worshippers through a wide range of perceptual and sensual inputs, his or her identity may have overwhelmed the blend, thereby reframing the worshippers' devotional intentions, needs, thoughts, and actions in that space in relation to the deceased's identity. Devotional books offered laypeople yet another opportunity to reconfigure religious meaning by means of rhythmic encounters. I interpret the Book of Hours as a pious space in which laypeople could exert their devotional agency materially and thereby foster specific sacred blends.

The Book of Hours: A Sensual Performance Space

The Book of Hours came into use in England in the late thirteenth century and functioned as a prayer book for the laity. According to

Jeremy Goldberg, testamentary evidence shows that Books of Hours became increasingly popular during the fifteenth century and were by far the most common service or devotional books that laypeople owned and the only books that regularly appear in the wills of artisans.[72] Goldberg's survey of registered wills from York dated between 1321 and 1500 reveals that Books of Hours—also called primers— account for a high proportion of all texts mentioned.[73] Less complex versions of breviaries and Psalters, these books are organized around the hours of the Virgin and usually begin with a calendar of saints' and feast days, followed by prayers to the Virgin and saints, the seven Penitential psalms, the Office of the Dead, and other liturgical offices.[74] Certain prayers, such as those directed to the Virgin or those said at the Elevation of the Host, often appear in the vernacular. Although many primers follow this model, until they were printed the general textual content was not standardized, and owners often personalized them in any number of ways based upon individual desires.[75] Consequently, although Books of Hours were often employed as part of institutionalized rituals in public spaces such as churches, they constitute devotional objects over which laypeople exercised a large degree of individualized control, especially in respect to their material design.[76]

As with alabaster sculptures, a medieval manuscript's devotional materiality only becomes apparent during live encounters. The gilded edges of the folios and the gold leaf of the illuminations do not sit on the page like reproduced images in modern books; instead, these elements impart a three-dimensional quality that moves out to the reader/user. Books were often made from parchment, animal skin that had been defleshed, stretched, and scraped smooth, and this material invests both texts and images with a fleshy presence. I propose that a Book of Hours constitutes a rhythmic site in which its users can encounter people and experiences, thereby prompting users to understand the book's sacred contents by means of living inside blends. A manuscript's material qualities shaped these encounters; therefore, physically altering a book influenced its rhythmic, perceptual potential.

Alterations are evident in a large percentage of lay devotional books. Eamon Duffy notes that of the three hundred Books of Hours in the Bibliothèque Nationale in Paris almost half have some type of annotation or addition, and that English owners quite commonly annotated their books. Although sometimes minor, these changes often involved adding devotional material, such as inscribed prayers or inserted images.[77] One book from York, commonly known as the

Pavement Hours, supplies us with a compelling example of this kind of devotional materiality. The Pavement Hours (York Minster Library Manuscript XVI.K.6; *ca*.1420) measures 215 x 162 mm, with writing space of approximately 150 x 108 mm.[78] The book contains thirty-seven pages with border decorations, two original large-scale miniatures, and twenty-nine historiated initials. It shows evidence of local use in such inclusions as a prayer to Richard Scrope and dedications in its calendar to the relics of York Minster and the Church of All Saints Pavement in York—incidentally, the location of the Corpus Christi cycle's final performance station. In addition, as Amelia Adams notes, the manuscript's original construction suggests an urge for personal adaptation, since a number of folios at the end of each gathering were originally left blank, presumably to accommodate later embellishments.[79] Some of these pages now contain texts and prayers added during the fifteenth century, while others remain bare. Besides textual additions, eight images were inserted into the manuscript, most of them sewn onto the top edges of folios and usually covering texts (see figure 4.1).[80] When only considered for their subject or iconographic content, most of the insertions do not relate obviously to the matter over which they were placed. However, as with York's pageants or objects donated to statues, I interpret this visual layering as prompting the book's users to slip into and out of different viewing positions, and, thus, to live in multiple sacred blends.

Throughout my analysis of the Pavement Hours I will use the pronoun "she" for convenience only. In fact, I suspect that many different people of both sexes used this book, a claim that scholars have made in respect to other Books of Hours.[81] People other than those who originally added these images also likely used the Pavement Hours, and this fact allows us to consider how the book accumulated layers of meaning over time.

The first insertions in the Pavement Hours occur as a cluster (see figure 4.2). A sixteen-line-high image of Saint Clare is sewn across the top margin of folio 26v, thereby placing it over the final folio of the prayer *Salve plaga lateris* and facing the beginning of the prayer said at the Elevation of the Host. Inserted between folios 26 and 27 is a large leaf, almost the size of a full folio, which contains an image of Saints Anthony, George, and Roch. Adams notes that this grouping of saints is uncommon and was most likely commissioned to reflect the personal desires of the owner.[82] The third insertion in this cluster—a small, three-line-high monogram of Jesus, an IHC enclosed in a heart—appears on folio 27r where it is sewn in place of the opening letter of the prayer recited at the Elevation of the Host.

DEVOTION AND CONCEPTUAL BLENDING 107

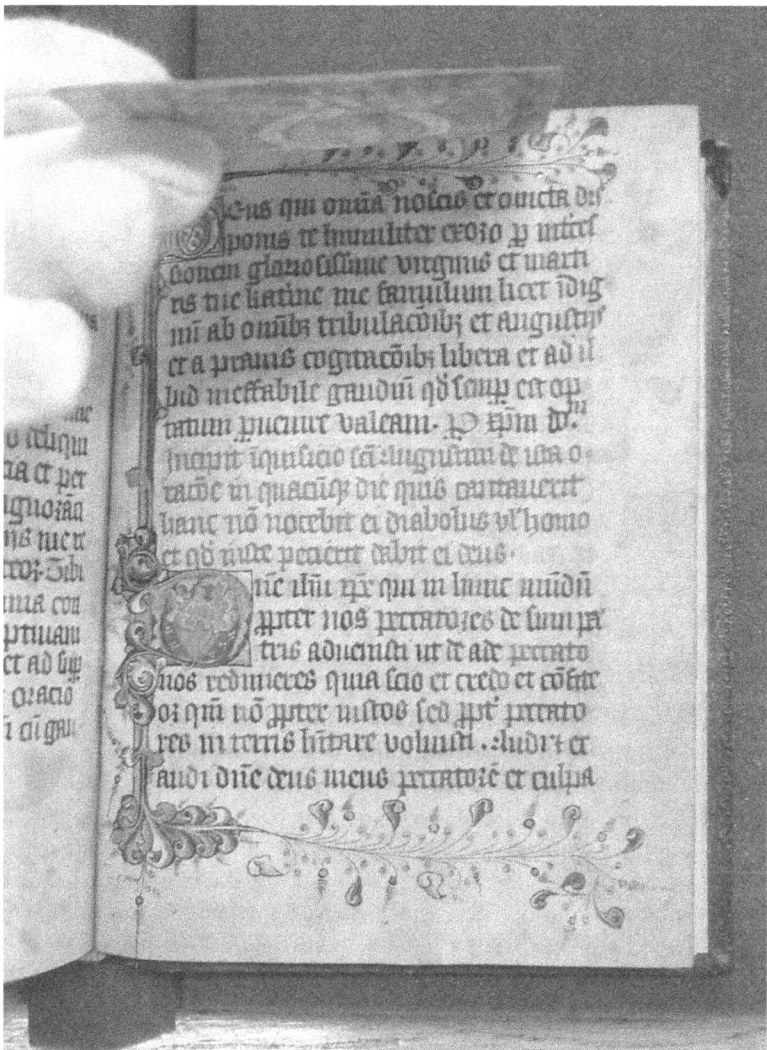

Figure 4.1 Lifting Face of Christ insertion, folio 94r, *Pavement Hours* (*ca.* 1420). York Minster Library, York, England.

This is the only insertion completely sewn into the manuscript and integrated into the existing design of a page.

These insertions appear at the moment in the liturgy that was most important to the layperson, the Elevation of the Host, suggesting that the owner felt the need to inscribe or mark this moment materially

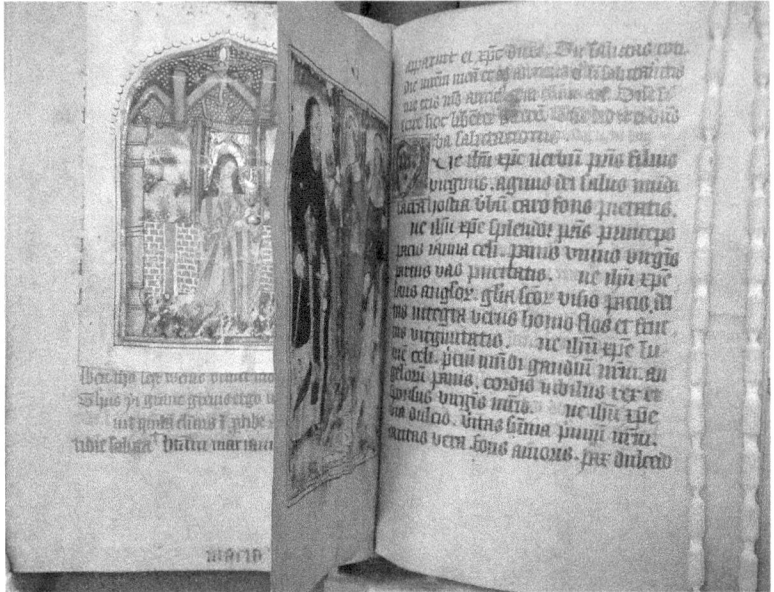

Figure 4.2 Folio spread of St. Clare, three male saints, and IHC insertions, fols. 26v–27, *Pavement Hours* (ca. 1420). York Minster Library, York, England.

as part of her pious practices. Although, as Adams points out, Saint Clare was often associated with the Host because she composed a prayer to the five wounds of Christ and was particularly devoted to the veneration of the Passion, the trio of male saints is not obviously related to this liturgical moment.[83] By marking the Elevation with an image that she found efficacious in her particular devotional life, the manuscript's owner structured this pivotal liturgical moment as a personal visual and material encounter, a tactic consonant with the late medieval laity's desire for live visual presence at the liturgical Elevation.

Most of the other insertions occur in isolation. A female saint holding a book and accompanied by a small animal is sewn into the top of folio 106r, covering seven lines of a prayer to God the Son that also appears on folios 83v–84r (see figure 4.3). Nobody has positively identified the subject of this image, though Adams posits that the animal is a lamb and the saint Agnes. The image's border pattern, different from the manuscript's decorative scheme, may indicate that it was purchased loose from a disassembled manuscript.[84] An insertion of Saint Christopher carrying the Christ Child appears close by,

Figure 4.3 Unidentified female saint insertion, folio 106r, *Pavement Hours* (ca. 1420). York Minster Library, York, England.

sewn across the top margin of folio 108r and over the prayer said at daybreak.

By placing these images over texts, the owner of the Pavement Hours does not reduce the text's value or erase it from the devotional encounter; instead, this act embellishes the textual content with associations and possibilities. Like items donated to statues, these insertions require viewers to navigate and hold in their minds multiple layers of meaning at once. The manuscript invites users to lift and lower images literally and thereby lift and lower ways of devotional seeing. In addition, as with clothing and jewelry donated to religious statues, these insertions establish material presence at specific sacred sites. Images appear throughout the Pavement Hours as part of its original construction, but the book's owner(s) purposefully placed these additions—which potentially interrupt the book's use—at specific textual or liturgical sites. In part, the insertions may have functioned as bookmarks or placeholders so that users could access meaningful places in the book quickly; the cluster at the Elevation prayer likely functioned in this way. Likewise, the unidentified female saint image might signal the significance of the prayer over which it was sewn. Its placement over the second and later copy of the prayer in the manuscript may also suggest that this version was used as the primary one.[85] The image highlights the prayer's value by tangibly inscribing it with material evidence of its past and present use.

The image of Saint Christopher carrying the Christ Child might function similarly. Christopher was a common subject of wall paintings and stained glass, and similar depictions are found in York's parish churches, such as All Saints Pavement and Holy Trinity Goodramgate. As with the female saint insertion, Adams argues that the different border style suggests that the image was purchased from a vendor. Christopher was considered the protector of travelers and therefore had particular resonance for merchants involved in seafaring expeditions. If such a merchant used this Book of Hours, he likely felt a special relationship with, and need to frequently turn to, both Christopher and the prayer that his image earmarks.

More fundamentally, these images may also materially insert the book's owner(s) into the blends of specific devotional moments and therefore into a subsequent user's experience in those blends. If purchased by or for a female user, the image of the female saint holding a book mirrors the reader herself and thereby sews her physical presence into the book's pages. If another of the manuscript's users was a merchant, the image of Saint Christopher stitched his profession—and therefore his identity—into a devotional context. The images of Saint Clare and of the three Saints placed at the Elevation accomplish the same thing. These insertions not only draw attention to specific prayers, but they also literally thread the book's owner into each prayer's use. The insertions give the lay owner perpetual physical presence at specific moments of prayer, as well as presence in the blends of worship that subsequent users of this book constructed and lived in.

The materiality—and, more specifically, the tactility—of these insertions are critical to how they actualized that presence. Alice Rayner argues that once staged in a theatre or a museum, objects are no longer identical to themselves, and their function is, in part, located in their real, tangible status, which marks their "disappearance from time past as well as their persistence into the present. In their double nature they are uncanny because one wonders about their reality even as they give sensory testimony."[86] Rayner uses Susan Stewart's analysis of the souvenir to explore this dual nature further. According to Stewart, souvenirs function as "traces of authentic experience...We do not need or desire souvenirs of events that are repeatable. Rather, we need and desire souvenirs of events that are reportable, events whose materiality has escaped us, events that thereby exist only through the invention of narrative."[87] As tangible images "staged" within a manuscript and containing the material traces of past experiences and identities, the Pavement Hours insertions function like souvenirs.

Two Passion insertions offer clear illustrations of how these "souvenirs" might generate layers of nonrepresentational meaning. The first is a fifteen-line-high printed image of the *Arma Christi* sewn along the top margin of folio 44v and over the last folio of the Gradual Psalms, which pilgrims often recited while traveling to Jerusalem (see figure 4.4). The accompanying text indicates that this image functioned as an indulgence granting 6,755 years off from Purgatory: "who sum euer deuoutely behoildith these armys of criste haith vi^m vii^c lv yer per-."[88] The other image, a narrative scene of Christ before Pilate, is sewn along the top of folio 45r, facing the *Arma Christi* and overlaying the opening folio of the Psalms of the Passion. That these insertions may have been acquired as pilgrimage souvenirs is suggested by the text on the *Arma Christi*, their placement at the Gradual Psalms, and their recycled parchment.

If these are indeed pilgrimage tokens, then they stand in place of—or ghost—the pilgrim, and their juxtaposition against the Psalms signifies the pilgrimage journey visually.[89] But these insertions not only alter the manuscript's visual program, they also reshape its rhythmic program; they ghost sensually as well. Using the book now occurs through and with the insertions and by extension the bodies to which these give tangible presence. The manuscript's devotional program has been reoriented in relation to that presence, with various sacred connotations and associations accumulating around and through it. Ultimately, the insertions integrate the pilgrim into the book's sacred rhythms.

Figure 4.4 Arma Christi insertion, folio 44v, *Pavement Hours* (*ca.* 1420). York Minster Library, York, England.

Mark Amsler describes a manuscript's material page as the "hinge of reading" that connected reader and text.[90] He suggests that the ways in which medieval laypeople manipulated a book's pages represented "strategies of medieval literate technology."[91] Sewing images into a book represents this kind of strategizing; insertions allowed the manuscript's owners to include themselves within sacred moments and, in so doing, to create blends that would continue to function when subsequent readers/users engaged them. As with other devotional items, the value of this manuscript is located not only in its representational elements, but is also found in the rhythmic encounters that took place between book and spectator.

Readers/users could physically manipulate the Pavement Hours insertions; however, even when they only looked at these insertions, never literally touching them, their encounters with these fleshy images were still sensual in nature. As I have argued with respect to other images and objects, regardless of what the user does physically to the insertion, it reaches out to her rhythmically.[92] Adams suggests that the Pavement Hours insertions "form an independent meditational focus" that, although related to the texts, ultimately drew attention and interest away from the textual elements.[93] Alternatively, I propose that these images engage the reader's/user's body in the textual contents more deeply and completely, by conveying rhythms that encourage users to interpret the book's devotional program through their bodies. They allow the manuscript's users to live in, and derive meaning from inside, blends that sustained the memories of previous owners/users of the book. Here, again, I see performance literacy operating. In the next chapter, I turn my attention to bodies in order to discuss the opportunities that arise when similar rhythmic encounters take place between live bodies in performance, and to suggest how these experiences may have impacted medieval lay visual piety.

Chapter Five

Pious Body Rhythms

York's Corpus Christi pageants functioned as material anchors, supplying spectators with both concrete images and concrete experiences of the Christian narrative and its abstract theological concepts.[1] But in addition to offering the audience an opportunity to see and, perhaps, "live in" these sacred images, the cycle also presented vision itself as a primary means of experiencing divine presence and power. In fact, by enacting for its audience some of the very same moments of visual piety in which those spectators were actively engaged, the cycle actualized not only religious images but also the act of religious seeing. In doing so, the cycle instructed its audience in "proper" ways to look at, and respond physically to, visual encounters with the divine.

Visual Anticipation in the York Cycle

Words associated with vision are ubiquitous in York's pageants, particularly in reference to Christ. For instance, *The Purification* uses visual metaphors to dramatize Symeon's desire to see Jesus and his joy when this finally happens. Symeon repeatedly proclaims his intense hope to "see that babe so bright" [se that babb so bright] (17.133).[2] Evidence of God's action or Christ's divinity frequently takes the form of light or brightness. When Jesus is brought to the Temple he is described as a "bright star that shines bright as day" [bright starne that shyneth bright as day] and "the blessed beam so bright" [the blyssed beam so bryght] (17.326; 328). In *The Nativity*, a light "that comes shining thus suddenly" [þat comes shynyng þus sodenly] (14.79) indicates to Joseph that Christ has been born. In *The Agony in the Garden and the Betrayal*, the soldiers have difficulty seeing Christ because they "are lost due to the brightness of this light" [are loste for leme of þis light] (28.258). One soldier threatens Christ by saying, "I will no more be frightened by the radiance of your countenance" [I will no more be abasshed for blenke of thy blee] (28.263). These lines may suggest that costuming or make-up, such as a mask painted gold, were used to highlight the sacred nature of visual encounters with Christ and to differentiate him from other mortal characters.[3]

Christ also uses visual terms when describing himself. In *The Baptism*, he calls himself a "mirror" [myrroure] for men and says that he must fulfill righteousness not only "in word but also in deed" [in worde but also in dede] (21.93; 130). This metaphor, or something similar, recurs in other York pageants, such as *The Temptation* ("their mirror may they make of me" [þare myrroure may þei make of me], 22.195) and *The Last Supper* ("Example of me ye shall take / Forever to heed in youth or old age" [Ensaumple of me take ȝe schall, / Euer for to ȝeme in ȝouþe and elde], 27.65–6). In *The Transfiguration*, not only do the words "seeing" and "sight" recur, but those who witness the Transfiguration describe it as an intense visual experience: "this brightness made me blind" [þis brightnes made me blynde] (23.191); "that cloud stunned us completely, / that came shining so radiantly, / Such a sight was never seen" [þat clowde cloumsed vs clene, / þat come schynand so clere, / Such syght was never sene] (201–3). Significantly, this pageant situates the cycle's medieval spectators as privileged visual witnesses alongside the disciples. Such witnessing also occurs in *The Baptism*; the angels tell John that during Christ's baptism,

> The heavens shall then be open,
> The holy ghost shall be sent down
> To be seen,
> The father's voice with great force
> Will be heard outright.
> (21.66–70)[4]

Some visible sign of the Holy Spirit may have accompanied the baptism, such as a dove, which often appears in iconography of the period. In *The Women Taken in Adultery/The Raising of Lazarus*, the audience witnesses the miracle of Lazarus raised from the dead, and the play ends with Jesus announcing that "those who have seen this sight / My blessing be with you" (24.208–9).[5] The language in these pageants implies that, like the characters, the spectators are participating in pious visual encounters.

Yet, the cycle does more than allow the audience to gaze upon enlivened images of biblical events. York's pageants also create scenarios that enhance visual piety. For instance, in *The Transfiguration* the medieval audience may actually see more of the biblical event than do the dramatized disciples. Although the disciples describe some visual elements—"His clothing is as white as snow / His face shines as the sun" (23.97–8)—they also remark upon their physical inability to see everything that has happened.[6] James says, "this brightness made me blind" (23.191), while Peter exclaims:

> Brother, whatever is that brightness?
> Such marvel was never before seen.
> It impairs my ability, I may not see,
> Such wondrous thing was never seen.
> (23.85–8)[7]

When Christ asks the characters to recount what they have seen, thereby indicating that their vision is a worthy record, they admit that they could not see every part of the event, in particular the face of God—"Ah, lord, why do you not let us see / Thy father's face in his splendor?" (23.217–18).[8] Jesus explains that to see God's face is to ask "over-grete degree" and they have not been granted "that grace" (23.219–20).

These lines complicate how we define the medieval spectator as visual participant in this play. A later scribal hand, interpolating stage directions into the play's text, designates God as "Father on a cloud" [Pater in nube] and indicates that clouds descended ("Hic descendunt nubes"). Admittedly, these notes may not accurately reflect the staging of the play, nor clarify for us exactly what the medieval audience saw. Perhaps, as suggested earlier, God appeared with a painted face or wearing a gilded mask. Regardless, whether or not the medieval audience saw a representation of God or his face, it seems likely that they were situated as privileged witnesses who saw more of the sacred event than did the disciples, who describe their own obstructed seeing. This juxtaposition likely intensified the spectator's visual encounter.

The pageants also create for the audience moments of visual anticipation. The expectation of Christ's presence onstage is particularly central to the pageant series that begins with *The Entry into Jerusalem* and ends with *The Ascension*. *The Entry* oscillates between a scene with Christ and a scene between the Porter and Burgesses. These men recount Christ's miracles and the Old Testament prophecies about a redeemer: "What prophets said in their proverbs, / All pertains to him" (25.153–4).[9] During the next hundred or more lines, these men grow increasingly eager to meet and see Christ: "For I desire to see him eagerly / And to honor him as his own man. / Since the truth I see" (25.220–2); "I long for him with fervent will / To see once, / I think from thence forth I shall / a better man be" (25.256–9).[10] The men express a physical desire to witness Christ's entry, a desire that comes to a head in the character Zaché, who climbs a tree in his desperation to see Christ pass by. Significantly, all these characters believe that seeing Christ will make them better people, implicitly acknowledging the visual encounter's sacred nature and transformative power.

By carefully controlling Christ's absence and presence onstage, the cycle cultivates an anticipatory devotional gaze among its spectators. As Christ is brought before a series of characters, care is taken in each scene either to place Christ before the eyes of the pageant's spectators or to keep him out of view. For instance, during the first 166 lines of *Christ Before Herod*, Herod expresses delight that he will finally see the famous prophet. Christ is not actually brought onstage until this anticipation has built to a climax, with Herod exclaiming, "Oh, my heart leaps for joy / To see now this prophet appear" (31.163–4).[11] *The Crucifixion* is perhaps the pageant that uses visual anticipation most effectively, with a dramatic sequence of approximately 65 lines in which the soldiers repeatedly attempt to lift Christ on the cross. This scene is particularly sophisticated in the way it orients the devotional gaze. The dramatic moment replicates the Elevation of the Host, a pivotal visual encounter in the lives of the late medieval laity, and the play's creators exploit this dramatic moment's devotional and dramatic potential by drawing out the experience for spectators. Moreover, during performances actors might prolong the anticipation by controlling changes in tempo.

Yet it is not simply the sight of Christ, but also his physical body, that characters, and thus the audience, anticipate. Like most theatrical performances, York's cycle is fundamentally theatre "of the body"—it is comprised of bodies and revolves around the display of bodies (in this case, Christ's body particularly). But the cycle was also staged as part of the Corpus Christi ("Body of Christ") event, and the language used in the pageants helps emphasize this fact, as well as foreground the body state shared by both the biblical characters/live actors and the audience members. Words such as "body" and "flesh" recur throughout the pageants. This vocabulary pattern begins in *The Fall of the Angels* when the character Deus opens the cycle with a lengthy speech in which he announces:

> I am gracious and great, God without beginning,
> I am maker unmade, all power is in me;

> I am life and the way unto salvation,
> I am foremost and first, as I bid shall it be.
> My blessing of my countenance shall be dazzling,
> And pouring forth, from harm to be protecting,
> *My body* in bliss abides forever,
> Endlessly, without any ending.
> (1.1–8; Emphasis mine)[12]

In this description of God as supernatural being—without beginning, maker unmade, the life and way to salvation—Deus places himself in a fleshy body, which remains in bliss without end.

Remarks about the bodied nature of the characters are used most frequently in reference to the Virgin Mary and Christ. In *The Annunciation and the Visitation*, the Angel tells Mary that "In chastity of thy body / Conceive and bear a child you shall" (12.157–8),[13] and Elizabeth refers to "the fruit [frute] of thy body" (12.207); the language focuses attention on Mary's fleshiness. In the play *Joseph's Trouble about Mary*, Mary's body becomes a site of contestation and contradiction.[14] This body reveals Mary's pregnancy to Joseph—"Thy womb is grown large, I think / You are with child" (13.95–6); "Her sides show that she is with child" (13.102)[15]—even as it attests to her chastity. The waiting women assert Mary's purity by saying:

> For truly no man ever came near her
> To shame her with evil *the body*
> Of this sweet person,
> For we have dwelt with her all the time
> And were never away from her day or night.
> Her keepers have we been
> And she always in our sight,
> Come no man between us
> *To touch that lady* so splendid.
> (13.114–22; Emphasis mine)[16]

Mary's physical body is undoubtedly chaste and without sexual stain, and the waiting women's surveillance corroborates this fact.[17] This emphasis on watching Mary's body may have served to ease cultural anxieties regarding Christ's conception. Likewise, in the pageant *The Nativity*, Christ's birth is staged virtually as a speech act:

> Now in my soul I have great joy,
> I am all clad in glorious comfort,
> *Now will be born of my body*
> *Both God and man together*

> Blessed must he be.
> Jesus my son that is so dear,
> Now born is he.
> (14.50–56; Emphasis mine)[18]

Once Christ enters the scene, he becomes a physical presence alongside Mary's own visible, present body.

York's pageants reinforce Christ's significance as an embodied image in various ways. Silence is used as a particularly powerful tactic. During the Passion pageants, characters repeatedly recount Christ's words, but as a dramatic figure onstage he remains largely silent. This choice underscores the importance of Christ's present, physical body as a devotional image. Those who interrogate Christ during the trial scenes want him to speak and incriminate himself, but his silence forces them to base their judgments solely upon his physical presence.[19] Alexandra F. Johnston points out that "At the centre of the play the Word falls silent," and she concludes that the York playwright(s) "exploited the concept of logos" and, by doing so, portrayed the Word as a silent, still center in contrast to the deceitful speech of Christ's interrogators.[20] However, although Christ is verbally silent, he is neither dramatically absent nor theatrically silent; Christ's physical body exudes rhythmic power whenever it appears onstage. Consequently, his silence may encourage viewers to engage those rhythms by means of performance literacy.

Characters onstage supplied the medieval audience with different examples of how to respond (appropriately and inappropriately) to this silent Corpus Christi. Three pageants in particular—*Christ Before Pilate I: The Dream of Pilate's Wife*, *Christ Before Herod*, and *Christ Before Pilate II: The Judgment*—present physical reactions to Christ's body as pivotal dramatic moments. When Christ is first brought before Pilate, the servant Bedellus, presented as exceptionally worthy and honest during the pageant, models proper devotional gestures. When ordered to fetch Christ, Bedellus replies,

> But first shall I honor you with mind and with will.
> This reverence I do you therefore,
> For people who were wiser than I,
> They honored you completely on high
> And with solemnity sang Hosanna to you.
> (30.311–15)[21]

The soldiers describe how, either during or after his lines, Bedellus honored Christ by means of devotional gestures: "this boy here before you full boldly was bowing / To honor [worshippe] this scoundrel" (30.318–19); "in your presence he prayed him of peace, / In kneeling on knees to this knave / He prayed him his servant to save" (30.320–2).[22] It is not simply Bedellus's pious words that the soldiers and high priests find offensive, but also the accompanying pious gestures that Bedellus directs toward Christ's present body.

Medieval spectators probably recognized Bedellus's actions as piety since they seem to duplicate devotional gestures common among the late medieval laity. The heresy trial of Margery Baxter of Norwich offers insight into the physical rituals that English laypeople used in parish churches. Although trial records are not always reliable sources, this document likely offers relatively accurate information about orthodox devotional activity. During the trial, Joan Clyfland recounted a conversation that she and two other women had with Margery:

> This witness then says that Margery asked her what she did in church every day. And she replied to her saying that first after her entrance into church, kneeling before the cross, she was accustomed to say five Paternosters in honour of the cross and the whole Ave Maria in honour of the Blessed Mary, mother of Christ.[23]

These rituals echo those that Reginald Pecock defends in his *Repressor of Over Much Blaming of the Clergy*. Describing laypeople's use of sacred images, Pecock writes that they "kneel before them, or pray before them, or cense before them, or set lights or lamps before them, or hold or bear [holde or bere] any such commemorative signs before them."[24] Similarly, Christ's live presence inspires Bedellus to kneel and pray. In addition, Bedellus describes how people of both high and low rank also responded physically to Christ's presence on Palm Sunday by running to him and calling "Hosanna, son of David."

Looking at Christ also prompts appropriate emotional responses from certain characters. *Christ Before Annas and Caiaphas*, which dramatizes Peter's denial of Christ, reinforces the potency of Christ's visible body. After his third denial, Peter sees Christ and says, "The look of his fair face so clear / With great sad sorrow shears my heart" (29.168–9).[25] Here, Christ's presence triggers an emotional gesture of self-examination, and the moment communicates a similar message as Bedellus's physical gestures: Christ's present body can induce appropriate devotional reactions. When Bedellus and Peter see Christ with their eyes, their bodies respond instinctively.

The pageant *Christ Before Herod* explores proper devotional gestures from a different angle. After a lengthy set-up, Christ is brought before Herod and told to "Kneel down here to the king on thy knee" (31.177).[26] When he does not comply, Herod accuses Christ of treating him without proper respect. Christ not only maintains this refusal to kneel, but also a refusal to speak. This aggravates Herod and his associates, who repeatedly ask Christ if he is crazy. The silence grows so frustrating that Herod and his courtiers begin to attack Christ's body in an attempt to control him. This is one of numerous instances in the cycle when authority figures, recognizing (and feeling threatened by) the power of Christ's body, try to suppress or manipulate its meaning through force.[27] In this example, Christ's body is dressed in white, which is said to befit "a deranged" [fonned] lad (31.351). This play may be modeling the refusal to perform devotional acts before profane images, while also reinforcing the idea that Christ's body is a visible symbol of power that others cannot fully control.

Christ's encounter with Pilate in *Christ Before Pilate II: The Judgment* maintains these themes. When Christ is onstage during this pageant, he is again mostly silent. This silence not only situates his body as the object of Pilate's and the Jewish high priests' scorn and anxiety, but also as the focus for the medieval spectator's devotional gaze. And yet, during this play, Annas and Caiaphas repeatedly try to persuade Pilate that Christ is a threat because of his dangerous language. In their own verbose tirades, the priests mention Christ's "speakings" [seggynges], "wordis," "expounding" [legyng], "tales," "speche," and "boasting" [blure] as evidence of his crime. Pilate initially finds these accusations suspect and warns the priests about their own use of false language ("For I like not your unrestrained language," 33.131).[28] When the priests cannot convince Pilate through this evidence, rather than bringing in Christ himself, they instead ask if they may call witnesses to give further testimony. Throughout this play, Annas and Caiaphas try to convince Pilate of Christ's crimes by means of language; however, the truth is ultimately revealed when Pilate makes visual contact with Christ. When Christ finally enters the scene, his presence provokes an involuntary reverential response from Pilate's body:

> Such a sight was never yet seen
> Come sit,
> My control was taken from me completely—
> I stood up, I could not restrain myself
> From honoring him in deed and in thought.
> (33.271–5)[29]

Pilate is so struck by the sight of Christ that his body uncontrollably springs up to honor him "in deed and in thought" [in wark and in witte]; Pilate's body immediately understands what his conscious mind does not.[30] This moment, which presents the lay body as a better judge of sacred truth than conscious reason, may also serve to endorse the devotional actions and gestures commonly displayed by lay worshippers. Furthermore, this scene vividly enacts the shift from the Old Testament's focus on the Word to the New Testament's focus on the flesh.

Unfortunately, we do not have the complete text for this pageant and therefore do not know how the trial of Christ and Barabbas was handled. Nevertheless, even without this material, the play's focus on seeing, responding to, and attempting to tame Christ's body is clear. Like Herod, when Pilate finally feels threatened by Christ ("To be king he claims [claymeth]," 33.329), he attacks his body, in this case commanding his soldiers to beat Christ. The lengthy scourging scene is narrated by the four soldiers performing the task, one of whom reiterates the goal of this assault on the flesh: "Thus we teach him to moderate his words" (33.400).[31] But for medieval spectators, when this body is beaten it only grows more powerful as it begins to resemble the familiar image of the suffering Christ. By the end of the play, the priests, their fears about Christ's compelling presence having been realized in Pilate's involuntary physical reaction, are eager to remove this body from the public space. Annas commands, "Draw him quickly away, deliver you, have done. / Go, do see him to death without further delay" (33.474–5).[32]

In these plays the body cannot be manipulated as easily as can rhetoric or logic. By spontaneously rising, Pilate's body reveals itself as the more accurate judge of divine truth—his body can differentiate truth from deceit even when his mind consciously cannot. This contrast between words and logic (which can be twisted by one's enemies) and the visible, present body (whether Christ's, which despite torture remains an indelible sign of divinity and truth, or the layperson's body, which repeatedly responds instinctively and appropriately to divine presence) reaches a climax in *The Death of Christ*. In this pageant Christ hangs from the cross, having already been crucified in the preceding play. Annas and Caiaphas continue to condemn Christ for his use of words and for what he convinced others to say about him: "With tricks yet spoke this Jew / And cursedly he called himself a king" (36.57–8); "And worst of all, / He made them call him / God's son" (36.63–5); "You displayed your tricks among many people; / But, wretch, you spoke thoughtlessly" (36.92–5).[33]

Shortly thereafter, Christ addresses the crowd. He tells spectators to look upon his crucified body and then guides them through a ritual of visual piety,

> You man that has sinned,
> Pay close attention to me.
> On a cross I am ragged and torn asunder,
> For the sake of your sinful soul;
> For your misdeeds I will repent.
> Here I remain, my back stretched out,
> Enduring this harm for your trespasses
> (36.118–24).[34]

The play ends with a final exemplar of proper devotional action. After wrapping and anointing Christ's body, Joseph of Arimathea kneels before it saying, "To thee, king, on knees here I kneel, / That readily you place me in bliss" (36.406–7).[35] Even when lifeless and broken, Christ's body still prompts physical enactments of piety.[36]

For characters who cannot see the divine image due to physical blindness, Christ's body acts as a remedy that miraculously restores their sight and, thus, expands their possibilities for devotional practice. When Pilate orders Longinus to pierce Christ's side with his sword, the water and blood that spills out from Christ's body gives Longinus his sight. Through this fluid, Christ's body literally extends out to touch the soldier, thereby enabling him to gaze upon the Crucifixion image. A similar miracle occurs in the *Entry* pageant when Christ looks at a blind man and restores his sight. These moments actualize both the physical power of Christ's body and the sacred contact this body makes with devout viewers when they gaze upon it, the very contact assumed by medieval visual theory.

The reality that both actor and audience are embodied not only creates a way for spectators to relate to salvation history, but it also provides an essential means by which they can derive meaning from that history. Patricia Cox Miller interprets certain characteristics of late ancient hagiographic imagery as emphasizing a mode of "visceral seeing." This mode creates "a stance for the beholder to occupy, a stance in which the senses have cognitive status and in which the intellect was materially engaged. This kind of embodied thoughtfulness was crucial to the experiential engagement of the beholder or reader with the saintly image."[37] Miller argues that the affective quality of these particular images "not only brings materiality and meaning very close together, it also demonstrates the close alignment of insistent physicality and equally insistent looking."[38] Viewers must acknowledge their bodies when encountering the image in order to comprehend its sacred meaning. Cognitive experiments reveal the sensorimotor basis for this kind of visceral seeing—on some level, perception appears to involve internal simulation. As Gallese explains, embodied simulation directly links agent and observer by allowing the observer to "penetrate" the agent's world and experience.[39] When characters' bodies respond instinctively to the presence of Christ— when Pilate leaps to his feet, Bedellus and Joseph of Arimathea kneel before Christ's body, the blind suddenly see—these reactions emphasize the body's role in devotional practices and assert its importance within sacred history. But the live performance of these reactions also triggers spectators to incorporate these responses to divine presence into their own lived experience. The cycle's devotional goals relied, in part, on the religious meaning that spectators derived through embodied simulation.

The Last Judgment's Call to Action

Many of the later pageants in York's cycle explore specific ways that laypeople must use their bodies actively to witness their faith.[40] For example, after Christ's Ascension, the disciples discuss their charge to "depart unto various countries / To preach throughout the whole world" (42.255–6).[41] They cannot dwell in their current place, but must "go from here" [wende vs hense] (42.263). In the opening monologue of the next play, *Pentecost*, Peter recounts how Christ commanded the disciples to preach and "bere wittenesse" (43.15), and the pageant ends with the disciples leaving to fulfill this duty. According to Richard Beadle's gloss, "bere" means to bear or carry. In this sense, witnessing implies carrying the message of Christ through one's body. For the disciples, witnessing constitutes a physical action. When Pilate rises or the blind receive sight, their bodies also effectively "bere wittenesse." At other times, witnessing takes the form of a change in perception or interpretation. For example, seeing the crucifixion events mentally transforms the Centurion, who then accuses Pilate and the high priests of slaying a "righteous man" [rightwise mane] (38.65). This change in attitude prompts a verbal witnessing—another way that characters "bere" Christ's message into the world.

Near the end of the cycle, this responsibility to witness is even more purposefully directed toward the medieval audience. *The Harrowing of Hell* and *The Last Judgment* pageants specifically assert the need for medieval Christians to "bere wittenesse" physically as part of their spiritual lives. *The Harrowing of Hell* presents a confrontation of bodies. Christ, having saved all believers "through buying with my blood" [thurgh bying with my bloode] (37.12), descends into Hell in order to reclaim God's people from eternal damnation. In some respect, *The Harrowing of Hell*'s premise works against theatre's strength as a representational mode: the play attempts to show a disembodied event through live physical action. Although it is Christ's spirit that enters Hell since, as he notes, "my body remains in the grave" [my bodie bidis in graue] (37.23), the audience watches an *embodied* Christ performing before them. The dialogue suggests that Christ's costume made him appear shining and bright, and therefore somewhat disembodied: "Now I see a sign of solace, / A glorious gleam to make us joyful" [Nowe see I signe of solace seere, / A glorious gleme to make vs gladde] (37.41–2); "This light comes from Christ" [þis light comes all of Criste] (37.57); "This light thou has provided" [þis light þou hast purueyed] (37.69). Nevertheless, considering the cycle's repeated emphasis on Christ's bodiliness up until this point, costumes and language would not be able to overcome the actuality of the actor's present body onstage. In addition, the character Belliall tells the devils to "Beat [Christ] hard / and make him go away" [Lay on hym þan hardely / And garre hym gange his gate] (37.143–4), a command that reinforces Christ's physical presence in Hell. Likewise, lines spoken by some of the characters refer to Christ's earlier bodiedness. For instance, Symeon remembers, "I had delight to associate with him / And embraced him affectionately with my hand" [I hadde delite with hym to dele / And halsed homely with my hande] (37.63–4). These allusions remind spectators of Christ's physical humanity.

    Although the pageant's subject is a supernatural disembodied event, the dramaturgical choices exploit the live, rhythmic encounter between actor and spectator in order to reinforce the play's call to action and underscore the message that witnessing requires a bodily "bearing forth." During this play, Christ explains that he has come to save all believers and that the prophets' words must be fulfilled through him (37.274). God's new law will therefore be fulfilled not only in Christ's death and resurrection, but also through the action of leading the souls from Hell. Satan assumes that he shall have more people in Hell than he has currently, since he is confident he can "pervert them quickly" (37.332) and teach men to disrespect "this law that you recently have set" (37.329).[42] Satan says, "I shall walk east and west, / And make them act much worse" (37.333–4). To prevent him from tempting Christians, Christ chains Satan ("Nay, fiend, thou shall be chained [feste]," 37.336) and commands him to "thy cell where you shall sit" (37.342).[43] This stage action visualizes and physicalizes the power struggle between good and evil that is the pageant's subject. Christ not only fulfills the Christian law of salvation by sacrificing his own body, but he also physically restrains the temptation and possibility for sin made actual by Satan's live body onstage. The dramatic action materially anchors the pageant's theological abstractions.

The Harrowing of Hell offers a striking example of how the action of bodies becomes, in Garner's words, the "currency of ludic exchange."[44] The doubled potentiality of the actor's body is a powerful theme in this play. Citing writers such as Augustine, Alan of Lille, and Robert Grosseteste, Suzannah Biernoff discusses how various medieval authors differentiate between the incorruptible, glorified body and the living, sinful flesh; York's *Harrowing* play stages this same distinction.[45] Placing Christ alongside Satan visually contrasts the tension ascribed to the human condition. And yet, in the harrowing story Christ and Satan do not represent bodies or even conditions of the body, but are instead potentialities. Christ chains Satan, not because he constitutes sinful flesh, but rather because he threatens humans by tempting them to sin. In Hell, Christ is not glorified flesh, but rather the opportunity to follow God's law and ultimately attain the eternal incorruptible body in Heaven. Christ and Satan do not represent states of the human condition, but are instead the contrasting possibilities available as part of that condition.

However, as physically present bodies onstage functioning as the currency of ludic exchange, the actors' bodies cannot ultimately be circumscribed as metaphors. During live performances the premise of the play's action—a disembodied event—cannot stand on its own; inevitably, meaning will accumulate around the actuality of the actors' bodies. Recognizing this fact, the pageant's creators may have taken advantage of the body's ability to make abstract ideas concrete and layered the onstage bodies with additional connotations in order to generate theological meaning. Consequently, during this play Christ and Satan symbolize abstract concepts (good and evil) as they simultaneously embody elements of the human condition, thereby offering spectators a way to interpret the actions of these characters as more than metaphor. In performance, Christ and Satan present spectators with two contrasting models of bodily conduct, two different ways to respond to God physically, and the actors may have used differing rhythms—variations in bodily control, comportment, and cadence—to emphasize this distinction.[46] These distinctions may have echoed prescriptions for bodily control found in medieval conduct literature or in texts such as Thoresby's *Lay Folks' Catechism*.

The *Harrowing* pageant offers medieval spectators a way to control their fleshiness in Christ's lines that describe the criteria for salvation:

> That my coming must be known,
> And to my sacraments pursue,
> My death, my resurrection, rightly understood—
> Whoever does not believe, they are not steadfast.
> Unto my doom I shall draw them,
> And judge them worse than any Jew.
> *And all that like to learn*
> *My law and live [leue] thereby*
> Shall never experience harm,
> But wealth, as is worthy.
> (37.315–24; Emphasis mine)[47]

According to Beadle, "leue" means both to live and to believe. Believing is therefore associated with living one's faith; in order to escape flesh's corruption, one must live the law of Christ. It is not enough to know and understand this law; one must also be a living witness of this law, bearing it forth through the body.

The cycle as a whole allows spectators to witness and experience the entire story of Christian history, sometimes even as confidantes, but at day's end *The Last Judgment* pageant confronts the audience with a decision about how they will respond in the future to what they have witnessed from the past. This final play encapsulates the cycle's overall salvation theme by designing a powerful physical memory intended to prompt proper action after the play concludes. Although the sacraments offered medieval Christians specific and codified ways to live God's law through their bodies, *The Last Judgment* pageant reminded lay spectators that everyday actions also constitute critical practices of belief. For this reason, I interpret this pageant as a meditation on the lived body.

The Last Judgment opens with Deus summarizing the day's/cycle's events. He emphasizes that Christ saved humanity with his "body bare" (47.30) and, through that body, "Example he gave them to win heaven" (47.38).[48] However, humankind has poorly repaid Christ's sacrifice by returning to its wicked ways. Deus has permitted humans to continue on this sinful, destructive path up until this point, but now he is sending his angels to earth to blow their trumpets and announce that "the time is come I will make an end" (47.64).[49] When the angels call all souls to God, they instruct them to "rise and fetch the flesh that was your companion" [rise and fecche youre flesh þat was youre feere] (47.86) and "body and soul with you bring" [body and sawle with ȝou ȝe bring] (47.91), lines that implicate the body in the judgment to come. As in the *Harrowing*, it is not sufficient to simply acknowledge Christ's example; believers must actively, physically imitate that example. Soul and body are both accountable at the final judgment.

The first wicked Soul describes how it not only rejected Christ's flesh ("we have his flesh forsworn," 47.119), but also that it "may bring forth no good deed" (47.123).[50] This soul realizes its error too late:

> Alas, that we such a life should lead
> That prepared us for this destiny
> Our wicked actions they will betray us
> That we believed never would become known.
> (47.127–30)[51]

This same character notes, "Our deeds are our damnation" (47.138). Similarly, a second damned soul says, "Our wicked actions we may not hide, / But on our backs we must bear them" (47.154–5), and implicates the entire body in its fate:

> Before us plainly are brought forth
> The deeds that we shall damn immediately
> That ears have heard, or heart has thought,
> Since any time that we may speak of,
> That foot has gone or hand has wrought,
> That mouth has spoken or eye has seen—
> This day very dearly then it is bought;
> Alas, it would be better had we never been born.
> (47.161–8)[52]

These souls are damned because they ignored Christ's earthly example, and the play overtly implicates the significance of bodily actions to their damnation. Christ reiterates this fact in another passage when he specifies that he will "judge folk far and near / By their deeds, wrong or right" (47.191–2). A few lines later, he says, "But, after their deeds, they shall have bliss or punishment" (47.200).[53] The text repeatedly emphasizes that at the final judgment God will assess the lives of Christians not based upon their thoughts or convictions, but instead by their deeds.

During performance, this evaluation of humankind reverberates through the spectator's body. As Clifford Davidson notes, plays about the final judgment "prove that late medieval Christianity did not merely look back at the events of past biblical history...[T]hey attempt to visualize what it would be like for the individual to be present at this final act of history."[54] But plays representing the final judgment do more than visualize this event; they also allow the audience to experience it firsthand. The performance offers spectators a chance to "live in" the final judgment and understand its meaning from inside the blend as they physically confront both the saved and the damned.

York's *Last Judgment* pageant ends with Christ speaking lines from the parable of the great judgment as he separates the saved from the damned (Matthew 25: 31–46). He recounts how the damned "never comforted me in my suffering" [neuere me comforte in my care] (47.318). When faced with the hungry, thirsty, "clothles," "harde presse," pained, or ill, the damned offered these people neither help nor pity. As I have said, the model of salvation offered in the play is one of lived bodies; how these bodies perform deeds and treat other bodies during their lifetimes will determine their fate at the end of time.[55] But rather than dramatize examples of these good or bad deeds, the pageant instead enacts their consequences—salvation and damnation. When Christ separates them, both groups receive equal time onstage, which allows the spectator to observe—and thus experience—both possible fates vicariously; direct address reinforces the immediacy of this encounter. According to neural mapping, spectators not only perceive, but also internally simulate both groups' responses: the physical fear of damnation, as well as the rush of joy at salvation. Performance literacy encouraged spectators to understand this pageant's theology by living in a blend of the final judgment and experiencing empathy with those who are judged by God.

As I mentioned in chapter one, empathy is not an emotion, but rather the precondition for establishing feelings for others, such as sympathy or antipathy. As Evan Thompson explains, for phenomenologists "empathy is a unique form of intentionality in which we are directed toward the other's experience."[56] Supplementing Edith Stein's description of empathy with evidence from cognitive science, Thompson proposes four empathetic processes or types of empathy.[57] The first involves the "involuntary coupling" of the living bodies of self and other that I have already discussed in relation to the mirror neuron system. The second process, cognitive empathy, is more active than the first and happens when we imaginatively transpose ourselves into another's place, a movement that allows us to exchange mental perspectives, thoughts, and feelings with another person. This process relates directly to theory of mind research, and is therefore related to embodied simulation. The third type of empathy involves the ability to grasp the experience of the other as other, thereby giving us the possibility of seeing ourselves from another's perspective.

The fourth process is where we begin to see empathy as the basis for developing feelings for another. Thompson describes this type of empathy as "the perception of the other as a being who deserves concern and respect," and he characterizes this empathy as moral;

> empathy in the moral sense is a basic cognitive and emotional capacity underlying all the moral sentiments and emotions one can have for another. The point here is not that empathy exhausts moral experience, for it certainly does not, but that empathy provides the source of that kind of experience and the entry point into it.[58]

In other words, empathy prepares the body—or, creates the potential—for other feeling states like sympathy.

Rather than happening in stages, Thompson argues that these four empathetic processes occur together and intertwine through the lived body as part of our "face-to-face intersubjective experience."[59] Although empathy is inarguably subjective, individualized, and enculturated,[60] theatrical devices may be able to coax spectators into certain empathetic relationships with actors/characters, and thereby shape their specific "entry points" into moral experience. In doing so, plays can encourage spectators to develop certain feelings over others. Moreover, because the feelings that emerge from empathy are incorporated into our embodied schema, empathy also supplies a basis from which meaning might subsequently emerge after the performance as a pattern *for* action that shapes real life decisions. Or, as Bruce McConachie succinctly states, "emotions generated through simulation change how people think."[61]

I proposed that the rhythmic experiences created by the cycle's staging conventions may have influenced how a spectator interacted with certain quarters of the city, such as Mickelgate, and with those who lived and worked in those same areas, in the months between cycle performances. So, too, after living in the blend of God's final judgment and developing empathetic relationships with the actors/characters, a spectator might feel a stronger motivation toward charity in the days and months following the performance.[62] Ultimately, such a post-performance response was crucial to the play's devotional agenda.

Cognitive science offers empirical evidence that the embodied actions seen in performances are simulated by and linger within the spectator's body, where they contribute to subsequent meaning construction. Medieval spectators not only "read" a pageant's devotional meaning, they also lived in it. However, I am not suggesting that all laypeople experienced devotional media in exactly the same ways, but have instead purposefully defined performance literacy as a tactic of consumption. As Claire Sponsler suggests, consumption is "indeterminate and open to conflicting understandings, with the effects on individuals being more plural than singular."[63] Because the viewer's body confronts an object/image/performance/space with its own experiential past, this mode of visual piety is variable. As McConachie argues,

> Cognitive theories supporting audience simulation and conceptual blending pose a major problem for spectatorial theories that emphasize the importance of reading representational meanings. Both cognitive theories suggest that spectators understand the world onstage not as an illusion, but as a different kind of reality when they are living in the blend of performance and mirroring the actions of actor/characters or looking at the setting of a production. Performance, it seems, mixes up our usual categories of actuality and make-believe all of the time.[64]

As I suggested in chapter one, certain religious authorities from the Middle Ages believed that this kind of mixing up had dangerous implications within the context of lay devotion. In the next chapter, I will examine moments in the York cycle when performance literacy's inherent uncontrollability may have complicated devotional meaning.

Chapter Six

Empathy, Entrainment, and Devotional Instability

The York cycle, with its many instances of pious seeing, seems to be the perfect performance to stage as part of Corpus Christi Day, a feast celebrated through the visible presentation and procession of the Eucharist. But the relationship between the cycle and the other Corpus Christi events was not always a comfortable one. Debate over the relationship between procession and play is evident as early as 1426 when Friar William Melton, according to an *A/Y* entry "a most famous preacher of the word of God," came to York and argued that the two events should be separated. The *A/Y* indicates that Melton

> commended the said play to the people in several of his sermons, by affirming that it was good in itself and most laudable; nevertheless, he used to say that the citizens of the aforesaid city and the other foreigners coming in to it during the said festival, attend not only to the play on the same feast, but also greatly to feastings, drunkenness, clamours, gossipings, and other wantonness, engaging the least in the divine service of the office of that day and that, alas, for that cause, they lose the indulgences granted to them in that matter by Pope Urban IV.[1]

Melton recommended "that this play should take place on one day and the procession on the other."[2] In agreement, the council decided that the plays "should be presented each year on the Wednesday which is the eve of the same feast, and that the procession should always be made solemnly on the day of the feast itself."[3] But a 1444 entry in the *B/Y Memorandum Book* specifies that the craft of Armourers brought forth their pageant "vpon corpus christi day," and a 1476 entry in the House Books indicates that by that date the city had moved the Corpus Christi procession to the Friday after the official feast day.[4]

The city separated pageants and procession, but the cycle is the event that remained on the feast day.

Playing the cycle on Corpus Christi Day framed it as a devotional event. Given that context, moving the Eucharistic procession to the following day may have encouraged the audience to apply to the Host the anticipation of seeing Christ that was modeled by the actors and practiced by the spectators the day before during the pageants. From one day to the next, their visual piety would slip from the actors' bodies to the Host, the actual body of Christ. York's community leaders may have recognized that the reverse order—placing the procession the day before the pageants—could confuse or disrupt this sequence of pious seeing, inadvertently encouraging people to *see* the bodies of the actors as they had *seen* the Eucharist the day before. Instead, playing the cycle on Corpus Christi day prompts the audience to engage this performance as a sacred event and to interpret the pageants' many examples of devotional seeing as precursors to their own visual encounters with the Host on the following day, when they would, perhaps, stand in the same places throughout the city as they had when watching the cycle.

However, in live performances no viewing position is ever entirely stable. Placing the cycle before the procession could not prevent the boundary between these two events from blurring, especially given how often these pageants draw attention to Christ's bodied presence onstage. Moreover, as I have reiterated throughout these chapters, York's religious performances were embedded within a larger, sophisticated network of lay visual piety; a vast range of things impacted each layperson's "way of seeing" the Corpus Christi pageants.

In particular, by the later Middle Ages lay devotional culture had developed into a highly affective one informed by medieval visual theories of sight as akin to touch. Devotional art and texts that focused attention on Christ's suffering body, as well as a growing emphasis on seeing the Eucharist, reinforced the notion that vision offered laypeople opportunities for bodily participation in, and identification with, the divine.[5] Although laypeople were not supposed to interpret these participatory and identificatory interactions as allowing them to become identical to Christ, Suzannah Biernoff notes that "ocular desire was something that required constant regulation, restraint, and sublimation" during the later Middle Ages.[6] In this chapter, I will argue that live performances of certain episodes in the cycle, especially those that exhibited Christ's suffering body, had the potential to challenge such visual regulation. In doing so, I return to the medieval anxieties about theatre that I analyzed in chapter one, but will suggest here that those who planned and performed York's Corpus Christi cycle may have used specific staging choices to address these very concerns about how performances "body forth."

Touching Divinity

Throughout the cycle's performance, the actors' physical actuality on stage, as well as various verbal references, continually reminds the audience of Christ's embodiment. This emphasis grows more pronounced during the Passion pageants, which tend to highlight Christ's humanity. For example, *The Agony in the Garden* concentrates attention on Christ's fleshiness by staging his fear and doubt. Christ admits, "My flesh is afraid due to doubt" [My flessh is full dredande for drede] (28.48), and then repeats a version of this line numerous times: "I feel by my terror that my flesh would quite gladly / Be gone from this trial" [I fele by my ferdnes my flessh wolde full fayne / Be torned fro this turnement] (28.89–90); "My flesh is very afraid and gladly would resist" [My flesshe is full ferde and fayne wolde defende] (28.105 and 28.130); "Now since my flesh is afraid, father I am glad / That my anguish and my torments are near an end" [Now if my flessh ferde be, fadir I am fayne / þat myne angwisshe and my noyes are nere at an ende] (123–4).[7] Christ's apprehension supplies the play with much of its dramatic action, and language choices firmly situate that apprehension in Christ's flesh.

But performances of *The Agony* also foreground Christ's bodiedness by presenting moments of physical contact between him and the other characters. The most obvious example is Judas's kiss, a moment of touch with biblical origins: "I would ask you for a kiss, master" [I wolde aske you a kysse maistir] (28.250). Furthermore, the staged confrontation between the soldiers and the disciples likely involved other instances of characters making physical contact with the actor playing Christ, and the play ends with remarks to this effect: "First Jew: Do, do lay your hands quickly on this scoundrel / Third Jew: We have hold of his miscreant in our hands" (28.301–2).[8] This pageant concludes with an image of Christ's body held fast.

Although *The Agony* supplies us with a particularly good example of how acts of touching highlight Christ's fleshiness, this tactic is employed throughout the cycle beginning the moment Christ appears onstage. During *The Nativity*, Mary holds and dresses Christ ("That I might take thee in my arms / And in this humble clothing clothe thee," 14.66–7) and the animals warm him with their breath ("The weather is cold as you may feel, / To keep him warm they are eager / With their warm breath," 14.129–31).[9] Other characters treat the Christ child with the same concern for physical comfort that the body of any infant should receive. Scenes of this nature continue throughout the Christ child pageants. Symeon holds the infant Christ in *The Purification* ("Come embrace me, the baby that is best born," 17.382; "That this sweet babe, that I in arms embrace," 17.392) and Joseph takes him from Mary's arms during their flight into Egypt ("And if you will ease your arm a bit / Give him to me, let me bear him awhile," 18.197–8).[10] Language and the accompanying actions remind the audience that Christ is made of real human flesh—a Corpus Christi theme. Of course, we can only trace examples of touch that are recorded or implied in the textual record. Many other moments may have occurred during live performances.

This use of touch is similar to what Brigitte Cazelles identifies in the thirteenth-century narrative *Vie de Saint Jehan Paulus*. Cazelles notes that during a recognition scene in this text "the fact that the spectacular is no longer a matter of *looking* at the saint's body, but of *touching* it, suggest[s] a treatment of the sacred focusing on the protagonist's corporeal rather than spiritual identity."[11] Likewise, when a character touches Christ in the York cycle this action directs the audience to contemplate Christ's human aspect, while also reinforcing for spectators the bodily state they share with the character/actor before them. Physical contact reminds the audience that the people they are watching, both the living actors and the sacred people from the past, are made of flesh and blood.

These physical interactions are critical to the cycle's devotional goals. Pamela King argues that moments of bodily contact, as when Mary holds up the infant during *The Nativity*, sustain the cycle's sacramental focus.[12] She identifies within the cycle text a striking attention to the details of these moments onstage, such as a stage direction in *The Last Supper* indicating that Christ washes his own hands ("Tunc lauat manus") after washing the feet of the disciples or the focus in *The Death of Christ* on preparing the body for burial.[13] In addition, King isolates how the post-Resurrection pageants in particular foreground Christ's bodiliness through words or staging.[14] The Passion pageants also contain a variety of physical encounters with Christ as his body is scourged, spat upon, pierced, forced to drag the heavy cross, crucified, and finally removed from the cross and prepared for burial. The language, blocking, and gestures in these plays maintain a focus on Christ's body.

Cognitive psychology suggests the potent sensorimotor impact of seeing these physical interactions. As with emotion and action, mirror neurons also respond to touch: the same cortex is activated whether a subject is touched, observes someone else being touched, or sees inanimate objects touching.[15] The interaction itself triggers the neurons; whether animate or inanimate, what is touched does not matter, as long as touch occurs.[16] Experiments indicate that a shared circuitry in our brain links our personal experience of touch with the corresponding event occurring to other animate beings or inanimate objects.[17] The authors of one study conclude that "when we witness touch, we do not just *see* touch but also *understand* touch through an automatic link with our own experience of touch." They suggest that this activation may reflect "an integration of other human beings or objects into our own embodied schema."[18]

Staged touch-encounters with Christ did not remain representational; instead, these enacted moments of touch traced (devotional) patterns into the spectator's embodied schema. Moreover, dialogue that described these moments may have allowed spectators who could not see the moment of touch to imagine it, thus prompting a similar neural simulation as would seeing the actual touch itself. In addition, scenes involving touch may have challenged claims regarding who could come into physical contact with Christ's body. The most germane instance occurs after Christ's birth in *The Nativity* pageant, when Mary recites a hail series and, the lines suggest, lifts the infant Christ: "Son, since I am a simple subject of yours, / Allow, sweet son I pray thee, / That I might take you in my arms / And in these humble garments clothe you" (14.64–67).[19] As I have already noted, various scholars have commented upon this dramatic gesture's powerful mnemonic value and resonance with the Elevation.[20] When, during the cycle's annual performance, a medieval layperson presumably performed this resonant act, it may have (advertently or inadvertently) validated ideas about the laity's right to unmediated contact with the divine. Presented by and before laypeople, this dramatic moment may have allowed spectators to "live in" the body of an authoritative figure who had direct physical access to the Corpus Christi.

Rhythmic Entrainment and Devotional Slippage

Physical interactions onstage prompted unconscious bodily activation and simulation through which spectators generated theological meaning. Although this audience response could be employed strategically to place spectators in particular empathetic relationships that reinforced orthodoxy, as I suggested with *The Last Judgment*, it could at times complicate efforts to regulate lay visual piety. This is especially the case during scenes in which violence is inflicted upon Christ's body. During the pageants following *The Agony in the Garden*, Christ's body is tortured in various ways, and these acts would have triggered embodied simulation in spectators. Since such simulation forms the basis for spectator empathy, the exact staging of these violent moments would help determine with whom spectators actually empathized. V. A. Kolve notes that during York's cycle, "a strange and disturbing mood is created the minute Christ is captured and the Passion begins: the stage is suddenly filled with noise, violence, rough laughter, talk of game."[21] As I mentioned in the previous chapter, Christ's stillness and silence in these moments accentuates the soldiers' raucous tone, and scholars have interpreted the impact of this juxtaposition in different ways. Kolve argues that York's scourging scene in *Christ Before Pilate II: The Judgment* translates the stage action "into everyday medieval terms, into a common children's game, called 'papse,'" and in doing so transforms the Passion violence into play in order to aesthetically control the image for the audience.[22]

I, too, recognize this element of game, but my conclusions about its reception are closer to those of Claire Sponsler, who contends that using play invites the audience to participate vicariously in the fun, since it is only a game, even as it emphasizes the soldiers' pleasure in tormenting Christ.[23] In scenes such as this, it is the transgressive characters—here the soldiers—who typically display the more engaging and attractive body rhythms.[24] Studies of how the brain processes musical rhythm can help to suggest this scene's potentialities when staged. Research demonstrates that auditory rhythm entrains our bodies. Data from experiments examining finger tapping to a randomly changing tempo show that "auditory rhythm communicates stable and precise interval-based temporal templates to the brain, to which the motor system has 'privileged' access even below levels of conscious awareness."[25] In other words, as Michael Thaut concludes, "neuronal activation patterns that precisely code the perception of rhythm in the auditory system spread into adjacent motor areas and activate the firing patterns of motor tissue."[26] Similar entrainment has been observed in studies of human conversation; W. S. Condon and W. D. Ogston's frame-by-frame analysis of videotaped conversations revealed that "speaker and hearer look like puppets moved by the same set of strings."[27] This same response has been observed in infants as early as twenty minutes after birth when they interact with their parents.[28] As R. Keith Sawyer contends, these studies "show that we are born with an ability to engage in rhythmically coordinated interpersonal interaction."[29]

The York cycle performances did include musical arrangements, but the poetic dialogue and physical actions onstage may also have been crafted to achieve a kind of musicality, as Kolve suggests with respect to the scourging scene. This could have been a mnemonic choice; as many of us know from experience, and cognitive science now confirms, we retain information much longer when we learn it through music. This is even true in cases of Alzheimer's disease and other neurological disorders: "data suggest that neuronal memory traces built through music are deeply ingrained and more resilient to neurodegenerative influences."[30] As Thaut says, "the brain that engages in music is changed by engaging in music."[31]

Music was threaded throughout medieval life and watching spectators visibly entrained by musical rhythms (heads nodding, feet tapping, bodies swaying) may have inclined those creating the York pageants to use musical rhythms strategically. Although brutal, if Christ's scourging was presented as a musical game, then the rhythms of the soldiers' bodies may have drawn the spectator's attentions away from Christ and, consequently, triggered embodied simulation of the soldiers; entrained by their physical rhythms, a spectator would— consciously or unconsciously—experience "living in" the bodies of the soldiers.[32] Staging violence as play could prompt spectators to incorporate the torturers' actions into their embodied schemata, a process facilitated by Christ's stillness and silence.

Although not all spectators may have vicariously fallen into "rhythm" with the soldiers' bodies, the spectacle of enjoyment and excess had the potential to overwhelm the visual field, thus promoting empathy with the soldiers over empathy with Christ. By foregrounding the "gaming" element of their actions, this empathetic entry point into moral experience could then encourage the audience to sympathize with the soldiers, rather than with Christ. If this was the play's explicit intention, the condemnatory tone of the next pageant is appropriately poignant; *The Road to Calvary* opens with a soldier directly challenging the audience to oppose Pilate's judgment: "And this day shall his death be ordained— / Let's see who dares say otherwise?" (34.20–1).[33] If, rather than resting their eyes meditatively upon the body of Christ and sympathizing with his experience, the cycle's spectators had instead directed their attention at the soldiers who were inflicting the pain—who may have held the scene's dramatic weight—and, thus, felt their bodies entrained by the rhythmic pleasure of a medieval pastime, then the opening lines of *The Road to Calvary* may be indicting the audience for this misdirected devotional gaze. The soldier's words remind spectators that if they did not "say otherwise" [saie naye] during the previous pageant, they are equally complicit in Christ's torment.

Specific staging choices may have been employed in York's two crucifixion pageants in order to regulate the spectator's empathetic relationships during reenactments of this incredibly pivotal sacred event. However, given the value of Christ's body as a central devotional image, and the way performative encounters could contradict or challenge orthodox interpretations of that body's meaning, these pageants may also reveal uncertainties about the ability to control reception of the crucifixion. Miri Rubin argues that engaging the body in religious rites creates anxiety specifically because physical engagement destabilizes meaning by making it subject to varied interpretations and translations. She describes how this was particularly the case in late medieval Eucharistic practices that involved physical rituals, like the Elevation of the Host:

> This type of eucharistic practice exerted inevitable pressure on the neatly designed mass of the liturgists and theologians. It exposes the living ritual not only in the material vulnerability of any sacramental exercise but through demonstration of the ways in which the clergy attempted to dramatise, vocalise, impress and cajole, in a complex dialectic of response to their audiences and to the exigencies of time and space. The balance of meanings presented in normative texts could never be fully achieved; the symbol was bound to be appropriated not only in the minds, but in the handling, seeing, and tasting of this very material artifact of divinity.[34]

Even authoritative clerical presence and command cannot entirely allay concerns.

The York cycle obviously did not offer its audience the actual body of Christ. Furthermore, various characteristics of the cycle, such as the fact that a different actor played Christ with each new pageant or the choice to spread the crucifixion events across two different pageants, helped to circumscribe how spectators devotionally engaged the pageants' images. Nevertheless, the laity regularly used the crucifixion image as part of their personal devotional practices and many of these activities infused elements of "liveness" into the layperson's meditative encounter with Christ's crucified body. In some cases, as Hans Belting argues with respect to the popular *Imago Pietatis* or Man of Sorrows image of Christ, viewer and image related to one another "mimetically."[35] Consequently, sermons and widely read devotional texts from this period, such as Nicholas Love's *The Mirror of the Blessed Life of Jesus Christ*, aimed to delineate the empathetic relationship between lay devotee and image. These media led laypeople toward an experience of sympathy with Christ, an orthodox relationship that they could subsequently apply within other devotional contexts.

Like performances, *The Mirror* situates the reader/listener as a visual witness to biblical events such as the Crucifixion, even using vivid language to describe Christ's physical experiences.[36] But texts such as this often overpower (and thereby constrain) these visceral embellishments through rhetoric. For example, after a richly detailed description of Christ on the cross, Love's text reads,

> You also if you behold well the lord, you may have means enough for the greatest compassion, seeing him tormented, from the sole of the foot up to the highest part of the head. There was in him no place nor part without passion.
>
> This is a pitying sight and a joyful sight. A pitying sight of him, because of that difficult passion that he suffered for our salvation, it is but a good sight for us, because it is by its means and effect that we have our redemption. Truly this sight of our lord Jesus hanging on the cross, by devout imagination of the soul, is very good for those creatures who, after long exercise of sorrowful compassion, feel sometimes such a great pleasure not only in the soul, but also in the body, that they understand it not, and which no man may know, but only he who by experience feels it. (Middle English transcription in note.)[37]

Although, as William Hodapp notes, texts like this one aimed to "break down time-space barriers" and make the Passion "immediate and present" for readers and listeners,[38] they also overtly directed the layperson to participate in the Passion images as witnesses, not to imagine themselves as the suffering Christ. The narrator describes Christ's body, thereby establishing an empathetic bond between listener/reader and Christ, but then decisively emphasizes the important distinction between the physical experiences of the devotee and Christ in order to encourage feelings of sympathy. In addition, *The Mirror* indicates that it is "devout imagination" that prompts "compassion" in the body and soul. This feeling is neither a manifestation of divine presence, nor complete understanding. Rather, the richly detailed descriptions that instantiate embodied simulation are rhetorically controlled in order to remind lay devotees that they can only ever achieve a sympathetic relationship with the crucified Christ. The prevalence of such devotional aids attests to the clerical desire to promote a specific lay relationship with this ubiquitous, and increasingly affective, sacred image.

It is not altogether surprising, then, that religious authorities responded warily to laypeople claiming direct, unmediated bodily access to Christ's experiences and suffering. *The Book of Margery Kempe* provides us with a good example of this kind of lay piety and the anxiety it provoked.[39] Kempe's devotional practices were well-known in the places she visited and they prompted much discussion among clergy and laypeople alike. Kempe's biography documents the perceived threat she posed to laypeople, as well as various accounts of clergy testing her and preachers sermonizing against her.[40] Kempe seems to have aroused passionate reactions because she claimed direct engagement with God through her bodily senses, rather than through clerical mediations and prescribed practices of communication.

The sensations Kempe experiences are repeatedly described by her biographer as "tokens" [tokenys].[41] According to the author's account, Christ tells Kempe that these "tokenys" are a sign that she is beyond needing clerical guidance and instruction: "There is no clerk in this world who can, daughter, teach you better than I can do, and, if you will be obedient to my will, I shall be obedient to your will. Where is a better token of love [charité] than to weep for your Lord's love?"[42] Kempe's bodily tokens function in a similar way as did the Virgin's girdle ("a token trewe") in *The Assumption of the Virgin* pageant—by manifesting divine power and presence in the material, physical realm, these tokens give laypeople direct access to that presence.

Kempe's devotional experiences are centered in her body and often triggered by seeing rituals or images:

> And there she came into a fine church where she beheld a crucifix, which was piteously portrayed and lamentable to behold, and through beholding of which, the Passion of our Lord entered her mind, whereupon she began to melt and utterly dissolve with tears of pity and compassion [gan meltyn and al to relentyn be terys of pyté and compassyown]. Then the fire of love kindled so quickly in her heart that she could not keep it secret for, whether she liked it or not, it caused her to break out in a loud voice and cry astonishingly, and weep and sob very terribly.[43]

This description could be used to illustrate all four of Evan Thompson's empathetic processes.[44] Kempe first sees a Passion image and then this Passion "entryd" her body and mind, triggering imaginative transposition. She then grasps Christ's experience, which ultimately gives her the moral perception from which sympathy for Christ can emerge. However, because these processes are manifested outwardly by her body, observers may have interpreted Kempe's responses as indicative of a suffering in, rather than a suffering for/with, Christ.

Kempe's biographer repeatedly explains how spiritual effects trace themselves into her physical flesh. Not only does the Holy Ghost manifest as a "fyer of lofe" in her breast, but Kempe also hears divine "sounds and melodies" [sowndys and melodiis] with "her bodily ears" [hir bodily erys], senses "sweet smells in her nose" [felt swet smellys wyth hir nose], and sees "with her bodily eyes many white things flying all about her on all sides, as thickly in a way as specks in a sunbeam" [wyth hir bodily eyne many white thyngys flying al abowte hir on every syde as thykke in a maner as motys in the sunne].[45] Kempe claimed that these overwhelmingly sensuous experiences traced themselves into her body, thereby guiding her toward unmediated religious knowledge and understanding.

I suspect that it was not only the body's prominent role in Kempe's devotional practices, but the particular emphasis placed upon that body's sensuality, that provoked concern. In the later Middle Ages, the senses were still viewed skeptically as potential entryways for vice and sin. Augustine's caution against sin was still relevant:

> This evil thing creeps stealthily through all the entrances of sense: it gives itself over to forms, it adapts itself to colors, it sticks to sounds, it lurks hidden in anger and in the deception of speech, it appends itself to odors, it infuses tastes, by the turbulent overflow of passion it darkens the senses with darksome affections, it fills with certain obscuring mists the paths of the understanding, through all of which the mind's ray normally diffuses the light of reason.[46]

Given the suspicion surrounding the senses, which, as I explained in chapter one, continued throughout the Middle Ages, it is no wonder that religious authorities were troubled by Kempe's claim of access to God through her senses without any clerical mediation to ensure that these were not experiences instigated by the devil.

Texts and sermons helped the laity navigate the human aspects of Christ's suffering during their pious activities. These aids aimed to help laypeople sympathize with Christ and see their own complicity in his suffering on the cross, but without identifying too strongly with Christ's passion and believing that they, too, could experience it fully. In this respect, embodied simulation—and the empathy it affords—would not pose a problem for medieval clerics. Empathy requires alterity; we feel responses like sympathy because empathy demands the self-other distinction necessary to generate a moral perception of the other.[47] Still, empathy can manifest itself visibly; emotive coupling and affective resonance illustrate that even during the initial coupling stage empathy is not always expressed exclusively at the sensorimotor level. As Thompson explains,

> In affective resonance, two or more individuals affect each other's emotional states. A classic example is crying in newborn infants (which is usually labeled with the misleading term *emotional contagion*)...Affective resonance also occurs when two individuals engage in direct interaction and one actively seeks to affect the other.[48]

Bruce McConachie explains that the research tracking these kinds of responses suggests that affective resonance in the theatre "is automatic and usually very quick."[49] Performances readily encourage such involuntary, automatic, and sometimes blatantly *visible* simulations.

Those individuals in the Middle Ages who questioned religious performance's devotional value would certainly have noted and criticized these very kinds of physical simulations. Clerics may have feared that, for those lay spectators who did not appear to progress from these emotionally driven reactions to more detached, sympathetic devotional responses, such passionate over-identification would obscure religious understanding; this is the very fear articulated in *A Tretise of Miraclis Pleyinge* when the author claims that people watching "miraclis pleyinge" "weep for the play of Christ's passion, failing to weep for their own sins and those of their children" [wepen for the pley of Cristis passioun, leevinge to wepen for the sinnes of hemsilf and of theire children].[50] As Sarah Beckwith asserts, York's *Crucifixion* pageant does not intend for the spectator to "merge with Christ in the identificatory theater of passion, not to become him, or to enter or be at one with him, but to *bear a terrible witness*."[51] Nevertheless, as enlivened and embodied devotional events, York's crucifixion pageants, which offered spectators a live, fleshy body enacting pain, may have triggered spectator responses that *appeared* to break through empathy's alterity. Such reactions to enactments of Christ's passion likely bolstered the belief that performances could destabilize the crucial demarcation between dramatic representation and sacred reality.

Empathy, Sympathy, and Christ's Body

Religious performances offered the medieval laity overt opportunities not only to encounter Christ's body, but also to understand the devotional relevance of that Corpus Christi by living in blends and bodies other than their own. It is likely that the pageants depicting Christ's crucifixion would provoke particularly visceral audience responses to this encounter because these plays present a body in pain. Stanton Garner, Jr. argues that when spectators watch plays that depict human suffering, they vicariously reexperience that pain through "a mimetic inhabiting of the suffering body."[52] Neurobiological evidence supports this notion of mimetic inhabiting; seeing pain inflicted on a person, or simply imagining someone's experience of pain, triggers embodied simulation of that same pain.[53] Although this supplies the foundation for empathy, it still involves an imaginative transposition—or slippage—into the other's body. Certain staging choices may have also stimulated (unconscious) visible rhythmic entrainment. These processes of simulation and entrainment are similar to notions about perception popular in late medieval theory. As I stated in chapter one, these ideas seem to influence at least some medieval anti-theatrical prejudice[54]; the author of *A Tretise of Miraclis Pleyinge* interprets the fact that laypeople often weep at the "pley" of Christ's Passion as evidence that they have "more compassion for pain than for sin" [more compassion of peine than of sinne].[55] Given the anxiety that surrounded appropriations of Christ's body in the later Middle Ages, I would argue that York's crucifixion plays were designed specifically to prevent, or at the very least to limit, the extent of these bodily responses to Christ's pain and suffering. Cognitive science can help to suggest the actual impact that certain performance choices made upon the medieval spectator's reception and interpretation of the cycle.

When Christ is onstage during *The Crucifixion*, he spends a large percentage of that time lying down as the soldiers fasten his body to the cross; one of the soldiers notes that the cross is on the ground (35.39) and that the "wretch on the length be laid" [ladde on lenghe be layde] (35.41). These lines imply that when the pageant was staged Christ was likely out of view to a large portion of the medieval audience. At the very least, Christ does not seem to be the central visual focus during much of the pageant's early action. In addition, Christ makes a brief appeal to God between lines 49 and 60, but does not speak again until line 253.

Over the course of the play's intervening action, the four soldiers vividly describe pulling Christ's arms, so that his body will fit the ill-made cross, and nailing him to the wood. The soldiers not only describe the pain they inflict upon Christ's body, but also the physical ache that this arduous work produces in their own bodies: "Great harm have I experienced, / My shoulder is out of joint" (35.189–90).[56] They also narrate those actions that would cause Christ physical pain: "Strike on then hard, for he who redeemed you. / Yes, here is a short, thick nail that will stiffly stand, / Through bones and sinews it shall be used" (35.101–3); "Fasten on a cord / And tug him in two, by his head and feet" (35.113–14); "The ropes have greatly increased his pains / Before he were to the holes pulled. / Yea, both sinews and veins are asunder / On each side, so have we seen" (35.145–8); "Let it down, so all his bones / Are now asunder on all sides" (35.223–4).[57] These lines were likely accompanied by the sounds of hammers striking nails or ropes stretching, and mirror neuron research suggests that these would have triggered spectators to mirror the actions that produced those sounds, in this case, to simulate the soldiers' actions.[58] Although a character's pain is mapped in the spectator's brain, for audience members at *The Crucifixion*, many of whom probably could not actually see Christ's reactions to the violence inflicted upon his supine body, this pain was only imagined and therefore not mapped onto the sensorimotor system. Instead, during much of the pageant, the sounds and rhythm of the dialogue likely entrained spectators, placing them into a closer empathetic relationship with the soldiers' actions, emotions, and pain, thereby prompting audience members to take on the soldiers' interests as their own.[59]

There seems to have been a lot vying for the audience's attention (and empathy) on this busy stage/wagon until finally, after numerous attempts and the expense of great effort, the soldiers succeed in raising the cross. This moment occurs around line 210, two-thirds of the way through the play's dialogue, and, as I have already noted, it iconographically replicates the Elevation of the Host. The crucified Christ now appears immobile and, for the most part, silent on the cross, which situates him as an image. This choice not only confronts spectators with the experience of physical presence at the event, but it also creates an abrupt aesthetic and rhythmic shift—a focal shift from the lively soldiers' bodies to the still crucified body. This dramatic choice makes spectators conscious that the pageant's primary dramatic action is now their own act of looking, an act understood in the Middle Ages to be alive with dynamic intercorporeal movement and impact.[60] Moreover, the sudden change in tone and rhythm may have, like the first lines in the *Road to Calvary* pageant, focused spectators on their own complicity.

The live display of a brutalized (medieval, probably layperson's) body on the cross may initially threaten distinctions between spectator and actor, as well as sacred and profane. But very quickly after the cross is raised, the pageant exerts direct control over the empathetic relationship between spectator and actor in ways similar to what I identified in *The Mirror*.[61] Christ's address from the cross interrupts the audience's moment of identification with the silent Corpus Christi: "Every man who walks by way or street, / Pay attention that you miss none of this affliction. / Behold my head, my hands, and my feet, / And truly understand anew, as you pass by" (35.253–6).[62] As the monologue continues, it evolves into an address to God:

> My father, who can relieve my suffering,
> Forgive these men that torment me.
> They know not what they perform;
> Therefore, my father, I ask,
> Let their sins never be visited upon them,
> But see that their souls are saved.
> (35.259–64)[63]

These words push back against the spectator's possible slippage into Christ's body; the lines acknowledge a common but distinct corporeality between spectator and religious image, a significant site of devotional meaning, but they then direct spectators toward a conscious meditation on their own blameworthiness and on Christ's suffering as a sacrifice for their salvation. The pageant thereby encourages spectators to live in a witness blend—they blend their experiences as living spectators in their everyday medieval streets into their experience of the crucifixion reenactment. However, because the actions they witness are not conceived as "fictions" by the audience in the traditional theatrical sense, Christ's direct address also assimilates into that "witness blend" the additional experience of live presence at the actual biblical event, an experience that each spectator's previous encounters with liturgy, sermons, art objects, devotional texts, and other pious practices had already cultivated. All the while, this densely loaded blend helps the spectator maintain a safe sympathetic distance from Christ's body on the cross.

The next pageant, *The Death of Christ*, must overcome similar problems with respect to Christ's suffering body onstage, but this play uses a somewhat different tactic to accomplish this. The pageant opens with a 117-line dialogue between Pilate, Annas, and Caiaphas, during which, as different verbal references imply, the actor playing Christ on the cross is likely a visible part of the stage picture. After this opening dialogue, Christ delivers his first monologue, followed by exchanges with Mary and the disciples. As Pamela King notes, while *The Crucifixion* is tightly focused on the crucifixion image, *The Death of Christ* adds more characters and context around that image.[64] Like the first crucifixion pageant, this play tries to situate the spectator in a stable, sympathetic viewing position, but here we also find other actors/characters modeling that position. As I noted in chapter five, Christ commands the audience (here, defined broadly) to see his body as a devotional image:

> You man that has sinned,
> Pay close attention to me.
> On a cross I am ragged and torn asunder,
> For the sake of your sinful soul;
> For your misdeeds I will repent.
> Here I remain, my back stretched out,
> Enduring this harm for your trespasses
> Who could you have shown more kindness
> Than I?
> Thus for your good
> I shed my blood.
> Mankind, mend your frame of mind,
> For bitterly I must buy your salvation.
> (36.118–30)[65]

Christ describes his body as beaten and broken, but the fact that he speaks so many lines from the cross as part of an outdoor performance, an event for which strong vocal projection would likely be a necessity, suggests that the actor on the cross did not enact bodily suffering very vividly during this pageant; over the course of the play, Christ speaks sixty lines total, including four thirteen-line monologues, before dying at line 260.[66] Moreover, although Christ draws attention to his corporeality, it is in order to explain how it serves a purpose for humanity as a means to salvation; like *The Mirror*, the monologue shrouds the physical in the rhetorical. Later in the play, Christ tells Mary not to look upon his body ("on me to look let thou not," 36.185), but demands everyone else's attention: "Mankind, make my kindness known, / True attention pay unto me, / And trust" (36.189–91).[67] He instructs the disciples to engage his body as a physically present devotional image. Such overt direction may have compelled spectators into empathetic relationships with those characters in the play who were modeling proper devotional viewing practices before a crucifixion image.

Throughout the rest of this pageant the audience hears from various other characters, witnesses Christ's final words and death on the cross, and sees the deposition enacted. Although some of these moments certainly focused attention on Christ's suffering and sacrificial flesh, thereby working at odds with the control mechanisms I have identified, it would perhaps be best to interpret both crucifixion pageants as offering audiences many different, supplementary (and sometimes competing) entry points into the crucifixion scene. As is the case during all performances, spectators likely moved into and out of various spectatorial positions when watching/hearing/experiencing these pageants, ultimately generating theological meaning by means of this shifting embodied simulation.

* * *

Performances of Christ's Passion seemed to bypass reason and directly engage the lay spectator's senses, a blatant challenge to clerical control over this highly sacred—but also complicated, continually resistant, and consequently unstable—image/event. A layperson "pleyinge" Christ on the cross in the live, unmediated, and, in many respects, unwieldy atmosphere of medieval York's Corpus Christi cycle must, then, have seemed particularly dangerous to behold. This was especially true given medieval visual theory. Like the cognitive theory of embodied simulation, medieval visual models propose that assimilation plays a fundamental role in how perceivers come to understand another person's actions and emotions. In the Middle Ages, physical entrainment and its impact on understanding was a very real moral, ethical, and spiritual concern; therefore, performance's powerful influence over the spectator's body may have suggested to some authorities that lay-controlled religious plays, like York's annual Corpus Christi cycle, had the potential to produce "unorthodox" interpretations and meaning more readily than could other media.

And yet, in these chapters I have argued that if we understand other religious media that were popular among the medieval laity as functioning like performances, and we analyze their reception through performance literacy, we can recognize how they, too, rhythmically engaged spectators. These other devotional forms—public rituals, objects, images, spaces, and books—also encouraged laypeople to construct and live in devotional blends that, like performance blends, mixed actuality and make believe, blurring the sacred past and the medieval present. Equally sensual and equally rhythmic, these media were also equally adept at lingering in the body as devotional modes of becoming.

Coda

Medieval Sensual Piety and a Few Twenty-First-Century Religious Rhythms

Whether they are discussing mental images, live performance events, or material objects and spaces, time and again writers in the Middle Ages call attention to the sensual nature of seeing, and to the moral, spiritual, and physical implications of that sensuality. Rather than reflecting medieval visual culture and visual piety, the discourse and practices involving images in the later Middle Ages might, therefore, be better understood as revealing medieval sensual culture and sensual piety. W. J. T. Mitchell has argued that the term "visual culture" is inexact because all media are in fact hybrids or mixed-media. Accordingly, he suggests that in analyses of images and their reception scholars should regard the senses as collaborative entities that "activate" one another.[1] To some extent and unwittingly, then, Mitchell is arguing for a return to the medieval theories of vision and visual media, which considered the entire sensory effect of an image in discussions of its function, use, and meaning. The full sensory impact of medieval performances and other devotional media has been the subject of the preceding chapters.

Studying the sensuality of medieval devotional culture has drawn my attention to certain religious practices and media that are popular among Evangelical Christians worshipping in the United States today. I believe one reason that many people find these contemporary phenomena spiritually efficacious and valuable is because they engage them through sensual piety. For instance, Praise Dance, "a form of worship that seeks to articulate the word and spirit of God through the body," is becoming increasingly popular in the United States.[2] Praise Dance comes in many forms that draw from a variety of traditions (including Ballet, Hip Hop Jazz, Calypso, and Tap) and is performed in many different worship and extra-worship contexts. The choreography may include sign language or symbolic gestures, but dancers sometimes take more improvisational approaches.[3]

Comments by both Praise dancers and spectators corroborate my suggestions about religious performance and embodied devotional meaning. As one dancer remarked, "Most of us are kinetic...Although the songs are saying the words, when you see it in our bodies it elevates the message. We're able to look into people's faces and feel what they're feeling. We're going through the same thing."[4] Praise Dance groups typically describe performers as "vessels" whose dances "touch" spectators' hearts and "open spiritual prison doors."[5] Praise Dance communicates theology through devotional rhythms that, although presented visually, are not experienced exclusively through the eye. As one spectator explained, "sometimes the physical moves me more than words. I respond better to the sensory experience."[6] Praise Dances entrain spectators and generate religious meaning, in great part, by allowing the spectator to live in the dancer's body. Although some audience members might move or clap along, it is not their own dancing, but instead the act of seeing other bodies engaged in religious movement, that ultimately produces the dance's spiritual meaning and relevance.

Using a medieval sensual approach may help us to recognize a diversity of ways that modern religious genres, such as Praise Dance, influence religious understanding. Like the medieval phenomena I examined in the preceding chapters, certain contemporary religious media allow believers to derive meaning from inside rhythmically constructed devotional blends. In this Coda, I will briefly suggest how my conclusions about performance literacy and sensual piety in the Middle Ages may also be relevant to the study of contemporary Evangelical devotional culture.

Rhythmic Proselytism

A wide variety of denominations fall under the Evangelical Christian rubric, but a central unifying tenet is the doctrine of salvation. Evangelical Christians see the world as fundamentally fallen and recognize Christ as the only hope for salvation. Until Christ's second coming, the Evangelical's mission is to spread this message of damnation and salvation—to witness.[7] Many Evangelical Christians witness by means of media designed to prompt spectators/users to live in blends that will function as powerful conversion experiences.

Although performance is not the only medium that can accomplish this goal, cognitive theory demonstrates that watching live theatre activates both our neural network and motor circuits. Understanding involves much more than "reading" a play's visual features; we also understand a performance based upon how we encounter, live in, and reenact it within us. Accordingly, performance spectatorship represents a deeply engaged mode of "active knowledge acquisition."[8] Some of the meaning we create is apparent immediately, while much of it remains embedded within us where it may continue to influence our interactions with and in the world. As I argued with respect to York's medieval pageants, this ability to function as a mode of becoming made performance a natural tool for witnessing to non-Christians.[9] In some respect, the cycle proselytized rhythmically.

Hell Houses, Christian-themed haunted houses that present images of sin, and some salvation, function in this same way. The first Hell House-type events were staged by Jerry Falwell in the 1970s, but adaptations are currently staged by churches across the country each autumn. The most well-known Hell House is probably the one presented annually by Trinity Church (Assemblies of God) in Cedar Hill, Texas. Trinity started staging its version in 1990, and George Ratliff's 2001 documentary *Hell House* follows the planning and production of Trinity's 2000 event.[10] Pastor Keenan Roberts, of New Destiny Christian Center in Colorado, began staging Hell Houses in the mid-1990s and now sells do-it-yourself Hell House Outreach Kits that contain a script, a sound effects CD, and a detailed instruction manual. In the fall of 2006, the theatre company Les Freres Corbusier presented a Hell House based on Roberts's kit at St. Ann's Warehouse in Brooklyn, New York. I attended this production and have also watched Ratliff's documentary; my analysis of Hell Houses is based primarily on these two examples.

Spectators at Hell Houses are led in small groups by a "devil" through various rooms in which different sinful activities and their consequences are enacted. This devil provides commentary throughout and between the scenes. In the Brooklyn production, scenes included a rave that results in a rape and suicide, an abortion, a school shooting, premarital teenage sex, and a gay marriage. The gay marriage episode evolved into a hospital scene in which one of the two gay men died of AIDS. After these vignettes, spectators walk through a vision of Hell in which various sinners are trapped, some of them visible under plexiglass flooring. Spectators, who likely simulated the characters' "sinful" actions during the preceding scenes, now live in a blend of these actions' consequences—damnation. After this walk through Hell, Satan greets spectators, but is quickly interrupted by Christ, who arrives to remind visitors that, unlike the characters they have just seen, they still have the opportunity to repent for their sins and avoid damnation. At this point, despite its attempt to create an "authentic" and un-ironic Hell House, Les Freres Corbusier chose not to end its production as Hell Houses typically conclude. Instead, spectators were led to a hoedown where they could snack on donuts and juice while listening to a live band performing Christian tunes.

Conventional Hell Houses end quite differently. In Ratliff's documentary, the audience enters a room where a minister greets them. The minister, telling them this is "not a scare tactic" or "a guilt trip," asks the group, "If you died tonight do you know where you would go or do you *think* you know where you would go?" He reminds them that if they just *think* they know, they are taking a chance with their eternal souls. The spectators are then given the chance to walk through a door into an adjoining room where people will pray with them as they repent and accept (or, recommit themselves to) Christ. The minister declares that choosing to walk through the door indicates they are ready "to get right with God" and are "through playing." The spectators have six seconds to decide before the door is shut. The documentary cuts to a new scene soon thereafter, but not before we hear the minister begin what sounds like a lecture directed at those who stayed in the room.

This ending confronts spectators with alternatives similar to those presented in York's *Last Judgment* pageant. Like York's pageant, Hell Houses enact two possible human fates—albeit with the grand majority of time devoted to the damned—before shifting the dramatic focus onto spectators and reminding them that this is not merely a theatrical fiction. Although Hell Houses offer visitors an opportunity to make an immediate, physical choice—to walk through the door, repent, and commit to Christ—I would argue that this response is not the production's ultimate objective; the creators likely realize that some of those who "repent" only do so out of momentary intimidation. A Hell House's success is not measured by these immediate reactions, but instead by the ongoing patterns of action and reflection that it is designed to embed within spectators. As with York's final pageant, Hell Houses give spectators an opportunity to "live in" damnation. This vicarious experience of suffering and pain is intended to direct spectators away from sinful conduct in the future. In this respect, each episode functions somewhat like Christ's scourging scene in the cycle—taking spectators along an empathetic journey that shifts abruptly from pleasurable body rhythms to moments of stark realization.[11] As one reviewer of the Brooklyn production noted, "Both Roberts and the Corbusier frères [*sic*] agree that probably no souls were saved in Brooklyn this October, but both also see their collaboration as a success. According to Roberts, 'Hell House' gave New Yorkers an opportunity to meet Jesus and to get acquainted with the risks of sin."[12] More than simple acquaintance, I suspect that Roberts and other Hell House producers believe that these performances' living images also embed the fear of sin's consequences within spectators, and, subsequently, impact (both consciously and unconsciously) how those same individuals will understand their personal relationship to those consequences when faced with similar temptations to sin in the future.

Those who plan Hell Houses perceive the design elements as critical to how these productions achieve their evangelical goals. This attention to material detail is illustrated by the Hell House Outreach Kit's extremely specific advice, such as to "purchase a meat product that closely resembles pieces of a baby" for the abortion scenes.[13] Admittedly, these elements are used to create a realistic aesthetic; in the documentary, one spectator said that she fainted during the abortion scene because it was too "lifelike" and reminded her of her two miscarriages. However, this materiality also reaches out rhythmically and engages the viewer's senses. In her article on Hell Houses, Barbara Brown Taylor writes, "their power is visceral. They bypass the mind." Alternatively, I would argue that their visceral power engages the mind very deeply—by triggering a neural response that simulates the staged actions and emotions within spectators, a Hell House performance encourages viewers to derive religious meaning from living in specific devotional blends.[14] The material design elements sensually enhance these blends by generating rhythms that embed patterns of devotional meaning and action in the spectator's body. Hell Houses are warnings traced into the body.

Of course, as I pointed out in chapter six, there is no way to monitor how these sensual patterns of meaning will ultimately impact spectators. Some spectators might feel exceptionally entrained by the rhythms of those characters performing sinful deeds, as Claire Sponsler argues may have been the case with Vice characters in medieval morality plays.[15] Those producing these events may be trying to limit and redirect this possibility by only depicting the sinful acts themselves very briefly. To me, the scenes in the Brooklyn production felt rushed and as if they never really settled into themselves. The only opportunity to gaze upon and thoughtfully consider the characters for any extended period of time was during the walk through Hell, where some of the same characters I had seen committing "sins" moments before were now suffering, alongside many others. Unlike the rest of the performance, during this section spectators walked one by one, rather than as a group, and were allowed to travel at their own pace. This shift in pace, tone, and structure encouraged me to connect vicariously with the characters when they were suffering the grave consequences of their actions and was perhaps a strategy meant to control the moments in the show I developed the strongest empathetic relationships with and, consequently, the blends I lived in most completely.

"Gilded with Truth": Creationist Museums

I have argued throughout this book that performance is not the only medium that creates these kinds of relationships with viewers and thus that promotes sensual piety. Religious theme parks and museums are also venues that generate religious meaning through material rhythms. The ways in which the creators and designers of these spaces describe their religious efficacy suggests that these venues utilize an iconic pop culture motif in order to embed a sensual faith experience in the bodies of visitors. Moreover, the familiarity of the genre (museum or theme park) encourages visitors to arrive in bodies open to living in the proffered blends.

Dinosaur Adventure Land is a creationist theme park in Florida that aims to teach the "truth" about dinosaurs from a creationist perspective. Its creator, Kent Hovind, a former public school science teacher turned minister, opened the park in 2001.[16] As a 2004 article about the park explains, "There are no mechanized rides at Dinosaur Adventure Land—no creationist-themed roller coasters, scramblers or even a ferris wheel—but instead, a simple discovery center and museum and about a dozen outdoor games, each of which has a 'science lesson' and 'spiritual lesson' posted nearby."[17] One of these games is the

> Nerve-Wracking Ball: a bowling ball on a rope, dangling from a tall tree branch. A child stands before the ball, and then a park guide gives it a shove from a specific angle, so that it comes careering back at the child's face only to stop just in front of it. The child wins if he does not flinch, proving he has "faith in God's laws"—in this case, that a swinging object will never come back higher than the point from which it took off.[18]

Although exhibits like this one are quite participatory, simply gaining access to a world that affirms creationist principles seems to be equally important to some visitors. As one guest remarked, "We've been to museums, discovery centers, where you have to sit there and take the evolutionary stuff... It feels good for [our children] to finally hear it in a public place, something that reinforces their beliefs."[19] A video on the park's website proclaims that Dinosaur Adventure Land "brings God's word to life" and thus offers "new inspiration, energy, and strength to thousands of children and adults from all walks of life."[20]

As its name suggests, Holy Land Experience, an Orlando theme park, also emphasizes the visitor's encounter with a faith-based environment. The park's website repeatedly describes Holy Land Experience as a "living" museum where the "combination of sights, sounds, and tastes will stimulate your senses and blend together to create a spectacular new experience."[21] Visitors walking through the museum's exhibits are meant to relive the sacred past through all of their senses. For this reason, decorum is also stressed; the Guest Conduct Policy begins, "We strive to promote a family friendly environment that glorifies God. Thank you in advance for dressing in modest and appropriate attire (fully clothed, shirts, shoes, etc.)."[22] The visual presentation of guests contributes to the theme park's sensual (and consequently, moral) aesthetic.

The Creation Museum represents by far the most extensive and spectacular of these venues. The museum is run by the evangelical Christian ministry group Answers in Genesis (AiG), which Ken Ham launched in 1979. Ham, who serves as AiG's president, founded and now directs the Creation Museum. AiG is committed "to proclaiming the Bible's literal history with logical reliable answers"[23]; the Creation Museum represents the perfect manifestation of this goal. This $27 million museum is located on the Kentucky, Indiana, and Ohio border, seven miles west of the Cincinnati/Northern Kentucky airport and therefore "within a day's drive (650 miles) of almost two-thirds of the U.S. population."[24] The museum opened in May of 2007 and had over 750,000 visitors in its first two years.[25] When I visited the museum in July of 2009, a one-day adult ticket was $21.95 and $11.95 for kids ages five–twelve; however, I was glad I took advantage of the two-day package ($29.95/$14.95). Even in two days I could only begin to scratch the surface.

Covering seventy thousand square feet, the museum's central attraction is the sixteen-exhibit, two-floor "Museum Experience Walk." This "Walk" includes a dinosaur dig site, fossil and science displays, a journey through biblical history, Noah's ark reconstruction, and various point/counterpoint exhibits. Animatronics, videos, and short films are scattered throughout it. The animatronics were created by a former Universal Studios Park designer.[26] In addition, the museum houses a special-effects theatre, a planetarium, a dinosaur den and fossil exhibit (visually similar to those in a traditional natural history museum), various food venues, and a gift shop. The museum grounds also contain a botanical garden, petting zoo, and picnic areas.

The museum's website exclaims: "Be prepared to experience history in a completely unprecedented way." It promises potential visitors live encounters with biblical history:

> The state-of-the-art 70,000 square foot museum brings the pages of the Bible to life, casting its characters and animals in dynamic form and placing them in familiar settings. Adam and Eve live in the Garden of Eden. Children play and dinosaurs roam near Eden's Rivers. The serpent coils cunningly in the Tree of the Knowledge of Good and Evil. Majestic murals, great masterpieces brimming with pulsating colors and details, provide a backdrop for many of the settings.[27]

Claims to truth constitute an important part of the Creation Museum's draw: "The Bible speaks for itself at the Creation Museum. The exhibit halls are gilded with Truth and the gardens teem with life. It is unique in presenting the scientific evidence for Creation alongside the obvious lies of the evolutionist propaganda. Clearly Christians do not need to be afraid of debate."[28]

Although the use of empirical data is essential to its mission, the Creation Museum ultimately produces and reinforces meaning through the sensual experience in which it embeds that data.[29] The museum presents an evidence-driven narrative, but, more importantly, it allows visitors to walk through and gaze upon a world that confirms their faith; visitors live in the creationist narrative. Museums, like performances, provide live sensual encounters. Consequently, I would argue that people arrive at museums as they do to performances, in bodies open to the museum's rhythmic possibilities. In this state of openness, visitors are more likely to embody a museum's overarching narrative. This may hold especially true for the Creation Museum, whose tagline—"Prepare to Believe"—implies as much. The familiar museum genre helps to encourage an open preparedness from both the believer and skeptic. And for those creationists who may not feel comfortable in a typical natural history museum, the very prominent animatronic display of dinosaurs alongside humans, which greets them in the lobby, may put them at ease. Moreover, while the inside of the venue feels like a traditional natural history museum, the exterior—as other scholars have noted—suggests a megachurch.[30] This choice might comfort and prompt openness among certain evangelical visitors.

Ham would likely agree that "living in the blend" is fundamentally the way his museum conveys meaning. He claims, "Parents say even little kids get the message because they experience it."[31] Certain reviewers seem to—if unconsciously—validate the museum's ability to achieve this objective. As Edward Rothstein asserts in his *New York Times* review,

> Whether you are willing to grant the premises of this museum almost becomes irrelevant as you are drawn into its mixture of spectacle and narrative... For the believer, it seems, this museum provides a kind of relief: Finally the world is being shown as it really is, without the distortions of secularism and natural selection.

But Rothstein also concludes his review with an image of bodily understanding, suggesting that even the skeptic "leaves feeling a bit like Adam emerging from Eden, all the world before him, freshly amazed at its strangeness and extravagant peculiarities."[32] Rothstein's words imply that the museum leaves spectators with a new way of interacting with, and thus understanding, the world.

I would argue that venues like the Creation Museum function in ways similar to performances. These spaces reenact a particular vision of sacred history through the bodies of visitors, particularly those of children, at whom many of the exhibits are specifically directed, and thereby instantiate embodied belief. The expectation is that these embodied beliefs will overpower opposing theories subsequently presented to these same children in books and other media. Those designing these spaces hope that, like a play, these venues will inscribe within children a more vividly actualized worldview than can books professing evolution specifically because these venues provide experiences of/in creationism. Moreover, as with religious performances, these patterns of understanding become the means by which these children will construct religious meaning in the future. Naomi Rokotnitz argues that some performances require spectators to take leaps of faith in response to what they see. Rather than blind faith, this kind of "belief" constitutes "an informed species of decision-making which takes account of—and trusts—embodied knowledge."[33] Like performances, these museums shape belief—or faith—in an ultimately inaccessible past through an actual kinetic experience of living in it; bodily knowledge assumes the status of truth. Visitors not only see a worldview made real and present, but they also experience it as a lived truth that can sustain their faith after they have left the museum.

Familiar Materialities

Kent Hovind created Dinosaur Adventure Land because he believed the theme park—a fixture of mainstream American culture—could serve as an effective means for promoting creationism outside the typical school curriculum. The idea that believers can, and even should, employ mainstream secular resources to impart sacred agenda is a central premise of the megachurch. Large, technologically augmented churches, megachurches began to appear in the United States in the 1970s. According to Anne C. Loveland and Otis B. Wheeler, this first-generation megachurch was aimed at adults born between the 1960s and 1980s who were raised in a culture that emphasized "visual communication, music, sensations, and feelings," more so than in previous generations.[34] These churches often integrated Praise Dancing, live music, or full-scale performances into their services.[35]

The arena-sized screens, state-of-the-art sound systems, and video projection systems found in many megachurch sanctuaries reflect what Loveland and Wheeler describe as a shift "from a participatory to a performance-oriented service."[36] But in addition to making spectacular services possible, these elements also create synesthetic worship experiences that draw congregants into a physical relationship with the space that is similar to what I identified in medieval parish churches. Although they may seem like very different spaces in some respects, the megachurch and medieval parish church environments function through comparable devotional principles.[37]

The sophisticated technology installed in megachurch sanctuaries allows worship leaders to control strategically the space's sensory aesthetic. For example, the acoustical system at Southeast Christian Church in Louisville can make the room "sound smaller" during a sermon and then " 'enlarge' it to sound like a cathedral when the Worship Choir sings."[38] But church leaders do not employ this technology solely to project, amplify, and enlarge; they also use it to generate pointedly sensual encounters for worshippers. For instance, projecting the lyrics to hymns and praise songs onto video screens is not merely a pragmatic choice; as Bo Emerson notes, projections eliminate the need for hymnals thus allowing worshippers to sing with their heads up.[39] In this posture, the worshipper's body is more open, which, perhaps, enables it to more readily engage the service's sensual dimensions and experience "flow." Flow, a term used in psychological theories to discuss play, as well as religious and artistic experiences, has been adopted by performance theorists. As Marvin Carlson explains, during flow, "reflexivity is swallowed up in a merging of action and awareness, a focus upon the pleasure of the present moment, and a loss of a sense of ego or of movement toward some goal."[40] The technology employed in megachurches affords congregants ways to feel the service with their whole bodies and thus experience devotional flow.

Some critics of megachurches disagree. Scott Thumma, on faculty at the Hartford Institute for Religion Research, argues, "The more you enhance and digitalize and alter the sound and all those sorts of things, the further it takes it from the lived reality."[41] Thumma seems to imply that technology is inherently artificial and therefore necessarily denigrates real or authentic religious experiences. I would propose instead that such material enhancements can call attention to the spectator's physical presence and therefore reinforce the "lived reality" of a worship experience. By giving texture to the massive sanctuary, technological additions imbue the worship encounter with degrees of sensuality that engage the parishioner's body. Such physical engagement may counter an inclination toward passivity that the space's large size might otherwise inculcate.

Although technology is still a staple of the megachurch aesthetic, in the last decade or so a new, more holistically minded breed of megachurch has developed. As Jonathan Mahler writes, "this is not the megachurch of the 1980's, where baby boomers turned up once a week to passively take in a 45-minute service...In many places, they operate almost like surrogate governments, offering residents day care, athletic facilities, counseling, even schools."[42] Radiant Church in Surprise, Arizona, exemplifies this "full service" megachurch:

> The foyer includes five 50-inch plasma-screen televisions, a bookstore and a café with a Starbucks-trained staff making espresso drinks. (For those who are in a rush, there's a drive-through latte stand outside the main building.) Krispy Kreme doughnuts are served at every service. (Radiant's annual Krispy Kreme budget is $16,000). For kids there are Xboxes (10 for fifth and sixth graders alone). "That's what they're into," [Radiant's founder Lee] McFarland says. "You can either fight it or say they're a tool for God." The dress code is lax: most worshippers wear jeans, sweats or shorts, depending on the season...Even

the baptism pool is seductive: Radiant keeps the water at 101 degrees. "We've had people say, 'No, leave me under,'" McFarland says. "It's like taking a dip in a spa."

Mahler concludes that "everything about Radiant has been designed to lure people away from other potential weekend destinations."[43]

Throughout history, incorporating everyday materialities into religious spaces has produced anxiety. In the Middle Ages, some authorities believed that layering a religious image with everyday clothes and accessories kept laypeople steeped in their flesh and unable to reach more elevated levels of religious seeing and understanding—laypeople "should be more spiritual and take less heed of such sensible signs."[44] Critics of megachurches sometimes echo these sentiments. Eddie Gibbs, a professor of church growth at Fuller Theological Seminary, argues, "worship that degenerates into a casual overfamiliarity is both presumptuous and embarrassing to those who see God from a transcendental perspective."[45] Alternatively, megachurch leaders and congregants contend that God is "constantly intervening in the everyday lives of human beings. And he could be encountered anywhere, not just in church."[46] Using popular, everyday synesthetic elements within the church helps to trace this particular theological message into the worshipper's body. Megachurch leaders and critics like Gibbs both recognize that those who engage these spaces "live in" a sacred/ everyday blend. However, to their advocates, integrating cafes and gyms into megachurches, and in this manner making them "look like a mall,"[47] does not de-sacralize the spiritual through "sensible signes"; instead, they believe that these elements sanctify the mundane. The sacred input frames the blend.

As with religious theme parks, the fact that elements of the megachurch space are familiar may encourage some people to arrive at worship in bodies that are more open to the religious message than they would be in a space less recognizable and "safe." Megachurch leaders believe this accessibility represents the first step toward achieving larger evangelical goals. As Mahler explains, McFarland has a long-term plan for his congregation that "involves much more than playing video games and eating doughnuts. He says that his hope—his expectation, really—is that casual worshippers will gradually immerse themselves in Radiant's many Christ-based programs...until they have eventually incorporated Christian values into every aspect of their lives."[48] Worded somewhat differently, "living in" a megachurch's blend embeds within a congregant's body patterns of faith that rather than rejecting the mundane or everyday, instead reshape these secular rhythms into sacred expressions of Christian faith.

* * *

Many pious Christians living in the United States today watch movies or television shows with religious themes, read novels based on sacred stories, and fill their homes with devotional images. Like the medieval laity, they use a variety of media to create sacred encounters that will enhance their faith. Medieval sensual piety may, therefore, supply us with ways to think about how these contemporary practices fulfill religious needs. Marcus Bull suggests that medievalism is not about studying the past in order to draw a direct link to the contemporary moment, but it is instead a process of understanding the medieval world by making "mental adjustments" that will help us set aside our own anachronistic perspectives and values.[49] In order to make these mental adjustments, Bull recommends that we examine the "mental spaces" that people lived in during the Middle Ages by asking questions that will expose our own "cognitive assumptions."[50] In the preceding chapters, I have suggested a way to adjust certain assumptions about how late medieval spectators saw religious performances, spaces, and objects. I interpret this mental adjustment as offering us some access to the mental spaces that medieval laypeople may have inhabited as part of their devotional lives. In this Coda, I have tried to demonstrate how a similar mental adjustment can also help us to better understand the ways in which certain contemporary religious media contribute sensually to today's culture of faith. The popularity of Praise Dance, Hell Houses, creationist theme parks and museums, and megachurches may reflect a longing among evangelical Christians similar to that of the late medieval laity. In both cases, sensual piety satisfies a desire for deeply engaged, bodily devotional experiences whose rhythms will linger in the body and "bere wittenesse" to faith.

Notes

Introduction

1. Aleksandra Wolska, "Rabbits, Machines, and the Ontology of Performance," *Theatre Journal* 57, no. 1 (2005): 85, 88.
2. Ibid., 91.
3. See Kathleen Ashley, "Sponsorship, Reflexivity and Resistance: Cultural Readings of the York Cycle Plays," in *The Performance of Middle English Cultures: Essays on Chaucer and Drama in Honor of Martin Stevens*, eds. James J. Paxson, Lawrence M. Clopper, and Sylvia Tomasch, 9–24 (Cambridge: Boydell and Brewer, 1998); Sarah Beckwith, *Signifying God: Social Relation and Symbolic Act in the York Corpus Christi Plays* (Chicago: University of Chicago Press, 2001); and Claire Sponsler, *Drama and Resistance: Bodies, Goods, and Theatricality in Late Medieval England* (Minneapolis: University of Minnesota Press, 1997).
4. There are certainly exceptions. Two recent publications that address this gap are: Theodore K. Lerud, *Memory, Images, and the English Corpus Christi Drama* (New York: Palgrave Macmillan, 2008) and various essays in *Visualizing Medieval Performance: Perspectives, Histories, Contexts*, ed. Elina Gertsman (Burlington, VT: Ashgate, 2008).
5. David Morgan, *Visual Piety: A History and Theory of Popular Religious Images* (Berkeley: University of California Press, 1998), 1.
6. The narrator in *Piers Plowman* recalls: "The ladies danced until the day dawned, / When the men rang bells to the resurrection—right then I woke, / And I called to Kytt my wife and Calote my daughter: / "Rise and go do honor to God's resurrection, / And creep to the cross on knees, and kiss it as if it were a jewel!" William Langland, *The Vision of Piers Plowman*, ed. A. V. C. Schmidt, 2nd ed. (London: J. M. Dent, 1995), 325.
7. Sarah Beckwith, *Christ's Body: Identity, Culture and Society in Late Medieval Writings* (London and New York: Routledge, 1993), 49–50.
8. Leonard E. Boyle, O.P., "The Fourth Lateran Council and Manuals of Popular Theology," in *The Popular Literature of Medieval England*,

ed. Thomas J. Heffernan (Knoxville: University of Tennessee Press, 1985), 31.
9. Eamon Duffy, *The Stripping of the Altars: Traditional Religion in England 1400–1580* (New Haven: Yale University Press, 1992), 53.
10. *The Lay Folks' Catechism, or the English and Latin Versions of Archbishop Thoresby's Instruction for the People*, eds. Thomas Frederick Simmons and Henry Edward Nolloth (London: Kegan Paul, Trench, Trübner and Co., 1901), 98. Original: "Our fadir the ercebisshop grauntes of his grace / Fourti daies of pardon til al that kunnes tham, / Or dos thair gode diligence for to kun tham."
11. Ibid., 96, 42.
12. Ibid., 70, 46, 52.
13. *The Book of Margery Kempe*, trans. B. A. Windeatt (New York: Penguin, 1985), 104 (original: I. 28.1565–71; 28.1585–8). For the original language, see *The Book of Margery Kempe*, ed. Lynn Staley, TEAMS Middle English Texts (Kalamazoo, Michigan: Medieval Institute Publications, 1996) available online at: http://www.lib.rochester.edu/camelot/teams/staley.htm.
14. Morgan, *Visual Piety*, 58. Morgan argues for an aesthetic of popular religious art viewing with characteristics that suggest an active encounter between believer and image.
15. Nicholas Love, *The Mirror of the Blessed Life of Jesus Christ: A Critical Edition Based on Cambridge University Library Additional MSS 6578 and 6686*, ed. Michael G. Sargent (New York: Garland Publishing, 1992). This text is an English translation of the *Meditationes Vitae Christi*, an early-fourteenth-century Latin text.
16. For a discussion of how crucifixion iconography was employed in late medieval England, see Beckwith, *Christ's Body*.
17. Sarah Stanbury argues, "One of the most striking and coercive features of both the *Meditationes* and of Love's *Mirror* is the use of the vocative, the voice of an invisible authority that not only orchestrates the story and commentary but also tells us how to see it, coaxing us to 'behold' landmark events in Christ's life." *The Visual Object of Desire in Late Medieval England* (Philadelphia: University of Pennsylvania Press, 2008), 178. In chapter six, I discuss Love's *Mirror* and Margery Kempe's devotional activities in greater detail.
18. See particularly Emile Mâle, *Religious Art in France, The Twelfth Century: A Study of the Origins of Medieval Iconography* (Princeton: Princeton University Press, 1978) and *The Gothic Image* (New York: Harper, 1958); and, M. D. Anderson, *Drama and Imagery in English Medieval Churches* (Cambridge: Cambridge University Press, 1963), 87–104. Pamela Sheingorn offers an overview and critique of the methodology employed in such studies in "On Using Medieval Art in the Study of Medieval Drama: An Introduction to Methodology," *Research Opportunities in Renaissance Drama* 22 (1979): 101–9.

19. *York Art: A Subject List of Extant and Lost Art Including Items Relevant to Early Drama*, ed. Clifford Davidson (Kalamazoo, MI: Medieval Institute Publications, 1978), iii.
20. For a critique of EDAM's mission, see Martin Stevens, "The Intertextuality of Late Medieval Art and Drama," *New Literary History* 22, no. 2 (Spring 1991): 318, 333–4.
21. Sheingorn, "On Using Medieval Art," 101–9; "Medieval Drama Studies and the New Art History," *Mediaevalia* 18 (1995): 143–62; "The Visual Language of Drama: Principles of Composition," in *Contexts for Early English Drama*, eds. Marianne G. Briscoe and John C. Coldeway (Bloomington: Indiana University Press, 1989), 173–91.
22. Sheingorn, "The Visual Language of Drama," 188.
23. As I will argue in chapter one, materiality is a particularly important element to consider with respect to medieval art. As Herbert L. Kessler writes, "Overt materiality is a distinguishing characteristic of medieval art...The materials do not vanish from sight through the mimicking of the perception of other things; to the contrary, their very physicality asserts the essential artifice of the image or object." *Seeing Medieval Art* (Ontario: Broadview Press, 2004), 19.
24. Robert Scribner describes piety as a "way of seeing" in "Popular Piety and Modes of Visual Perception in Late Medieval and Reformation Germany," *Journal of Religious History* 15 (1989): 456.
25. Here are just a few texts published on this subject in the last decade: Madeline H. Caviness, *Visualizing Women in the Middle Ages: Sight, Spectacle, and Scopic Economy* (Philadelphia: University of Pennsylvania Press, 2001); Mary C. Erler and Maryanne Kowaleski, eds., *Gendering the Master Narrative* (Ithaca and London: Cornell University Press, 2003); A. B. Mulder-Bakker, ed., *Seeing and Knowing: Medieval Women and the Transmission of Knowledge* (Turnhout: Brepols, 2004); Christine Peters, *Patterns of Piety: Women, Gender and Religion in Late Medieval and Reformation England* (Cambridge: Cambridge University Press, 2003); Pauline Stafford and Anneke B. Mulder-Bakker, eds., *Gendering the Middle Ages* (Oxford: Blackwell Publishers, 2002); and the *New Trends in Feminine Spirituality Series* published by Brepols.
26. Caroline Bynum, *Fragmentation and Redemption: Essays on Gender and the Human Body in Medieval Religion* (New York: Zone Books, 1991); *Holy Feast and Holy Fast: The Religious Significance of Food to Medieval Women* (Berkeley: University of California Press, 1987).
27. Sponsler, *Drama and Resistance*, 53.
28. Anna Dronzek, "Gendered Theories of Education in Fifteenth-Century Conduct Books," in *Medieval Conduct*, eds. Kathleen Ashley and Robert L. A. Clark (Minneapolis: University of Minnesota Press, 2001), 142.

29. Ibid., 143. See also Sponsler, *Drama and Resistance*, 50–74; and Felicity Riddy, "Mother Knows Best: Reading Social Change in a Courtesy Text," *Speculum* 71, no. 1 (January 1996): 66–86.
30. Robert L. A. Clark, "Constructing the Female Subject in Devotion," in *Medieval Conduct*, eds. Kathleen Ashley and Robert L. A. Clark (Minneapolis and London: University of Minnesota Press, 2001), 173–4.
31. See particularly *Performance and Cognition*, eds. Bruce McConachie and F. Elizabeth Hart (New York: Routledge, 2006); *Staging Philosophy: Intersections of Theater, Performance, and Philosophy*, eds. David Krasner and David Z. Saltz (Ann Arbor: University of Michigan Press, 2006); and the December 2007 issue of *Theatre Journal* dedicated to work on performance and cognition. Various medieval scholars are also using cognitive theory. See Anne L. Clark's essay "Why All the Fuss About the Mind? A Medievalist's Perspective on Cognitive Theory," in *History in the Comic Mode: Medieval Communities and the Matter of Person*, eds. Rachel Fulton and Bruce Holsinger (New York: Columbia University Press, 2007), 170–81. The increasing number of conference sessions and the inception of the "Medieval Cognitive Literary and Scientific Studies" organization at the 2009 Medieval Congress at Western Michigan University reflect a growing interest in cognitive science among medievalists.
32. Bruce McConachie, "Metaphors We Act By: Kinesthetics, Cognitive Psychology, and Historical Structures," *Journal of Dramatic Theory and Criticism* 8, no. 2 (1993): 23–45; "Approaching Performance History Through Cognitive Psychology," *Assaph* 10 (1994): 113–22; "Doing Things with Image Schemas: The Cognitive Turn in Theatre Studies and the Problem of Experience for Historians," *Theatre Journal* 53 (2001): 569–94; and *Engaging Audiences: A Cognitive Approach to Spectating in the Theatre* (New York: Palgrave Macmillan, 2008).
33. Bruce McConachie, "Preface," *Performance and Cognition: Theatre Studies and the Cognitive Turn*, eds. Bruce McConachie and F. Elizabeth Hart (New York: Routledge, 2006), ix.
34. Evan Thompson, *Mind in Life: Biology, Phenomenology, and the Sciences of the Mind* (Cambridge: Harvard University Press, 2007), 14. For Mark Johnson's recent work in this area, see *The Meaning of the Body: Aesthetics of Human Understanding* (Chicago: University of Chicago Press, 2008).
35. Shaun Gallagher and Dan Zahavi, *The Phenomenological Mind: An Introduction to Philosophy of Mind and Cognitive Science* (London and New York: Routledge, 2008), 5, original emphasis. They also explain various changes that have motivated "a reconsideration of phenomenology as a philosophical-scientific approach," among these the notion of "embodied cognition," which took hold in the 1990s, and the progress in neuroscience (5).

36. McConachie, "Doing Things," 583. This is why, according to McConachie, "certain kinds of plays fashion certain groups of spectators and vice versa" (ibid.).
37. Ibid., 571. McConachie tackles the issue of how cultural practices shape audience engagement in *Engaging Audiences* (121–83). He asserts, "Regarding culture, the mind/brain is neither 'hard-wired' for certain cultural responses nor is it a 'blank slate' or passive recorder that facilitates the direct transmission of individual and social experiences into memory. Rather... 'the ecological brain' both enables and constrains perceptions and practices, leading enculturated humans to a range of cultural-historical possibilities" (122).
38. Naomi Rokotnitz, "'It is required/You do awake your faith': Learning To Trust the Body Through Performing *The Winter's Tale*," in *Performance and Cognition: Theatre Studies and the Cognitive Turn*, eds. Bruce McConachie and F. Elizabeth Hart (New York: Routledge, 2006), 140.
39. In *Drama and Resistance*, Claire Sponsler also examines how medieval visual theory impacted lay devotional practices with images across genres. I see my work as building upon some of her conclusions. For example, Sponsler writes, "Like devotional images in books of hours, cycle plays asked from the spectator an imaginative projection into the representation such that the acts of spectatorship and participation were blurred" (151). As I will explain in chapters one and four, the theories of mirror neuron responses and conceptual blending reveal a cognitive basis for such blurring.
40. There has been a significant amount of research on the art and architecture of medieval York, including *York Art*, edited by Clifford Davidson, and the Royal Commission's Inventories of Historical Monuments in York. I have used Royal Commission on Historical Monuments, *An Inventory of the Historical Monuments in the City of York. Volume Three: Southwest of the Ouse* (London: Her Majesty's Stationary Office, 1972) and *An Inventory of the Historical Monuments in the City of York. Volume Five: The Central Area* (London: Her Majesty's Stationary Office, 1981).
41. E. K. Chambers, *The Mediaeval Stage*, 2 vols (London: Oxford University Press, 1903).
42. Harold C. Gardiner, *Mysteries' End* (New Haven: Yale University Press, 1946); V. A. Kolve, *The Play Called Corpus Christi* (Stanford: Stanford University Press, 1966); Rosemary Woolf, *The English Mystery Plays* (London: Routledge and Kegan Paul, 1972).
43. Martin Stevens, *Four Middle English Mystery Cycles: Textual, Contextual, and Critical Interpretations* (Princeton: Princeton University Press, 1987); R. M. Lumiansky and David Mills, *The Chester Mystery Cycle: Essays and Documents* (Chapel Hill and London: University of North Carolina Press, 1983); Peter W. Travis, *Dramatic Design in the Chester Cycle* (Chicago and London: University of

Chicago Press, 1982); Patrick J. Collins, *The N-Town Plays and Medieval Picture Cycles* (Kalamazoo: Medieval Institute Publications, 1979).
44. In *Four Middle English Mystery Cycles*, Martin Stevens identifies the York cycle as "more nearly a communal enterprise than any other extant English cycle" (17). Richard Beadle describes how York's cycle "contrasts variously with the eclectic approach to the cycle structure adopted by the compiler of the N-town manuscript, or Chester's self-conscious attempt to recreate the genre in a form appropriate to the changing times of the sixteenth century, or the radical experimentations with the individual components of the cycle found in the plays of the Wakefield Master." See "The York Cycle," in *The Cambridge Companion to Medieval English Theatre*, ed. Richard Beadle (Cambridge: Cambridge University Press, 1994), 89.
45. Alexandra F. Johnston and Margaret Rogerson, eds., *Records of Early English Drama: York*, 2 vols (Toronto: University of Toronto Press, 1979), xix. My work relies heavily on the archival evidence compiled in these volumes. Although they represent the first volumes in the *REED* series and therefore maintain more restrictive criteria for dramatic evidence than later volumes, they offer an extraordinary collection of references to dramatic activity from public and ecclesiastical records. Unless specified, all English modernizations are my own and I use the Middle English transcriptions as they appear in these volumes. I use Johnston and Rogerson's English translations of Latin texts, but also include the page numbers of their transcriptions of the Latin originals in parentheses in the citation. Although there has been much thoughtful criticism of the *REED* series, this project's contribution is immense. For a constructive examination of *REED*, see Theresa Coletti's "Reading REED: History and the Records of Early English Drama," in *Literary Practice and Social Change in Britain 1380–1530*, ed. Lee Patterson (Berkeley: University of California Press, 1990), 248–84, and Patricia Badir's response, "Playing Space: History, the Body, and Records of Early English Drama," *Exemplaria* 9, no. 2 (Fall 1997): 255–79.
46. I am not suggesting that an exact reconstruction of the medieval performance could ever take place. However, York's topography still provides the pageant route, with many medieval buildings and churches along its path. As Eileen White admits, "it is still possible to walk the streets of York that contained the procession of wagons and by their shape and size dictated the style of performance, and sense a link between the old and the new tradition" (75). "Places to Hear the Play: The Performance of the Corpus Christi Play at York," *Early Theatre* 3 (2000): 49–78.
47. The Guilds of York, "York Mystery Plays," http://www.yorkmysteryplays.co.uk/index.htm.

48. British Library Additional Manuscript 35290 contains the nearly complete text of the cycle, assembled sometime between 1463 and 1477. This manuscript, intended to be the official record of the text, was a public document and apparently compiled from guild prompt copies of the plays.
49. The other two manuscripts are the *B/Y Memorandum Book*, a later companion volume to the *A/Y* that is comprised in large part of guild ordinances, and the *E Memorandum Book*, which contains guild ordinances after 1573.
50. Johnston and Rogerson, *York*, xix.
51. Ibid., 3. Revisiting the *A/Y* with a digital camera, Meg Twycross has identified previously unseen erasures and emendations that shed further light on the continually shifting life of the York cycle. In respect to this particular 1376 entry, she discovered that it "is written over an erasure in a different ink and different, later, hand, and that the accepted dating of the earliest record of the York cycle is therefore, to say the least, unsafe" (113). She suggests that, at this point, the hand looks like "one which appears later in the Memorandum Book, from the 1390s" (129). "The *Ordo paginarum* Revisited, with a Digital Camera," in "*Bring furth the pagants*": *Essays in Early English Drama Presented to Alexandra F. Johnston*, eds. David Klausner and Karen Sawyer Marsalek (Toronto: University of Toronto Press, 2007), 105–31.
52. Johnston and Rogerson, *York*, 701 (15). Source: *A/Y Memorandum*.
53. Alexandra F. Johnston argues that these plays were presented on wagons in the same processional format as the Corpus Christi cycle, and most scholars believe that both the Creed and Pater Noster plays were divided into smaller pageants that coincided with the petitions. See Johnston, "The Plays of the Religious Guilds of York: The Creed Play and The Pater Noster Play," *Speculum* 50 (1975): 55–90. See also Sue Powell, "*Pastoralia* and the Lost York Plays of the Creed and Paternoster," *European Medieval Drama* 8 (2004): 35–50.
54. Duffy, *Stripping of the Altars*, 67.
55. Johnston and Rogerson, *York*, 693 (6). The guild was also responsible for maintaining "a certain drawing which hangs above a column in the cathedral church aforesaid, next to the above candelabrum and depicts the layout and usefulness of the Lord's Prayer", [864 (646)].
56. Ibid., 757 (80). The <...> surrounding words indicate that these are damaged or lost letters. The (...) surrounding letters or words indicate blank spaces in the original manuscript where writing might be expected.
57. Beckwith, *Signifying God*, xvi.
58. Ibid., 3.
59. Jeffrey Jerome Cohen and Bonnie Wheeler, "Becoming and Unbecoming," in *Becoming Male in the Middle Ages*, eds. Cohen

and Wheeler (New York and London: Garland Publishing, 1997), xviii.

One   Performance Literacy

1. *The Book of Margery Kempe*, trans. B. A. Windeatt (New York: Penguin, 1985), 186 (I.60.3492–5). For the original language, see *The Book of Margery Kempe*, ed. Lynn Staley, TEAMS Middle English Texts (Kalamazoo, Michigan: Medieval Institute Publications, 1996) available online at: http://www.lib.rochester.edu/camelot/teams/staley.htm.
2. Ibid., 104 (I.28.1565–68).
3. James H. Marrow, "Symbol and Meaning in Northern European Art of the Late Middle Ages and the Early Renaissance," *Simiolus* 16 (1986): 152, original emphasis.
4. Scholars of medieval drama who have attended to performance's visual contributions to lay devotional culture include: Gail McMurray Gibson, *The Theater of Devotion: East Anglian Drama and Society in the Late Middle Ages* (Chicago: University of Chicago Press, 1989); Victor I. Scherb, *Staging Faith: East Anglian Drama in the Later Middle Ages* (Madison: Fairleigh Dickinson University Press, 2001); Theodore K. Lerud, *Memory, Images, and the English Corpus Christi Drama* (New York: Palgrave Macmillan, 2008); Glenn Ehrstine, *Theater, Culture, and Community in Reformation Bern, 1523–1555* (Leiden, Boston, and Köln: Brill, 2002); and "Framing the Passion: Mansion Staging as Visual Mnemonic," in *Visualizing Medieval Performance: Perspectives, Histories, Contexts*, ed. Elina Gertsman (Burlington, VT: Ashgate, 2008), 263–77.
5. Beth Williamson, "Altarpieces, Liturgy, and Devotion," *Speculum* 79, no. 2 (April 2004): 381, 387.
6. Eamon Duffy, "Late Medieval Religion," in *Gothic Art for England 1400–1547*, eds. Richard Marks and Paul Williamson (London: V&A Publications, 2003), 57.
7. Ibid., 40. Comments by an Italian visitor to England in 1497 reflect this characteristic of lay piety: "Although they all attend mass every day, and say many Paternosters in public, the women carrying long rosaries in their hands, and any who can read taking the office of our Lady with them and with some companion reciting it in the church verse by verse in a low voice after the manner of churchmen, they always hear mass on Sunday in their parish church." "A Relation...of the Island of England...about the Year 1500," in *Women in England c. 1275–1525: Documentary Sources*, ed. P. Jeremy P. Goldberg, trans. C. A. Sneyd (Manchester and New York: Manchester University Press, 1995), 283.
8. David Saltz, "Infiction and Outfiction: The Role of Fiction in Theatrical Performance," in *Staging Philosophy: Intersections of*

Theater, Performance, and Philosophy, eds. David Krasner and David Saltz (Ann Arbor: University of Michigan Press, 2006), 203.
9. Mark Johnson, *The Body in the Mind* (Chicago: University of Chicago Press, 1987), 104.
10. For example, scholars have argued that the N-town manuscript was compiled for a reader. See Martin Stevens, *Four Middle English Mystery Cycles: Textual, Contextual, and Critical Interpretatións* (Princeton: Princeton University Press, 1987), 184, 191. Darwin Smith makes similar conclusions about a medieval copy of *Pierre Pathelin*. See *Maistre Pierre Pathelin-Le Miroir d'Orgueil* (Saint-Benoît-du-Sault: Tarabuste Editions, 2002).
11. As David Morgan asserts, a popular religious image is not "a neutral or a blank slate, an unresistant medium that receives whatever believers wish to see limned there." *Visual Piety: A History and Theory of Popular Religious Images* (Berkeley: University of California Press, 1998), 122.
12. A frequently quoted story from the early seventeenth century recounts an old man who, when quizzed on his knowledge of Christ, replied "I think I heard of that man you spake of, once in a play at Kendall, called Corpus Christi play, where there was a man on a tree, and the blood ran down." "The Life of Master John Shaw," in *Yorkshire Diaries and Autobiographies in the Seventeenth and Eighteenth Centuries*, ed. Charles Jackson (Durham: Andrews and Company, 1877), 139. Another example appears in the late-fifteenth-century Dutch play *Mariken van Nieumeghen* when a young girl is persuaded to repent her sins after attending a public play that advocates repentance. This episode also appears in the sixteenth-century English version of this play: *Mary of Nemmegen*, ed. Margaret M. Raftery (Leiden: Brill, 1991).
13. Simon Shepherd, *Theatre, Body and Pleasure* (London and New York: Routledge, 2006), 36–7.
14. Stanton B. Garner, Jr., *Bodied Spaces: Phenomenology and Performance in Contemporary Drama* (Ithaca and London: Cornell University Press, 1994), 12.
15. Paul Stoller reviews Husserl's contribution to phenomenology in "Rationality," in *Critical Terms for Religious Studies*, ed. Mark C. Taylor (Chicago: University of Chicago Press, 1998), 249.
16. Many scholars working with cognitive theory have also found Husserl's approach problematic. Although Evan Thompson's earlier work took this position, Husserlian phenomenology figures centrally in *Mind in Life*. Thompson devotes an appendix to explaining this attitudinal shift. *Mind in Life: Biology, Phenomenology, and the Sciences of the Mind* (Cambridge: Harvard University Press, 2007), 413–6.
17. Maurice Merleau-Ponty, *Phenomenology of Perception*, trans. Colin Smith (1945; New York: Routledge and Kegan Paul, 1962; reprint, London and New York: Routledge, 2005), xii.

18. Ibid., 239.
19. Garner, *Bodied Spaces*, 4.
20. Ibid., 5.
21. Stoller, "Rationality," 252.
22. Shepherd, *Theatre*, 85.
23. Ibid., 90.
24. Ibid., 78–82.
25. Ibid., 94–5.
26. Nelson Goodman, "Pictures in the Mind?" in *Image and Understanding: Thoughts about Images, Ideas About Understanding*, eds. Horace Barlow, Colin Blakemore, and Miranda Weston-Smith (Cambridge: Cambridge University Press, 1990), 362–3.
27. Shaun Gallagher and Dan Zahavi, *The Phenomenological Mind: An Introduction to Philosophy of Mind and Cognitive Science* (London and New York: Routledge, 2008), 28.
28. Ibid., 30.
29. Thompson, *Mind in Life*, 358. Francisco J. Varela first outlined this approach in "Neurophenomenology: A Methodological Remedy for the Hard Problem," *Journal of Consciousness Studies* 3 (1996): 330–50. As Gallagher and Zahavi explain, neurophenomenology, as defined by Varela, originally signified "an approach to the neuroscience of consciousness that incorporates the phenomenological methodology outlined in the Husserlian tradition. In recent years, however, the term has been used in a much looser sense to signify any kind of appeal to first-person data in combination with data from neuroscience." *Phenomenological Mind*, 41.
30. Thompson, *Mind in Life*, 14.
31. At the end of part one of *Mind in Life*, Thompson asserts, "If we follow Merleau-Ponty's lead, but combine it with the more recent developments reviewed in this chapter and the previous one, then we can begin to envision a different kind of approach to matter, life, and mind from objectivism and reductionism. Starting from a recognition of the transcendental and hence ineliminable status of experience, the aim would be to search for morphodynamical principles that can both integrate the orders of matter, life, and mind, and account for the originality of each order. This approach is precisely what Varela envisioned in calling for a 'neurophenomenology' in mind science" (87). Thompson offers an excellent overview and analysis of Merleau-Ponty's work that connects it with the concerns of cognitive theory in *Mind in Life*, 3–87.
32. Johnson, *Body in the Mind*, 175.
33. Suzannah Biernoff, "Carnal Relations: Embodied Sight in Merleau-Ponty, Roger Bacon and St Francis," *Journal of Visual Culture* 4, no. 1 (2005): 39–40.
34. Robert S. Nelson, "Descartes's Cow and Other Domestications of the Visual," in *Visuality Before and Beyond the Renaissance: Seeing*

as Others See, ed. Nelson (Cambridge: Cambridge University Press, 2000), 1–21.
35. Michael Camille, "Before the Gaze: The Internal Senses and Late Medieval Practices of Seeing," in *Visuality Before and Beyond the Renaissance: Seeing as Others See*, ed. Robert S. Nelson (Cambridge: Cambridge University Press, 2000), 208.
36. David C. Lindberg, *Theories of Vision from Al-Kindi to Kepler* (Chicago and London: University of Chicago Press, 1976), 104–21.
37. Ibid., 109.
38. Roger Bacon, *The Opus majus of Roger Bacon*, 3 vols, ed. John H. Bridges (London, 1900; Reprint, Frankfurt: Minerva-Verlag, 1964), 2: 52; as quoted in Lindberg, *Theories of Vision*, 115.
39. Ibid., 2: 71–2; as quoted in Lindberg, *Theories of Vision*, 113.
40. Suzannah Biernoff, *Sight and Embodiment in the Middle Ages* (New York: Palgrave, 2002), 75, emphasis mine.
41. Biernoff remarks, "As a scientist [Bacon] is attentive to the world of sensible forms; as a Christian he cannot dispense with a realm of pre-existent, universal and immutable truths" (ibid., 84).
42. Biernoff explains, "The images of the visible world reproduced in the eyes and brain are, for Bacon as for Aristotle, *material* images. The idea of the disembodied mind having visual experiences is an oxymoron in this context because the sensitive soul is embodied." "Carnal Relations," 42, original emphasis.
43. Ibid. Claire Sponsler also discusses the impact of medieval visual theory on the use of devotional images by the laity. She writes, "meditation on images was understood as offering immediate access to the 'real' thing. Images were not viewed as abstract illusions but rather as ways of perceiving the religious world and so providing a route to direct sensory experience from which the worshiper might otherwise be shut off" (122–3). *Drama and Resistance: Bodies, Goods, and Theatricality in Late Medieval England* (Minneapolis: University of Minnesota Press, 1997), 121–6.
44. Biernoff, "Carnal Relations," 48. Biernoff argues, "In medieval sources, and in Merleau-Ponty's writings, 'flesh' exceeds the visible body. Sight lends the flesh an intersubjective dimension; it literally carries carnality outside the viewer's corporeal envelope and into the world" (ibid., 45).
45. Merleau-Ponty, *Phenomenology of Perception*, 325.
46. Thompson, as well as Gallagher and Zahavi, discuss the mirror neuron system. Thompson, *Mind in Life*, 393–7; Gallagher and Zahavi, *Phenomenological Mind*, 177–81.
47. Giacomo Rizzolatti, Laila Craighero, and Luciano Fadiga, "The Mirror System in Humans," *Mirror Neurons and the Evolution of Brain and Language*, eds. Maxim I. Stamenov and Vittorio Gallese (Amsterdam and Philadelphia: John Benjamins, 2002), 37–59.

48. Vittorio Gallese and George Lakoff, "The Brain's Concepts: The Role of Sensory-Motor System in Conceptual Knowledge," *Cognitive Neuropsychology* 22, no. 3/4 (2005), 463. It is important to highlight the fact that not all of the neurons that fire when we execute an action also fire when we perceive that action; only a percentage of our brain cells function as mirror neurons. As Amy Cook notes, in order for the conversation between the sciences and humanities to be "mutually fruitful, it is important for both sides to recognize the limits, as well as the potential, of the theories and findings" and not to overstate the possibilities that cognitive theories offer. See "Interplay: The Method and Potential of a Cognitive Science Approach to Theatre," *Theatre Journal* 59, no. 4 (2007): 591.
49. Gallese and Lakoff, "The Brain's Concepts," 464.
50. As Gallese explains, experiencing an emotion like disgust and "witnessing disgust expressed by the facial mimicry of someone else both activate the same neural structure." "Embodied Simulation: From Neurons to Phenomenal Experience," *Phenomenology and the Cognitive Sciences* 4, no. 1 (2005): 39.
51. Ibid., 39, 37.
52. It is important to recognize that mirror neuron system (MNS) research is still developing and that the evidence is far from conclusive. Recent articles have challenged the notion of action understanding through the MNS in humans or questioned the existence of an MNS in humans entirely. See Gregory Hickok, "Eight Problems for the Mirror Neuron Theory of Action Understanding in Monkeys and Humans," *Journal of Cognitive Neuroscience* 21, no. 7 (2008): 1229–1243; and Angelika Lingnau, Benno Gesierich, and Alfonso Caramazza, "Asymmetric fMRI Adaptation Reveals No Evidence for Mirror Neurons in Humans," *Proceedings of the National Academy of Sciences* 106, no. 24 (2009): 9925–9930. Other scholars have challenged these positions. For example, Christian Keysers explains that currently there is "no individual piece of evidence generally accepted as definitive, but quite a lot of indirect evidence for human mirror neurons has been reported" (R971). He contends that "for each experiment that fails to find evidence for mirror neurons in humans there is at least one that succeeds," and notes that in recent fMRI experiments testing for evidence of mirror neuron response in humans "three of the four experiments that tried found such an effect. Given statistics that limit false positives to <5%, this ratio of 3:4 is strong evidence for the existence of human mirror neurons" (R972). However, although some preliminary research has linked the MNS to empathy and emotion, Keysers admits that further studies are needed, and he calls for caution when applying such preliminary data to suggest higher cognitive functions (R972–R973). Christian Keysers, "Mirror Neurons," *Current Biology* 19, no. 21 (2009): R971–R973.

53. Vittorio Gallese, "The Roots of Empathy: The Shared Manifold Hypothesis and the Neural Basis of Intersubjectivity," *Psychopathology* 36 (2003): 174.
54. Gallese, "Embodied Simulation," 35.
55. Making a similar point, Phillip B. Zarrilli suggests that "the actor's body is a site that generates representation, as well as experience, for both self and other," and that the actor's experience constitutes "one's being-in-the-world." "Towards a Phenomenological Model of the Actor's Embodied Modes of Experience," *Theatre Journal* 56, no. 4 (2004): 664. Zarrilli's recent work draws upon research into human perception and cognition. See "An Enactive Approach to Understanding Acting," *Theatre Journal* 59, no. 4 (2007): 635–47.
56. Gallese and Lakoff, "The Brain's Concepts," 456.
57. George Lakoff and Mark Johnson, *Philosophy in the Flesh: The Embodied Mind and its Challenge to Western Thought* (New York: Basic Books, 1999), 13.
58. Ibid., 19.
59. This approach is especially compatible with visual culture's shift from analyzing a visual work to analyzing vision itself.
60. Vittorio Gallese, Morris N. Eagle, and Paolo Migone, "Intentional Attunement: Mirror Neurons and the Neural Underpinnings of Interpersonal Relations," *Journal of the American Psychoanalytic Association* 55, no. 1 (2007): 143.
61. Kai Vogeley and Albert Newen, "Mirror Neurons and the Self Construct," in *Mirror Neurons and the Evolution of Brain and Language,* eds. Maxim I. Stamenov and Vittorio Gallese (Amsterdam and Philadelphia: John Benjamins, 2002), 136.
62. Gallese, Eagle, and Migone, "Intentional Attunement," 143.
63. Ibid., 144.
64. Ibid.
65. Ibid., 151.
66. Thompson, *Mind in Life*, 393. In chapters five and six, I examine Thompson's larger theory of empathy in which he argues that while empathetic understanding occurs at the level of involuntary coupling, it is also established through other cognitive responses.
67. Bruce McConachie, *Engaging Audiences: A Cognitive Approach to Spectating in the Theatre* (New York: Palgrave Macmillan, 2008), 72.
68. Ibid.
69. Thompson argues, "For me to perceive the other—that is, for the other's bodily presence to be perceptually disclosed to me—the open intersubjectivity of perceptual experience must already be in play. Thus one's actual experience of another bodily subject is based on an *a priori* openness to the other. For the same reason, the intersubjective openness of consciousness cannot be reduced to any contingent and factual relation of self and other, for this openness belongs to

the very structure of subjectivity in advance of any such encounter." *Mind in Life*, 385.
70. Biernoff, *Sight and Embodiment*, 82.
71. Ibid. Robert Pasnau also discusses this characteristic of medieval visual theory in *Theories of Cognition in the Later Middle Ages* (Cambridge: Cambridge University Press, 1997), 43. For example, Thomas Aquinas posited that "in the case of seeing, the pupil is altered through the species of a color." Aquinas, *Commentary on Aristotle's De anima*, trans. K. Foster and S. Humphries (London: Routledge, 1951), Lectio 14 on Book II, paragraph 417. As quoted in Biernoff, *Sight and Embodiment*, 82.
72. Biernoff, *Sight and Embodiment*, 100, original emphasis.
73. Jean Gerson, "Treatise against *The Romance of the Rose*," in *Jean Gerson: Early Works*, trans. Brian Patrick McGuire (New York: Paulist Press, 1998), 388, emphasis mine.
74. Augustine, *The Confessions*, trans. Henry Chadwick (Oxford and New York: Oxford University Press, 1992), 10.33.
75. Johnson, *Body in the Mind*, 19, 205; Gallese, "Embodied Simulation," 23–48.
76. Johnson, *Body in the Mind*, 20. Johnson uses Ulric Neisser's definition of schema.
77. Ibid., 21, original emphasis.
78. Tobin Nellhaus, "Performance Strategies, Image Schemas, and Communication Frameworks," in *Performance and Cognition: Theatre Studies and the Cognitive Turn*, eds. Bruce McConachie and F. Elizabeth Hart (New York: Routledge, 2006), 83.
79. Ibid., 82.
80. Biernoff suggests that "Studying historical accounts of embodied vision helps us to make sense of the power that images have exercised." "Carnal Relations," 44.
81. Portions of this section appeared in "The Material Bodies of Medieval Religious Performance in England," *Material Religion: The Journal of Objects, Art, and Belief* 2, no. 2 (2006): 204–32.
82. *A Tretise of Miraclis Pleyinge*, ed. Clifford Davidson (Kalamazoo, MI: Medieval Institute Publications, 1993). My modernizations of the *Tretise* were made using Davidson's extensive glossary.
83. Lawrence Clopper summarizes these arguments in *Drama, Play, and Game: English Festive Culture in the Medieval and Early Modern Period* (Chicago: The University of Chicago Press, 2001), 63–107.
84. Jonas Barish, *The Antitheatrical Prejudice* (Berkeley: The University of California Press, 1981); Glending Olson, "Plays as Plays: A Medieval Ethical Theory of Performance and the Intellectual Context of the *Tretise of Miraclis Pleyinge*," *Viator* 26 (1995): 195–221.
85. Clopper, *Drama, Play, and Game*, 63–107.
86. Olson, "Plays as Plays," 206.

87. Sponsler, *Drama and Resistance*, 76. While Sponsler analyzes this characteristic of the treatise in relation to misbehavior and carnivalesque play, I am interested in its relationship to pious intention and devotional response.
88. *A Tretise of Miraclis Pleyinge*, 96, 104.
89. Ibid., 98, 99.
90. Ibid., 97.
91. Ibid., 101.
92. Ibid., 102.
93. Ibid., 102, emphasis mine.
94. Ibid., 104.
95. Ibid., 107.
96. Ibid.
97. Ibid., 109.
98. Theodore K. Lerud also examines Augustine's views on theatre, noting that Augustine's mistrust of theatre is informed by his mistrust of the senses. See *Memory*, 15–23.
99. Augustine, *On Genesis: Two Books on Genesis Against the Manichees and On the Literal Interpretation of Genesis*, trans. R. J. Teske (Washington, D.C.: Catholic University Press, 1991), 2: 186–215.
100. Biernoff, *Sight and Embodiment*, 25.
101. Augustine, *The Confessions*, 10.35. For the original Latin text, I have used the online reprint of *Augustine: Confessions*, text and commentary by James J. O'Donnell (New York: Oxford University Press, 1992), for the Stoa Consortium 1999, http://www.stoa.org/hippo/.
102. Ibid., 3.1.
103. Ibid., 3.2, 3.3.
104. Garner writes that for early-twentieth-century modernists such as Gordon Craig and Adolphe Appia, "the actor's body threatened the stage's formal autonomy through its non-aesthetic physiology, its independent sentience, the various ways by which it registers its living presence…[it] posed a danger to the aesthetic enterprise through its insistent naturalism." *Bodied Spaces*, 57. I would argue that for the medieval theologian the spectator's body similarly threatened the devotional aesthetic because of its "insistent naturalism," which was believed to focus devotion on the flesh, rather than on the spirit. A moral objection to sensory interactions appears in medieval discourse on other sense experiences. For instance, Mary Carruthers analyzes uses and meanings of the term sweetness (suavis; dulcis) arguing that in the Middle Ages there rests a degree of ambivalence within this much used term. In particular, she describes how because sweetness can reside in things that are not good for us, it underscores how the physical, sensing body cannot always distinguish pleasure from evil. See "Sweetness," *Speculum* 81, no. 4 (2006): 999–1013.

105. Donnalee Dox, *The Idea of the Theater in Latin Christian Thought: Augustine to the Fourteenth Century* (Ann Arbor: University of Michigan Press, 2004), 14. Dox teases out the various ways in which Augustine employed and critiqued theatrics. For example, she demonstrates how "in *Soliloquies, Sermons, On Christian Doctrine,* and *Concerning the Teacher,* Augustine uses theater much more neutrally, to investigate the problem of truth and falsity writ large" (38). Dox's excellent study examines various conclusions about ancient theatre made by writers up to the fourteenth century. She notes that writers after Augustine did not have first-hand experience of the Greco-Roman theatrics they were theorizing, which perhaps suggests why discussion of theatricality's sensuality is largely missing from these later analyses. Significantly, the final text that Dox engages—Bartholomew of Bruges' *Brevis expositio supra poetriam Aristotelis* (1307)—begins to address issues of theatricality that would become central in treatises from subsequent centuries. Bartholomew's commentary on Aristotle's *Poetics* acknowledges the presentational elements of ancient poetry and thus its material form in the world of the senses, thereby linking the kinds of knowledge that poetry offers to experiences of its material form. Dox identifies in Bartholomew "an emerging consciousness of the theatrical presentation of dramatic poetry" (121).
106. Ibid., 17.
107. Dox notes, "Augustine finds that the counterfeit emotions of the theater fail to provoke proper Christian compassion...Pity remains lodged in the soul of the observer, with no outlet other than the enjoyment of the emotion itself and with no reinforcement of Christianity's ethical demands for compassion." *Idea of the Theater*, 17. Here we find Augustine—unlike cognitive theory—implying that simulated emotions provoked by theatre are unreal. However, his vocabulary suggests that he did believe they had a very real, material presence.
108. Mary Thomas Crane uses cognitive theory to explore theatrical criticism in Early Modern England. Analyzing "documents of control, as well as antitheatrical tracts and plays themselves" Crane notes that "a range of words with very different connotations, emerges." Among these are the terms "keep, use, exercise," which emphasize "the process of performance and its material effects on both actors and audience." "What was performance?" *Criticism* 43, no. 2 (Spring 2001). In Expanded Academic ASAP [database online]. Accessed September 3, 2009.
109. Original: "Nam quod legentibus scriptura, hoc idiotis praestat pictura cernentibus, quia in ipsa etiam ignorantes vident quid sequi debeant, in ipsa legunt qui litteras nesciunt; unde et praecipue gentibus pro lectione pictura est." Latin and English translation as cited in Celia Chazelle, "Pictures, Books, and the Illiterate: Pope

Gregory I's Letters to Serenus of Marseilles," *Word and Image* 6 (1990): 139–40.
110. Ibid., 138.
111. For connections between iconoclasm and anti-theatrical prejudice, see *Iconoclasm vs. Art and Drama*, eds. Clifford Davidson and Ann Eljenholm Nichols (Kalamazoo: Medieval Institute Publications, 1989); and Michael O'Connell, *The Idolatrous Eye: Iconoclasm and Theater in Early Modern England* (Oxford: Oxford University Press, 2000).
112. Theodore K. Lerud, "Quick Images: Memory and the English Corpus Christi Drama," in *Moving Subjects: Procession Performance in the Middle Ages and the Renaissance*, eds. Kathleen Ashley and Wim Hüsken (Amsterdam and Atlanta: Rodopi, 2001), 215. Lerud develops these ideas further in *Memory, Images, and the English Corpus Christi Drama*, especially in chapter five.
113. Reginald Pecock, *The Repressor of Over Much Blaming of the Clergy*, ed. Churchill Babington (London: Longman, Green, Longman, and Robert, 1860), 163, 214.
114. Ibid., 152. Original: "thei meenen and feelen that this ymage is the Trinyte, or that thilk ymage is verili Iesus, and so forth of other."
115. Ibid., 220–1.
116. Ibid., 221. Original: "whanne a quyk man is sett in a pley to be hangid nakid on a cros and to be in semyng woundid and scourged."
117. Lerud, *Memory*, 61.
118. British Library Add. 24202 contains *A Tretise of Miraclis Pleyinge* (fols 14r–17v) and *Tretyse of Ymagis* (fols 26r–28v). I will refer to these texts as *Tretise* and *Ymagis* hereafter. A transcription of the Middle English *Ymagis* is published as "Images and Pilgrimages," in *Selections from English Wycliffite Writings*, ed. Anne Hudson (Toronto: University of Toronto Press, 1997), 83–8.
119. "Images and Pilgrimages," 83.
120. Ibid.
121. Ibid.
122. Ibid.
123. Ibid., 84.
124. Ibid. *A Tretise of Miraclis Pleyinge*, 107, 109. Original: "fleysly pley is not leveful with the gostly werkis of Crist and of his seintis"; "goinge backward fro dedis of the spirit to onely signes don after lustis of the fleysh."
125. "Images and Pilgrimages," 83.
126. Ibid., 84.
127. Ibid.
128. Sara Lipton, "'The Sweet Lean of His Head': Writing About Looking at the Crucifix in the High Middle Ages," *Speculum* 80, no. 4 (October 2005): 1173.

129. Ibid., 1200, 1175.
130. Ibid., 1201.
131. Herbert Kessler describes how in the Middle Ages "many materials were selected because they seemed, in their very nature, to negotiate between the world of matter and the world of spirit." *Seeing Medieval Art* (Ontario: Broadview Press, 2004), 29.
132. "Images and Pilgrimages," 84.
133. Kessler, *Seeing Medieval Art*, 19–42.
134. J. Giles Milhaven, "A Medieval Lesson on Bodily Knowing: Women's Experience and Men's Thought," *Journal of the American Academy of Religion* 52, no. 2 (1989): 356–7.
135. Ibid., 360, 355. Milhaven builds on Joanna E. Ziegler's analysis in *Sculpture of Compassion: The Pietà and the Beguines in the Southern Low Countries c. 1300–c. 1600* (Rome: Institut Historique Belge de Rome, 1992). Ziegler's aim is "to pursue the exchange between material (object) and the immaterial (feeling), and to explore the construction of emotions through art" (15).
136. In their study of material possessions, Mihaly Csikszentmihalyi and Eugene Rochberg-Halton assert "in all cases where actual physical objects become associated with a particular quality of the self, it is difficult to know how far the thing simply reflects an already existing trait and to what extent it anticipates, or *even generates*, a previous nonexistent quality." *The Meaning of Things: Domestic Symbols and the Self* (Cambridge: Cambridge University Press, 1981), 28, emphasis mine.
137. "Images and Pilgrimages," 84.
138. Ibid., 85.
139. Ibid., 86.
140. Ibid., 87.
141. Ibid., 86.
142. Alice Rayner, "Presenting Objects, Presenting Things," in *Staging Philosophy: Intersections of Theater, Performance, and Philosophy*, eds. David Krasner and David Z. Saltz (Ann Arbor: University of Michigan Press, 2006), 187–8.
143. Ibid., 185. Rayner builds on Martin Heidegger's theory of "thingness" and uses his example of the jug to distinguish between the object put before us and thingness.
144. Ibid., 195.
145. McConachie, *Engaging Audiences*, 83. Using neuroscientific evidence, Pierre Jacob and Marc Jeannerod suggest that seeing is the product of interplay between two visual systems. Looking at inanimate elements uses a system that creates "visual perceptions," while the system that processes actions generates "visuomotor representations"; simply put, seeing an object and seeing someone pick up an object trigger different visual systems. Jacob and Jeannerod, *Ways of Seeing: The Scope and Limits of Visual Cognition* (Oxford: Oxford

University Press, 2003), xi–xvi. Watching theatre requires spectators to switch seamlessly between these two systems, something McConachie examines in "Falsifiable Theories for Theatre and Performance Studies," *Theatre Journal* 59, no. 4 (2007): 561–3.
146. David Freedberg and Vittorio Gallese, "Motion, Emotion and Empathy in Esthetic Experience," *Trends in Cognitive Sciences* 11, no. 5 (2007): 200. For the debate on this issue, see Roberto Casati and Alessandro Pignocchi, "Mirror and Canonical Neurons are not Constitutive of Aesthetic Response," *TRENDS in Cognitive Sciences* 11, no. 10 (2007): 410, and Freedberg and Gallese's response, "Mirror and Canonical Neurons are Crucial Elements in Esthetic Response," *TRENDS in Cognitive Sciences* 11, no. 10 (2007): 411.
147. Freedberg and Gallese, "Motion, Emotion and Empathy," 200–1.
148. Ibid., 201. At a 2007 panel discussion entitled "Eye of the Beholder," in which both Freedberg and Gallese participated, Freedberg discussed work he and another neuroscientist were undertaking that examined how viewer responses change based upon visual medium. He explained, "we've been using transcranial magnetic stimulation, and we found that the motor evoked potentials for muscles—this is the realm of automaticity—when you observe a Michelangelo are greater than when you observe a photograph" (8). Transcript of "Eye of the Beholder," April 23, 2007, The Philoctetes Center, New York, NY, http://philoctetes.org/Past_Programs/Eye_of_the_Beholder.
149. Freedberg and Gallese, "Motion, Emotion and Empathy," 202.
150. Work by cognitive-evolutionary psychologists can help us explore this idea further. Research reveals that as children we begin to think of plants, animals, and humans as having immutable "essences," but that we do not ascribe these same essences to objects or artifacts. Instead, we tend to think of objects in terms of function. In her article "Essentialism and Comedy," Lisa Zunshine provides a brief review of the scholarship in this area. Zunshine suggests that it is in part because the set of essentialism-enabled inferences that we "use to deal with living things is very different from that for dealing with artifacts" that we find plays and stories involving "domain-crossing" so compelling (105, 106). "Essentialism and Comedy: A Cognitive Reading of the Motif of Mislaid Identity in Dryden's *Amphitryon* (1690)," in *Performance and Cognition: Theatre Studies and the Cognitive Turn*, eds. Bruce McConachie and F. Elizabeth Hart (New York: Routledge, 2006), 97–121. Zunshine draws heavily upon Susan Gelman's work, particularly *The Essential Child: Origins of Essentialism in Everyday Thought* (Oxford and New York: Oxford University Press, 2003). Although this research indicates that we process living things/people and objects differently, as Zunshine's article illustrates, the cognitive evidence also reveals the creative possibilities that can

emerge when our essentialist-assumptions about living things and our assumptions about objects blend. She also points out that a degree of "nervousness" surfaces "precisely because the 'essence' that we attribute to individuals cannot be captured" (113). My work in subsequent chapters is, in part, an examination of the potential enjoyment and anxiety that can arise from such blending, especially when it involves devotional media.
151. Roger Bacon maintained, righteous men "turn away their senses as far as possible from all species of delectable things...lest the species multiplied into the senses should compel the spirit to serve carnal allurements." Bacon, *Opus majus*, 1: 241; as quoted in Biernoff, *Sight and Embodiment*, 104.
152. Rayner writes, "the thing is not a product of the mind but an otherness that is recognized as having its own, for lack of a better phrase, life process." "Presenting Objects," 186.
153. Biernoff, *Sight and Embodiment*, 104.
154. David Z. Saltz, "Infiction and Outfiction: The Role of Fiction in Theatrical Performance," *Staging Philosophy: Intersections of Theater, Performance, and Philosophy*, eds. David Krasner and David Z. Saltz (Ann Arbor: University of Michigan Press, 2006), 215, 214.
155. Ibid., 203.
156. In his article analyzing William Wordsworth's ethics of the thing, Adam Potkay examines the way the term "thing" had been employed before Wordsworth. According to Potkay, "in Old English there is no term such as *object*, for a material entity...From this linguistic detail we can surmise that medieval Germanic-language speakers...did not in general conceive of material objects in a delimited physical sense, as separate from events, from the constitution and frame of that which is and comes to be, from the transcendental condition for knowing what little we can know of systems or stories that exceed our comprehension." For example, he notes how in *Beowulf* "'thing' designates narrative that is not fully known and gestures toward the unknowability of larger chains of events." Moreover, the *Oxford English Dictionary* indicates that it is not until William Blackstone's mid-eighteenth-century use of the term that we have "the first clear example of *thing* as a 'being without life or consciousness; an inanimate object, as distinguished from a person or living creature.'" Potkay, "Wordsworth and the Ethics of Things," *PMLA* 123, no. 2 (2008): 394.
157. Katherine Zieman, "Reading, Singing and Understanding: Constructions of the Literacy of Women Religious in Late Medieval England," in *Learning and Literacy in Medieval England and Abroad*, ed. Sarah Rees Jones (Turnhout: Brepols, 2003), 101.
158. Ibid., 103, 101. In relation to medieval nuns, Zieman constructs a notion of "liturgical literacy" that "could draw upon a number of learned abilities, from those we might qualify as musical (such as

solmization), to phonetic decoding skill, to mnemonic techniques, to a variety of grammatical proficiencies" (106).
159. Keyan G. Tomaselli and Arnold Shepperson remind us that "people simply are not *born* literate: they *become* more or less literate as they develop their endowments into talents through education...Everyday people get on with life as they encounter it, draw on their experience as a basis for getting along, and make it all intelligible by virtue of the fact that what they do *works for them.*" "'Speaking in Tongues, Writing in Vision': Orality and Literacy in Televangelistic Communications," in *Practicing Religion in the Age of the Media: Explorations in Media, Religion, and Culture*, eds. Stewart M. Hoover and Lynn Schofield Clark (New York: Columbia University Press, 2002), 348–9, original emphasis.
160. Gallese, "Eye of the Beholder," 7. Gallese also asserts that "there is already plenty of evidence showing that the degree and intensity to which such mirroring mechanisms can be evoked during, for example, observation of different actions, emotions or sensations, is potently driven by the personal experiential history of the individual displaying these responses. There are beautiful studies done on professional dancers, for example, which clearly exemplify that if you're a classical ballet dancer and if you watch classical ballet, as opposed to Capoeira, your mirror neuron system is more driven by the observation of classical ballet than when you observe Capoeira, and the other way around" (7).
161. As Mary Thomas Crane and Alan Richardson note, a number of cognitive philosophers "leave room for the 'emergence' of agency through the massive integration of neural activity." "Literary Studies and Cognitive Science: Toward a New Interdisciplinarity," *Mosaic* 32, no. 2 (1999). In Expanded Academic ASAP [database online]. Accessed September 3, 2009.
162. Michel De Certeau, *The Practice of Everyday Life*, trans. Steven Rendall (Berkeley: University of California Press, 1984), xix, 173.
163. One could argue that this kind of seeing through the body served to perpetuate the trend toward a more visceral faith that began among mystics in the twelfth and thirteenth centuries. Caroline Bynum argues that mystical writing from this period expresses a desire for encounters with God and that "such desire is not only *for* bodies; it is lodged *in* bodies." "Why All the Fuss about the Body? A Medievalist's Perspective," *Critical Inquiry* 22 (August 1995): 26. The connection between body and desire found in these texts also invaded lay pious practices. Anne L. Clark's essay "Why All the Fuss About the Mind? A Medievalist's Perspective on Cognitive Theory," in *History in the Comic Mode: Medieval Communities and the Matter of Person*, eds. Rachel Fulton and Bruce Holsinger (New York: Columbia University Press, 2007), 170–81, uses cognitive theory to respond to and build upon Bynum's conclusions.

164. Kathleen Ashley argues that the metaphor of the tactic "allows us to see medieval dramatic performances as always a reinterpretation or adaptation of traditional myths and ideologies." I am suggesting that it also allows us to see the performance encounter as a reinterpretation or adaptation of the laity's traditional role in devotion and devotional seeing. See Ashley, "Contemporary Theories of Popular Culture and Medieval Performances," *Mediaevalia* 18 (1995): 9. Claire Sponsler also employs de Certeau's theory of consumption to analyze how medieval laity used devotional (including dramatic) images. See Sponsler, *Drama and Resistance*, xiv, 122.
165. In some ways, performance literacy is related to the educational concept of disciplinary literacy: "Disciplinary literacy is based on the premise that students can develop deep conceptual knowledge in a discipline only by using the habits of reading, writing, talking, and thinking which that discipline values and uses" (8). See Stephanie McConachie, et al., "Task, Text, and Talk," *Educational Leadership* 64, no. 2 (2006): 8–14. Similarly, I would situate the elements of visual, material, and performance culture that I analyze in these chapters within a shared discipline of lay devotion. Performance literacy involved certain habits of seeing, thinking, and engaging, and, I would argue, laypeople could only gain a full conceptual understanding of the larger discipline of lay devotion if they adopted these very habits as part of their pious practices. Thanks to Bruce McConachie for pointing out this relationship.
166. Oliver Gerland, "From Playhouse to P2P Network: The History and Theory of Performance under Copyright Law in the United States," *Theatre Journal* 59, no. 1 (2007): 92–3.
167. Aleksandra Wolska, "Rabbits, Machines, and the Ontology of Performance," *Theatre Journal* 57, no. 1 (2005): 88.
168. Biernoff notes that in the most prevalent medieval models, "perception involves a process of becoming, a period of gestation if you like, as the sensitive organs of the mind and body are assimilated with their objects." *Sight and Embodiment*, 102.
169. During the later Middle Ages, York had a clear sense of itself as an historically significant city. York was self-governing, the seat of England's other archbishopric, second only to Canterbury, and by the late fourteenth century had the second largest population in England estimated at fifteen thousand. As Peter Meredith writes, "it was clearly a city proud of its history and its status and jealous of its privileges." "The City of York and its 'Play of Pageants,'" *Early Theatre* 3 (2000): 23.

Two Material Devotion

1. See Peter Burke, *Eyewitnessing: The Uses of Images as Historical Evidence* (Ithaca: Cornell University Press, 2001); Michael Ann

Holly, *Past Looking: The Historical Imagination and the Rhetoric of the Image* (Ithaca: Cornell University Press, 1996); David Freedberg, *The Power of Images: Studies in the History and Theory of Response* (Chicago: University of Chicago Press, 1989); and John Berger, *Ways of Seeing* (London: Penguin Books, 1972).
2. V. S. Ramachandran and Sandra Blakeslee, *Phantoms in the Brain: Probing the Mysteries of the Human Mind* (New York: Quill, 1998), 59. Their experiments also reveal that we sometimes project our own sensations onto external objects and assimilate them into our own body image, even when those objects, such as tables or chairs, have little resemblance to our bodies (58–62).
3. Suzannah Biernoff explains, "medieval vision had a kinaesthetic dimension. It involved a sensation of movement." *Sight and Embodiment in the Middle Ages* (New York: Palgrave, 2002), 97.
4. Eamon Duffy, *The Stripping of the Altars: Traditional Religion in England 1400–1580* (New Haven: Yale University Press, 1992), 328. On memory in will-making practices, see Robert N. Swanson, *Religion and Devotion in Europe, c. 1215–1515* (Cambridge: Cambridge University Press, 1995), 191–234, 322–9.
5. Various scholars have analyzed medieval wills as examples of identity performance, and the funerals they describe as public performances. For example, see Gail McMurray Gibson, *The Theater of Devotion: East Anglian Drama and Society in the Late Middle Ages* (Chicago: University of Chicago Press, 1989), 67–106; and Gail Camiciotti Del Lungo, "Performative Aspects of Late Medieval Wills," *Journal of Historical Pragmatics* 3, no. 2 (2002): 205–27.
6. This is the same period for which we have records of York's cycle performances. I surveyed over three hundred wills from the York diocese, concentrating on those made by people who identified themselves as members of parish churches in the city. I considered evidence from two sources: Registers of the Exchequer and Prerogative Court of the Archbishops of York, held at the Borthwick Institute (hereafter BI Reg., followed by volume and folio numbers) and Registers of the Peculiar Jurisdiction of the Dean and Chapter, held at the York Minster Library (hereafter D&C Reg., followed by volume and folio numbers). Indices for these collections are published as: F. Collins, ed., *Index of Wills etc. from the Dean and Chapter of York, 1321–1636*, Yorkshire Archaeological Society Record Series 38 (1907) and F. Collins, ed., *Index of Wills in the York Registry, vol. 1, 1389–1514 & vol. 2, 1514–1553*, Yorkshire Archaeological Society Record Series 6 & 11 (1891 and 1899). I reviewed microfilm copies of the original manuscripts for every will that I cite. All modernized English translations of Middle English wills are mine, unless otherwise noted. I use published transcriptions of Middle English and translations of Latin when available, and will specify when these are my own. My primary sources for transcriptions are the *Testamenta Eboracensia* series,

Surteees Society: vol. I, wills up to 1429 (1836); vol. II, 1429–67 (1855); vol. III, 1467–85 (1865); vol. IV, 1485–1509 (1869); vol. V, 1509–34 (1884); vol. VI, 1534–50 (1902) (hereafter *TE*, followed by volume and page number), and *Some Early Civic Wills of York*, ed. R. Beilby Cooke, compiled from York Architectural Society Reports and Papers, 8 vols (1906, 1911, 1913, 1914, 1915, 1916, 1917, 1919) (hereafter Cooke, followed by year and page number). While extremely useful, these volumes do not always include the full text of a will and are therefore problematic when not used in conjunction with the manuscript originals.
 7. Clive Burgess, "Late Medieval Wills and Pious Convention: Testamentary Evidence Reconsidered," in *Profit, Piety and the Professions in Later Medieval England*, ed. Michael Hicks (Gloucester: Alan Sutton, 1990), 17.
 8. Ibid., 18.
 9. Peter Heath, "Urban Piety in the Later Middle Ages: The Evidence of Hull Wills," in *The Church, Politics and Patronage in the Fifteenth Century*, ed. R. B. Dobson (New York: St. Martin's Press, 1984), 210.
10. P. Jeremy P. Goldberg, "Lay Book Ownership in Late Medieval York: The Evidence of Wills," *The Library* 16, no. 3 (September 1994): 182. There are several gaps in York's medieval probate records. In addition to smaller interruptions, the Borthwick evidence has large gaps from October 1408 to March 1417, and from January 1418 to May 1426.
11. Clive Burgess notes that a meager will may indicate that the testator died "with his wishes and estate well in order and with widow and parish prepared for what was to be done, rather than suggesting lack of funds or apathy toward religion." "Late Medieval Wills," 21.
12. For an introduction to the typical features of late medieval wills from York and customary funeral practices, see P. S. Barnwell, "'Four hundred masses on the four Fridays next after my decease.' The Care of Souls in Fifteenth-Century All Saints', North Street, York," in *Mass and Parish in Late Medieval England: The Use of York*, eds. Barnwell, Claire Cross, and Ann Rycraft (Reading: Spire Books, 2005), 57–87. For funeral practices in late medieval England, see also Duffy, *Stripping of the Altars*, 301–76.
13. Thomas Bracebrig, 4 September 1436, proved 10 May 1437 (BI Reg. 3 fols 487v–490r)
14. Duffy, *Stripping of the Altars*, 332.
15. John Dautre, 20 May 1458, proved 14 August 1459 (BI Reg. 2, fols 413r–414r): fol. 413r. Original: "coram ymagine Sanctissimi Johannis Baptistae quem prae ceteris Sanctis a juventute mea in maximo ardoris amore habuissem" (*TE* 2, 230–1).

16. John Mirk, *Mirk's Festial: A Collection of Homilies by Johannes Mirkus*, vol. 1, ed. Theodor Erbe (London: Kegan Paul, Trench, Trübner, 1905; Kraus Reprint, 1987), 297.
17. Both wax candles and torches are stipulated in wills. According to Duffy, torches refer to flaring lights made with thick plaited wicks and a mixture of resin and wax. *Stripping of the Altars*, 96.
18. Bracebrig, 487v.
19. Ibid. These include candles placed before images of the Virgin Mary, St. John the Baptist, and St. Anne, and one maintained before the Crucifix in the Rood loft.
20. P. S. Barnwell and Claire Cross note, "at their deaths virtually all of the more prosperous York testators paid for the four orders of friars to celebrate Masses for the welfare of their soul." "The Mass in its Urban Setting," in *Mass and Parish in Late Medieval England: The Use of York*, eds. Barnwell, Cross, and Ann Rycraft (Reading: Spire Books, 2005), 23.
21. Barnwell, "'Four hundred masses,'" 60.
22. Ibid., 62. "Placebo" refers to the first line in the office of Vespers of the dead ("I shall please the Lord in the land of men") from Psalm 116 verse 9, and "Dirige" is the first word of the antiphon at the office of Matins for the dead, taken from Psalm 5 verse 8. The line reads "Dirige, Domine, Deus Meus, in conspectus tuo viam meam" (Direct my way in your sight, O Lord my God).
23. Anne Bagnall Yardley, *Performing Piety: Musical Culture in Medieval English Nunneries* (New York: Palgrave Macmillan, 2006), 113, 114. Yardley builds on Clifford Flanagan's "Medieval Liturgical Processions in Semiotic and Cultural Perspectives," in *Moving Subjects: Procession Performance in the Middle Ages and the Renaissance*, eds. Kathleen Ashley and Wim Hüsken (Amsterdam and Atlanta: Rodopi, 2001), 35–51.
24. Pilgrimage by proxy was "a common occurrence in wills from all over England up to and beyond the break with Rome." Duffy, *Stripping of the Altars*, 193. Pilgrimage by proxy stipulations appear in: Dame Jane Chaumerleyn (dated 1502; BI Reg. 6 fols 34v–35v); John Cowper (dated 1518; BI Reg. 9 fol. 71v); Thomas Batley (dated 1521; BI Reg. 9 fol. 217v); and Thomas Strangwayes (dated 1525; BI Reg. 9 fols 343v–344r).
25. Duffy, *Stripping of the Altars*, 193.
26. Barnwell, "'Four hundred masses,'" 63; Duffy, *Stripping of the Altars*, 361–2.
27. Drew Leder, *The Absent Body* (Chicago and London: University of Chicago Press, 1990), 124–5.
28. Miri Rubin, *Corpus Christi: The Eucharist in Late Medieval Culture* (Cambridge: Cambridge University Press, 1991), 243.
29. Ibid., 247–8.

30. *The Register of the Guild of Corpus Christi in the City of York*, ed. R. H. Skaife (London: Mitchell and Hughes, 1872).
31. Alexandra F. Johnston and Margaret Rogerson, eds., *Records of Early English Drama: York*, 2 vols (Toronto: University of Toronto Press, 1979), 701 (15).
32. Ibid., 702 (15).
33. Ibid., 777 (109).
34. Ibid., 780 (117).
35. Ibid., 283.
36. Ibid., 735 (51).
37. Ibid., 736 (52).
38. Ibid., 735 (51).
39. Ibid., 736 (52).
40. Maintaining the prescribed processional order seems to have become more challenging during the late fifteenth and sixteenth centuries. Multiple entries in the House Books outline penalties for those who do not attend the procession and describe efforts to regulate the event more closely. In addition, disputes between guilds regarding the processional order appear repeatedly throughout the civic record. A disagreement between the Cordwainers and Weavers continued for many years. In 1492 the Cordwainers were ultimately fined because they did not carry their torches in the procession as ordered to by the mayor and common council. Other disputes arose as well, such as a 1530 disagreement between the Carpenters and the Joiners and Carvers. See Johnston and Rogerson, *York*, 186, 166, 252.
41. Funeral custom involved taking the body to the church "the day before the burial, and for the coffin, sometimes draped in a pall, to be surrounded by a timber frame, or hearse, which held candles." Later that same day the first part of the Office of the Dead was performed, which consisted of the Placebo. An overnight vigil was held, followed, the next day, by the second part of the Office (the Dirige) and, later that day, the Requiem Mass. At that point, the body was usually taken out of the coffin for burial. Barnwell, "'Four hundred masses,'" 62.
42. Bracebrig, 489v; my transcription; translation from Cooke, 1915: 14.
43. Ibid.
44. Guaranteeing that a funeral procession would take place during daylight hours was a more pressing concern for those living in northern cities, such as York, where winter days are extremely short. Memory of the plague may have included stories about the logistical need to conduct many funeral processions after daylight.
45. This organization was first established in 1357 as the fraternity and guild of Jesus Christ and the Blessed Virgin Mary, associated with the parish church of St. Crux. Between 1358 and 1361, the fraternity built a guildhall on the Foss River, which still stands today. The

guild was associated with the Mercers' craft from its earliest years and by 1420 more than two-thirds of the men working in the guild's hospital were Mercers; however, other professions are represented among testamentary gifts to the guild. Because the religious guild seems to have offered a fertile beginning for the Mercers' guild, but was always open to a wider range of professions, any analysis of the Mercers' pageant must acknowledge the variety of individuals who may have contributed to the play's design and performance (including the guild's female members), and also how the Mercers' organization was simultaneously secular and sacred in nature. D. M. Palliser, *Company History* (York: The Company of Merchant Adventurers of the City of York, 1998), 4; David Crouch, *Piety, Fraternity and Power: Religious Gilds in Late Medieval Yorkshire, 1389–1547* (York: York Medieval Press, 2000), 139–40.
46. Palliser, *Company History*, 5. Kate Crassons analyzes how the Mercers' guild documents and *Last Judgment* pageant present poverty, charity, and community. See "The Challenges of Social Unity: The *Last Judgment* Pageant and Guild Relations in York," *Journal of Medieval and Early Modern Studies* 37, no. 2 (Spring 2007): 305–34.
47. For detailed analyses of this indenture, see Alexandra F. Johnston and Margaret Dorrell, "The Doomsday Pageant of the York Mercers, 1433," *Leeds Studies in English* 5 (1971): 29–34; Johnston and Dorrell, "The York Mercers and their Pageant of Doomsday, 1433–1526," *Leeds Studies in English* 6 (1972): 10–35; Peter Meredith, "The Development of the York Mercers' Pageant Waggon," *Medieval English Theatre* 1 (1979): 5–18.
48. Johnston and Rogerson, *York*, 55. Original: "A Pagent With iiij Wheles helle mouthe iij garments of iij deuels vj deuelles faces in iij Vesernes Array for ij euell saules þat is to say ij Sirkes ij paire hoses ij vesenes & ij Chauelers Array for ij gode saules þat ys to say ij Sirkes ij paire hoses ij vesernes & ij Cheuelers ij paire Aungell Wynges with Iren in þe endes...A cloud & ij peces of Rainbow of tymber Array for god þat ys to say a Sirke Wounded a diademe With a veserne gilted A grete coster of rede damaske payntid for the bakke syde of þe pagent...iiij squared to hang at þe bakke of god iiij Irens to bere vppe heuen iiij finale coterelles & a Iren pynne A brandreth of Iren þat god sall sitte vppon when he sall sty vppe to heuen With iiij rapes at iiij corners."
49. Stanton B. Garner, Jr., *Bodied Spaces: Phenomenology and Performance in Contemporary Drama* (Ithaca and London: Cornell University Press, 1994), 89.
50. A three-play series related to the death of the Virgin appears at the end of the cycle: *The Death of the Virgin*, *The Assumption of the Virgin*, and *The Coronation of the Virgin*. The series appears between the pageants *Pentecost* and *The Last Judgment*. Originally there were four plays in this group, but *The Funeral of the Virgin*, also known as

the "Fergus" play, does not survive. For work on contemporary staging of these plays, see John McKinnell, "Producing the York *Mary* plays," *Medieval English Theatre* 12 (1990): 101–23.
51. Original: "Rise Marie, þou maiden and modir so milde"; "Come vppe to þe kyng to be crouned." *The York Plays*, ed. Richard Beadle (London: Edward Arnold, 1982), cited by play number and line numbers. For modern translations of a selection of York's pageants, see Richard Beadle and Pamela M. King, eds., *York Mystery Plays: A Selection in Modern Spelling* (Oxford: Clarendon Press, 1984). Beadle's new edition of the plays is currently forthcoming: *The York Plays*. Volume 1: The Text, ed. Richard Beadle. Early English Text Society, supplementary series 23 (Oxford: Oxford University Press, forthcoming).
52. Original: "For to my tales þat I telle þei are not attendinge"; "I schall þe schewe / A token trewe / Full fresshe of hewe, / My girdill, loo, take þame þis tokyn."
53. Johnston and Rogerson, *York*, 709 (23).
54. Mary's Assumption is described in an apocryphal book attributed to John the Evangelist. *The Golden Legend*, a collection of saints' lives compiled around 1260 by Jacobus de Voragine, provides us with a version of the Assumption narrative that handles Thomas's doubt differently: "Thereupon Mary's soul entered her body, and she came forth glorious from the monument and was assumed into the heavenly bridal chamber, a great multitude of angels keeping her company. Thomas, however, was absent, and when he came back refused to believe. Then suddenly the girdle that had encircled her body fell intact into his hands, and he realized that the Blessed Virgin has really been assumed body and soul." Jacobus de Voragine, *The Golden Legend: Readings on the Saints*, vol. 2, trans. William Granger Ryan (Princeton: Princeton University Press, 1993), 82.
55. Andrew Sofer, *The Stage Life of Props* (Ann Arbor: University of Michigan Press, 2003), 17.
56. Ibid., 18, 19.
57. Original: "Petrus: Itt is welcome iwis fro þat worthy wight, / For it was wonte for to wappe þat worthy virgine. / Jacobus: Itt is welcome iwis from þat lady so light, / For hir wombe scho wrappe with it and were it with wynne / Andreas: Itt is welcome iwis fro þat saluer of synne, / For scho bende it aboute hir with blossome so bright. / Johannes: Itt is welcome iwis from þe keye of our kynne, / For aboute þat reuerent it rechid full right."
58. Alice Rayner, "Presenting Objects, Presenting Things," in *Staging Philosophy: Intersections of Theater, Performance, and Philosophy*, eds. David Krasner and David Z. Saltz (Ann Arbor: University of Michigan Press, 2006), 191.
59. Original: "Now knele we ilkone / Vppone oure kne"; "To þat lady free."

60. Rayner, "Presenting Objects," 192, original emphasis.
61. Ruth Evans also discusses how this play associates the girdle with Mary's body. She argues that the pageant sexualized the girdle with the apostles treating it "almost as a fetish, dwelling on its proximity to Mary's body" (210). "When a Body Meets a Body: Fergus and Mary in the York Cycle," in *New Medieval Literatures*, eds. Wendy Scase, Rita Copeland, and David Lawton (Oxford: Clarendon Press, 1997), 193–212. Although I interpret the degree of fetishism in this pageant as related to the girdle's status as a devotional object, rather than as a sexualized object, these readings are not mutually exclusive. A variety of medieval practices involving saints' relics can be interpreted as simultaneously devotional and sexual in nature. For a collection of hagiographic material, see Thomas Head, ed., *Medieval Hagiography: An Anthology* (New York: Routledge, 2001).
62. Girdles were valued as mnemonic objects, bequeathed by and to both men and women, and often decorated to enhance their memorializing capabilities. For instance, Beatrix Santon bequeaths a small girdle ornamented with silver letters to John Haliwell, her clerk and relation. Beatrix, wife of Thomas Santon, citizen and draper, York, 10 March 1405, proved 15 Mar 1405 (BI Reg. 3 fols 246r–v): 246v. Girdles are mentioned in fifteen of the wills in my survey.
63. Rayner, "Presenting Objects," 196. Rayner uses this phrase in respect to the work of Tadeusz Kantor.
64. Richard Marks, "An Age of Consumption: Art for England c. 1400–1547," in *Gothic Art for England 1400–1547*, eds. Richard Marks and Paul Williamson (London: V&A Publications, 2003), 15.
65. Susan Foister, "Private Devotion," in *Gothic Art for England 1400–1547*, eds. Richard Marks and Paul Williamson (London: V&A Publications, 2003), 334–6. Eamon Duffy discusses—and in part refutes—arguments about "laicisation" as they pertain to Books of Hours. See *Marking the Hours: English People and their Prayers 1240–1570* (New Haven and London: Yale University Press, 2006).
66. Susan Foister, "Paintings in Sixteenth-Century English Inventories," *Burlington Magazine* 123, no. 938 (May 1981): 273–82. Foister lists a number of terms used for images that appear in late-fifteenth- and sixteenth-century inventories including: "costryngs" (a common type of hanging), "hanging payntd," "pageant" (Foister suggests that this denotes a smaller type of painted hanging), "ymage," "table" or "tabelet," and "picture."
67. Annas Thomson, 5 Oct 1546, proved 21 Oct 1546 (D&C Reg. 3 fols 16r–v): 16r. Original: "paynted clothe hanging in my halle having one pieta upon it"; "one paynted clothe hanging at my bedside having upon it one Image of our Ladie"; and "one of the lityll paynted clothe that hang in my bed" (my transcription).
68. P. M. Stell and Louise Hampson outline the standard format used for medieval English inventories, as well as medieval monetary values, in

Probate Inventories of the York Diocese 1350–1500 (York: Unpublished typescript, 2005), 3–7, 11. Bound copies of the typescript are available through the York Minster Library. Monetary values in York's medieval records are given in pre-decimal notation. Four farthings equaled one penny (d.); twelve pennies totaled one shilling (s.); and, twenty shillings equaled a pound (£1). Sometimes values are given in marks, with one mark typically worth 13s. 4d.

69. Ibid., 5–7.
70. Foister, "Paintings," 278.
71. Stell and Hampson, *Probate Inventories*, 155. Original: Borthwick Institute of Historical Research, Dean and Chapter of York, Original Wills, 1383–1499. "Chapman" usually denotes either dealer or peddlar, which means there is a chance that Gryssop may have sold images himself. Although I use their translations, I reviewed the original manuscripts for those inventories that I cite from Stell and Hampson.
72. Ibid., 314–15. Original: Borthwick Institute of Historical Research, Dean and Chapter of York, Original Wills, 1383–1499.
73. Ibid., 287. Original: York Minster Library, Probate Jurisdiction, Inventories, L1(17)6.
74. Ibid., 159–70. Original: York Minster Library, Probate Jurisdiction, Inventories, L1(17)44.
75. Ibid., 192–223. Original: York Minster Library, Probate Jurisdiction, Inventories, L1(17)17.
76. William Revetour, 2 August 1446, codicil 11 August 1446, proved 3 September 1446 (BI Reg. 2 fols 137v–138v): 138r.
77. Revetour's performance-related entries appear in Johnston and Rogerson, *York*, 68. For a Latin transcription and English translation of Revetour's entire will, see Alexandra F. Johnston, "William Revetour, Chaplain and Clerk of York, Testator," *Leeds Studies in English* 29 (1998): 153–71.
78. "Quemdam librum vocatum le Crede Play cum libris & vexillis eidem pertinentibus." Revetour, 138v; transcription and translation Johnston and Rogerson, *York*, 68 (746).
79. Ibid.
80. Ibid.
81. Revetour, 138r–v. Transcription from Johnston, "William Revetour," 161; translation 169.
82. Revetour, 138v. Transcription from Johnston, "William Revetour," 165–7; translation 171.
83. Thomas Wod, draper and alderman, Hull, 3 November 1490, proved 25 Nov 1491 (BI Reg. fols 402v–403v): 403r. The term "bed" usually refers to bedding. This is almost certainly the case here, since Wod uses the phrase "Arras work" typically employed in wills to indicate a rich style of tapestry fabric associated with Arras, France. Stell and Hampson, *Probate Inventories*, 349, 347.

84. Katheryne the Countes of Northumberlande, widow of the Earl of Northumberland, 14 October 1542, proved 9 November 1542 (BI Reg. 11 fols 638r–v): 638v. Original: "a rynge of golde to remember and pray for me" (Transcription *TE* 4: 168).
85. David Freedberg and Vittorio Gallese, "Motion, Emotion and Empathy in Esthetic Experience," *Trends in Cognitive Sciences* 11, no. 5 (2007): 197–203. Alice Rayner suggests something similar when she argues that the surfaces of objects offer a degree of "tactility" that can exceed visibility and representational modes of signification. "Presenting Objects," 195.
86. Johnston and Rogerson, *York*, 16. See also *The York Play: A Facsimile of British Library MS Additional 35290, together with a Facsimile of the Ordo Paginarum Section of the A/Y Memorandum Book, and a Note on the Music by Richard Rastall*, eds. Richard Beadle and Peter Meredith (Leeds: University of Leeds, School of English, 1983).
87. Johnston and Rogerson, *York*, 703 (17).
88. Ibid., 707 (22).
89. Ibid., 708 (23).
90. Ibid., 109.
91. "And concerning the rent of the first station, it is let to William Catterton and others beyond the station of the common clerk." Johnston and Rogerson, *York*, 801 (187). Source: City Chamberlains' Rolls. See also Peter Meredith, "John Clerke's Hand in the York Register," *Leeds Studies in English* 12 (1981): 245–71.
92. Johnston and Rogerson, *York*, 722 (37). Richard Beadle discusses possible reasons for this performance change in "The York Cycle," in *The Cambridge Companion to Medieval English Theatre*, ed. Richard Beadle (Cambridge: Cambridge University Press, 1994), 100–2.
93. Johnston and Rogerson, *York*, 722 (37).
94. Ibid., 722 (37).
95. A similar concern is expressed in the Banns to the Chester cycle. Although the 1609 Banns describe Chester's pageants as "set forth apparently to all eyes," the anxiety over reception expressed here is directed at the performance's verbal cues: "Condemn not our matter when simple words you hear / which convey at this day little sense or understanding." Lawrence Clopper, ed., *Records of Early English Drama: Chester* (Toronto: University of Toronto Press, 1979), 240, 241. Peter Meredith identifies in these words an "awareness of the old-fashionedness of the language at Chester" that, over the years, would have caused it to sound different to audiences, something he believes may also have been the case in sixteenth-century York. See "The City of York and its 'Play of Pageants,'" *Early Theatre* 3 (2000): 27. As the English language transformed during the cycle's lifetime, to some degree York's laity must have recognized that the pageant texts were no longer, if they had indeed ever been, stable sites of meaning. For commentary on the York cycle's inherent textual

instability, see Pamela M. King, "The York Cycle and Instruction on the Sacraments," in *Learning and Literacy in Medieval England and Abroad*, ed. Sarah Rees Jones (Turnhout: Brepols, 2003), 178; and *The York Mystery Cycle and the Worship of the City* (Cambridge: D. S. Brewer, 2006), 182.

96. Johnston and Rogerson, *York*, 732 (47–8). For work on this lost pageant and the laughter it provoked, see Evans, "When a Body Meets a Body," 193–212.
97. Johnston and Rogerson, *York*, 732 (48).
98. Ibid., 732–3 (48).
99. The Masons may have been unhappy for other, less devotional or performance-oriented reasons. For instance, they may have wanted to finish early so that they could take part in the day's other festivities. Yet, because their concern about daylight is juxtaposed against concerns about the pageant's sacred, devotional goals, I would argue that, at least when presenting their case, they framed the issue of daylight as a concern about the audience's ability to see the pageant and thereby receive its spiritual benefits.
100. David Morgan, *Visual Piety: A History and Theory of Popular Religious Images* (Berkeley: University of California Press, 1998), 48.
101. Seth Lerer identifies in medieval drama "a growing self-consciousness about the theatricality of theater." " 'Representyd now in yower syght': The Culture of Spectatorship in Late Fifteenth Century England," in *Bodies and Disciplines: Intersections of Literature and History in Fifteenth-Century England*, eds. Barbara Hanawalt and David Wallace (Minneapolis: University of Minnesota Press, 1996), 34. For instance, according to the extant production records from the Gréban-Michel *Passion*, presented at Mons from July 5 to 12, 1501, this performance had spectacular visual effects, including devices that caused blood to pour from Christ's wounds and fire-throwing machines. See *Le livre de conduite du régisseur et le compte des dépenses pour le Mystère de la Passion joué à Mons en 1501 (The Director's Handbook and the Expense Record for the Mystery of the Passion Performed at Mons in 1501)*, ed. Gustave Cohen (Paris: Champion, 1925). For primary evidence about staging medieval religious performances, much of which concerns visual elements, see Peter Meredith and John E. Tailby, *The Staging of Religious Drama in Europe in the Later Middle Ages: Texts and Documentation in English Translation* (Kalamazoo: Medieval Institute Publications, 1982).

Three Claiming Devotional Space

1. York's Minster is both a cathedral, a term applied to the principal church within a bishop's diocese that houses the episcopal throne,

and a Minster, which denotes a church attached to a monastery. The cathedral is dedicated to St. Peter and is often referred to in wills as the cathedral church of St. Peter.
2. John H. Harvey, "Architectural History from 1291 to 1558," in *A History of York Minster*, eds. G. E. Aylmer and Reginald Cant (Oxford: Clarendon Press, 1977), 149–92; R. B. Dobson, "The Later Middle Ages, 1215–1500," in *A History of York Minster*, 44–109.
3. A number of wills from York include bequests to the head of Richard Scrope, which was kept as a relic at his shrine near the city's Clementhorpe neighborhood, and these donations (such as girdles, jewelry, torches, and beads) attest to the strength of his cult in the city and diocese. For examples, see Katherine de Craven, 1418 (BI Reg. 3 fols 613r–v); John Dautre, 1458 (BI Reg. 2, fols 413r–414r); Isabell Bruce, 1477 (BI Reg. 5 fol. 17v); and Alison Clark 1509 (D&C Reg. 2 fols 82r–83v).
4. Dobson, "The Later Middle Ages," 108.
5. Ibid.
6. The present boss in the Minster is a reproduction made from John Browne's drawing of the fourteenth-century original. For an image and description, see *York Art: A Subject List of Extant and Lost Art Including Items Relevant to Early Drama*, ed. Clifford Davidson (Kalamazoo, MI: Medieval Institute Publications, 1978), 100.
7. Sara Lipton, " 'The Sweet Lean of His Head': Writing About Looking at the Crucifix in the High Middle Ages," *Speculum* 80, no. 4 (October 2005): 1202. I discuss Lipton's analysis in chapter one.
8. Katherine French, *The People of the Parish: Community Life in a Late Medieval English Diocese* (Philadelphia: University of Pennsylvania Press, 2001), 20. Eamon Duffy lists various objects for which parishioners were responsible. *The Stripping of the Altars: Traditional Religion in England 1400–1580* (New Haven: Yale University Press, 1992), 132–4.
9. French, *People of the Parish*, 173.
10. A. G. Dickens, ed., "Robert Parkyn's Narrative of the Reformation," *English Historical Review* 62 (1947): 58–83. Parkyn's will, dated March 16, 1568, appears in the York Probate Registry and indicates that he was a parish priest in Adwick, near Doncaster. See BI Reg. 19 fols 54v–55r.
11. "Robert Parkyn's Narrative," 66. My modern translation of the Middle English.
12. Ibid., 68, 68–9.
13. Ibid., 74.
14. Ibid., all excerpts from 68, except the final quotation from 75.
15. Ibid., 80.
16. Paul Binski, "The English Parish Church and Its Art in the Later Middle Ages: A Review of the Problem," *Studies in Iconography* 20 (1999): 3, 18.

17. Royal Commission on Historical Monuments, *An Inventory of the Historical Monuments in the City of York. Volume Five: The Central Area* (London: Her Majesty's Stationary Office, 1981), 6. Most of the medieval parish glass can be found in All Saints Pavement, Holy Trinity Goodramgate, St. Martin Coneystreet, St. Michael-le-Belfry, and St. Michael Spurriergate. St. Denys' Walmgate houses York's only extant example of thirteenth-century glass in a parish church.
18. Rachel Fulton makes a similar point in her article "Praying with Anselm at Admont: A Meditation on Practice," *Speculum* 81, no. 3 (2006): 700–33. Analyzing prayers as experiences, Fulton attempts to "use" medieval prayers herself as one mode of inquiry. She writes, "it is extremely difficult, if not impossible, to handle such artifacts as prayers without experiencing something of their intended effect. Some readers may find this unsettling, not what they are used to in reading an academic article" (707).
19. P. S. Barnwell notes, "All Saints' stands in the middle rank in the 1524 Lay Subsidy," which suggests that by the end of the Middle Ages this parish was average in terms of wealth. " 'Four hundred masses on the four Fridays next after my decease.' The Care of Souls in Fifteenth-Century All Saints', North Street, York," in *Mass and Parish in Late Medieval England: The Use of York*, eds. Barnwell, Claire Cross, and Ann Rycraft (Reading: Spire Books, 2005), 60.
20. The size and color of the chancel's hammerbeam angels may have made them visible to some of the laity standing in the nave.
21. Barnwell, " 'Four hundred masses,' " 70–7. A chantry was an office established for a priest in a specific chapel or altar within a church. The priest's duty was to offer prayers and Masses for the souls of its founder and any others whom the founder named. See Clive Burgess, "For the Increase of Divine Service: Chantries in the Parish in Late Medieval Bristol," *Journal of Ecclesiastical History* 36 (1985): 46–65.
22. Duffy, *Stripping of the Altars*, 95.
23. Ibid., 112.
24. Miri Rubin, *Corpus Christi: The Eucharist in Late Medieval Culture* (Cambridge: Cambridge University Press, 1991), 49–63. Eamon Duffy argues that the effectiveness of the large veil used during Lent to completely conceal the high altar from the laity "derived from the fact that it obscured for a time something which was normally accessible." *Stripping of the Altars*, 111.
25. Duffy, *Stripping of the Altars*, 97–9.
26. Eamon Duffy notes that although a rich array of altars and chantries is usually associated with larger churches and cathedrals, "even small churches had their quota of altars for the celebration of gild and chantry Masses, all crammed into the nave." *Stripping of the Altars*, 113.
27. Ibid., 112. Duffy also describes how these side altars made use of the rood screen "as the backdrop" for the Mass (113).

28. *The Pricke of Conscience*, ed. Richard Morris (Berlin: A. Asher, 1863; London: Philological Society, 1863).
29. Barnwell, "'Four hundred masses,'" 81.
30. Reginald Bawtre, 21 Nov 1429, proved 21 Nov 1429 (BI Reg. 2 fols 572r–v).
31. Barnwell, "'Four hundred masses,'" 81. Clara Barnett, "Memorials and Commemoration in the Parish Churches of Late Medieval York," 2 vols (PhD diss., University of York, 1997), 326.
32. According to E. A. Gee, an inscription originally under the images in the window's eastern donor panel reads "Rogeri Henrison et Cecilie uxoris ejus. Abel Hesyl et Agnete...et omni fidelium defunct." An inscription under the images in the center donor panel reads "et dni. H. Hesyl." Gee, "The Painted Glass of All Saints' Church, North Street," *Archaeologia* 102 (1969): 161, 162.
33. Barnwell, "'Four hundred masses,'" 81.
34. Ibid., 77; French, *People of the Parish*, 170–3.
35. French, *People of the Parish*, 162. French analyzes the English parish church's "architecture of community" and suggests the ways in which design relates to social and devotional functions. For instance, she writes, "As the laity filled their nave with pews, chapels, and side altars, they shaped the route of the liturgical processions and compelled the clergy to acknowledge their social concerns, while caring for their spiritual ones" (155). See ibid., 142–74.
36. Duffy, *Stripping of the Altars*, 96.
37. Corine Schleif, "Hands that Appoint, Anoint and Ally: Late Medieval Donor Strategies for Appropriating Approbation Through Painting," *Art History* 16, no. 1 (March 1993): 1–32.
38. Alice Rayner notes that "the staging of things put them in process, traveling between a gathering of objects from the world, showing them in the transit of performative present, and still allowing their embeddedness in signification to trail along." "Presenting Objects, Presenting Things," in *Staging Philosophy: Intersections of Theater, Performance, and Philosophy*, eds. David Krasner and David Z. Saltz (Ann Arbor: University of Michigan Press, 2006), 189.
39. This practice of dressing a saint's statue in layers of clothes and accoutrements is exactly the kind of devotional activity to which the *Ymagis* author objects. Original will Katherine de Craven, 20 July 1418, proved 28 Jan 1419 (BI Reg. 3 fols 613r–v): 613v; Latin translation from Cooke 1913: 314–17.
40. Mary E. Fissell, "The Politics of Reproduction in the English Reformation," *Representations* 87 (Summer 2004): 54.
41. Brian Spencer, *Pilgrim Souvenirs and Secular Badges* (London: Stationery Office, 1998). Spencer notes that by the fifteenth century such souvenirs included "religious pictures, statuettes of saints, votive figurines, candles and candleholders, as well as secular and

heraldic badges, bells, whistles and other knick-knacks, which had nothing to do with the shrine concerned" (5).
42. Pamela King, *The York Mystery Cycle and the Worship of the City* (Cambridge: D. S. Brewer, 2006), 136.
43. Some medieval devotees believed that Christ and the Virgin animated the pictures and sculptures depicting them. They sometimes addressed sacred images as persons and even attributed sensitive faculties to images. Suzannah Biernoff, *Sight and Embodiment in the Middle Ages* (New York: Palgrave, 2002), 135, 212. See also Richard Trexler, *Church and Community 1200–1600: Studies in the History of Florence and New Spain* (Rome: Storia e Letteratura, 1987).
44. French, *The People of the Parish*, 155.
45. John Schofield, "Urban Housing in England, 1400–1600," in *The Age of Transition: The Archaeology of English Culture 1400–1600*, eds. David Gaimster and Paul Stamper (Oxford: Oxbow Books, 1997), 140–1.
46. P. Jeremy P. Goldberg, "Household and the Organisation of Labour in Late Medieval Towns: Some English Evidence," in *The Household in Late Medieval Cities, Italy and Northwestern Europe Compared*, eds. Myriam Carlier and Tim Soens (Louvain-Apeldoorn: Garant, 2001), 59–70; Judith M. Bennett, *Ale, Beer and Brewsters in England: Women's Work in a Changing World, 1300–1600* (Oxford: Oxford University Press, 1996).
47. Felicity Riddy, "Looking Closely: Authority and Intimacy in the Late Medieval Urban Home," in *Gendering the Master Narrative*, eds. Mary C. Erler and Maryanne Kowaleski (Ithaca and London: Cornell University Press, 2003), 217.
48. According to Riddy, these "demands of the body" included "eating, sleeping, washing, getting dressed and undressed, preparing the food and clearing it away; raising the children; tending the sick and the dying" (ibid., 222).
49. Ibid.
50. For work on the development of an idea of "one's own body" and its relationship to sacrality, see Alain Boureau, "The Sacrality of One's Own Body in the Middle Ages," *Yale French Studies* 86 (1994): 5–17.
51. W. L. Hildburgh, "Folk-life Recorded in Medieval English Alabaster Carvings," *Folklore: Transactions of the Folk-lore Society* 60, no. 2 (1949): 252.
52. Francis Cheetham, *English Medieval Alabasters: With a Catalogue of the Collection in the Victoria and Albert Museum* (Oxford: Phaidon, 1984), 13–17.
53. F. Collins, ed., *Register of the Freemen of the City of York from the City Records, 1272–1558* (London: Surtees Society, 1896), 177, 183, 185, 187, 194, 213, 246.

NOTES

54. Richard Marks, "An Age of Consumption: Art for England c. 1400–1547," in *Gothic Art for England 1400–1547*, eds. Richard Marks and Paul Williamson (London: V&A Publications, 2003), 22. The *Records of the Borough of Nottingham*, Volume 3, ed. S. G. Johnson (London and Nottingham: Bernard Quaritch and Thomas Forman and Sons, 1885) contains a number of cases that appear to involve alabasters. An April 1492 action prices a head of Saint John the Baptist at 5 shillings (22), and a January 1500 appraisement lists six heads of John the Baptist as worth 8 pennies (74). The 1402 probate inventory of John de Scardeburgh includes an alabaster image of Mary Magdalene worth 2 shillings. P. M. Stell and Louise Hampson, *Probate Inventories of the York Diocese 1350–1500* (York: Unpublished typescript, 2005), 53.
55. Susan Foister, "Paintings in Sixteenth-Century English Inventories," *Burlington Magazine* 123, no. 938 (May 1981): 275.
56. Pamela Sheingorn identifies several visual principles functioning in both medieval art and drama, including framing, juxtaposition, and recapitulation. "The Visual Language of Drama: Principles of Composition," in *Contexts for Early English Drama*, eds. Marianne G. Briscoe and John C. Coldeway (Bloomington: Indiana University Press, 1989), 173–91.
57. Although we cannot suggest an "ideal" position for the alabaster viewer that remained consistent for every interaction with the piece—a viewer may have stood in various locations with respect to an image placed in the home—the performance viewer's perspective was variable in much the same way. Both genres offered laypeople opportunities to choose viewing positions for themselves before sacred images.
58. For examples, see Francis Cheetham, *Alabaster Images of Medieval England* (Woodbridge: Boydell Press, 2003), numbers 90–95. The Victoria and Albert Museum collection contains a number of Ascension alabasters, most of which follow the basic design I described earlier. Images and descriptions of these pieces are available through the V&A's online collection (http://collections.vam.ac.uk/) using museum numbers A.113-1946; A.144-1946; A.147-1946; A.27-1950; A.54-1935. An especially good example in the collection is an early-fifteenth-century panel, museum number A.112-1946. This panel, which once formed part of an altarpiece, was later reappropriated as an independent sculpture and placed in a wooden box. See: http://collections.vam.ac.uk/indexplus/result.html?_IXFIRST_=1&_IXSS_=_IXFIRST_%3d1%26_IXINITSR_%3dy%26%2524%253dIXID%3d%26_IXACTION_%3dquery%26%2524%253dIXOBJECT%3d%26_IXMAXHITS_%3d15%26%252asform%3dvanda%26%2524%253dIXNAME%3d%26_IXSESSION_%3dJ5nFLcURf3e%26%2524%253dIXPLACE%3d%26_IXadv_%3d1%26search%3dsearch%26%2524%253dIXMATERIAL%

3d%26%2524%253ds%3dascension%26%2524%253dop%3dAND%
26_IXFPFX_%3dtemplates%252ft%26%2524%253dsi%3dtext%26%
2524%253dIXFROM%3d%26%2524%253dIXTO%3d%26%2524%
253ddelflag%3dy&_IXACTION_=query&_IXMAXHITS_=1&_
IXSR_=Ls6ONwoHMWO&_IXSPFX_=templates%2ft&_
IXFPFX_=templates%2ft

59. The 1433 inventory for *The Last Judgment* describes that pageant's raising machinery as, "A brandreth of Iren þat god sall sitte vppon when he sall sty vppe to heuen With iiij rapes at iiij corners." Alexandra F. Johnston and Margaret Rogerson, eds., *Records of Early English Drama: York*, 2 vols (Toronto: University of Toronto Press, 1979), 55. Something similar may have been used in the *Ascension* and *Assumption of the Virgin* pageants.
60. For analysis of this image in medieval art and drama, see Pamela Sheingorn, "The Moments of Resurrection in the Corpus Christi Plays," *Medievalia et Humanistica* 11 (1982): 111–29.
61. According to Francis Cheetham, the first reference to a Saint John Head alabaster appears in the May 15, 1432, will of Isabella Hamerton, the widow of a York merchant and chapman (BI Reg. 3 fols 345v–346v). Hamerton gives John Branthwate, a chaplain, a number of items, among them "unum lapidem alabastri, secundum formam capitis Sancti Johannis Baptistae" (346v, my transcription). For a few examples of such bequests, see: Alice Grymmesby, 1440 (BI Reg. 2 fols 17v–18r), Johannet Holme, 1488 (BI Reg. 5 fol. 335), and Mawde Shawe, 1532 (BI Reg. 11 fol. 278v).
62. Images of different Head of John the Baptist panels are reproduced in Cheetham's 1984 catalogue *English Medieval Alabasters*, numbers 243–56.
63. Francis Cheetham, *Medieval English Alabaster Carvings in the Castle Museum of Nottingham* (Nottingham: Art Galleries and Museums Committee, 1962), 49.
64. Rubin, *Corpus Christi*, 315.
65. Ibid.
66. Original: "abill to fullfill þis dede certayne"; "holy gost schalle doune be sente." *The York Plays*, ed. Richard Beadle (London: Edward Arnold, 1982), cited by play number and line numbers.
67. Original: "fullfillid in worde but also in dede."
68. Henk Van Os, *The Art of Devotion in the Late Middle Ages in Europe, 1300–1500*, trans. Michael Hoyle (Princeton: Princeton University Press, 1995), 12.
69. David Freedberg and Vittorio Gallese, "Motion, Emotion and Empathy in Esthetic Experience," *Trends in Cognitive Sciences* 11, no. 5 (2007): 197–203.
70. Mary Carruthers's work on memory demonstrates the many different layers of interpretation that a single medieval text or image often invited users to contemplate simultaneously. See *The Book of Memory:*

A Study of Memory and Medieval Culture (Cambridge: Cambridge University Press, 1990); *The Craft of Thought: Meditation, Rhetoric, and the Making of Images, 400–1200* (Cambridge: Cambridge University Press, 1998).
71. Herbert L. Kessler, *Seeing Medieval Art* (Ontario: Broadview Press, 2004), 108–9.
72. One such diptych is only 20.3 x 9.5 cm (Van Os, *Art of Devotion*, Plate 1), while the Head of John alabaster I analyzed is 42.7 x 53.3 cm (including box with wings open).

Four Devotion and Conceptual Blending

1. Gilles Fauconnier and Mark Turner, *The Way We Think: Conceptual Blending and the Mind's Hidden Complexities* (New York: Basic Books, 2002), 102.
2. Ibid., 103.
3. Ibid., 102–4.
4. Ibid., 104.
5. Ibid., 205.
6. Ibid.
7. Ibid., 206.
8. Ibid., 207.
9. Ibid., 266–7.
10. Ibid., 267.
11. This decision suggests that the community was prepared to perform this play on relatively short notice. Royal visitors to York include: Richard II, Henry VI, Edward IV, Richard III, Henry VII, Princess Margaret (Henry VII's daughter), and Henry VIII. Alexandra F. Johnston and Margaret Rogerson, eds., *Records of Early English Drama: York*, 2 vols (Toronto: University of Toronto Press, 1979), 130–1.
12. Ibid., 137–52.
13. Lorraine Attreed, "The Politics of Welcome: Ceremonies and Constitutional Development in Later Medieval English Towns," in *City and Spectacle in Medieval Europe*, eds. Barbara A. Hanawalt and Kathryn L. Reyerson (Minneapolis: University of Minnesota Press, 1994), 215.
14. Johnston and Rogerson, *York*, 139.
15. Ibid.
16. Ibid., 140. Original: "To you henrie I submit my Citie key and Croune / To reuyll and redresse your dew to defence / Neuer to this Citie to presume ne pretence / Bot holy I graunt it to your gouernaunce / as A principall parcel of your inheritaunce / Please it I besuch you for my remembrance / Seth that I am prematiue of your progenie / Shew your grace to this Citie with such Abounedance / As the reame may recouer in to prosperitie."

17. Ibid. "With oon concent knowing you yer sufferaine and king."
18. Ibid., 142.
19. Gordon Kipling, *Enter the King: Theatre, Liturgy, and Ritual in the Medieval Civic Triumph* (Oxford: Clarendon Press, 1998), 134–9.
20. Fauconnier and Turner, *The Way We Think*, 30.
21. Fauconnier and Turner use graduation ceremonies to exemplify "compression achieved by blending," that is then further "compressed into an abiding material anchor that you take with you and hang on the wall: your diploma" (ibid., 30–1).
22. Rhonda Blair, "Image and Action: Cognitive Neuroscience and Actor-Training," in *Performance and Cognition: Theatre Studies and the Cognitive Turn*, eds. Bruce McConachie and F. Elizabeth Hart (New York: Routledge, 2006), 176, 177, emphasis mine. See also Blair, *The Actor, Image, and Action: Acting and Cognitive Neuroscience* (London: Taylor & Francis, 2008).
23. Blair, "Image and Action," 182, original emphasis; 182–3.
24. For example, an *A/Y* entry regarding the Tailors' guild notes that "four searchers will collect each year within the city the proper amount from each man of the said guild for the support of their pageant of Corpus Christi." Johnston and Rogerson, *York*, 690–1 (4).
25. Ibid., 696 (10). Source: *A/Y Memorandum*.
26. For instance, the Plasterers fined members 40d. to the Chamber and 40d. to their pageant if they employed apprentices for terms shorter than seven years. The Parchmentmakers fined their members 40d. for preventing searches, to be divided equally between the common purse and their pageant. Johnston and Rogerson, *York*, 16, 39. Source: *A/Y Memorandum*.
27. P. Jeremy P. Goldberg, "Craft Guilds, The Corpus Christi Play and Civic Government," in *The Government of Medieval York: Essays in Commemoration of the 1396 Royal Charter*, ed. Sarah Rees Jones (York: University of York and Borthwick Institute of Historical Research, 1997), 148–9.
28. Heather Swanson, *Medieval British Towns* (New York: St. Martin's Press, 1999). See also R. B. Dobson who argues that the cycle developed as a way for the overseas merchant elite to exert control over York's commercial life. "Craft Guilds and City: The Historical Origins of the York Mystery Plays Reassessed," in *The Stage as Mirror: Civic Theatre in Late Medieval Europe*, ed. Alan Knight (Cambridge: D. S. Brewer, 1997), 91–105.
29. Goldberg, "Craft Guilds," 157.
30. Sarah Beckwith, *Signifying God: Social Relation and Symbolic Act in the York Corpus Christi Plays* (Chicago: University of Chicago Press, 2001), 53. See also Margaret Aziza Pappano, "Judas in York: Masters and Servants in the Late Medieval Cycle Drama," *Exemplaria* 14, no. 2 (October 2002): 317–50; and Gervase Rosser, "Crafts, Guilds

and the Negotiation of Work in the Medieval Town," *Past and Present* 154 (1997): 3–31.
31. Johnston and Rogerson, *York*, 697 (11).
32. After 1517, when this body was patented as the "Common Council," it was composed of two representatives from each of the thirteen "major crafts" and one representative from the fifteen "minor crafts." Meetings of the civic council were normally attended by the mayor, Council of Twelve (made up of the twelve aldermen), and the Council of Twenty-four (whose life-term memberships were limited to ex-sheriffs). The Common Council did not convene regularly, though it sometimes met to protest the actions taken by the senior Councils or to present its concerns to these bodies. Johnston and Rogerson, *York*, xiii. See also Sarah Rees Jones, "York's Civic Administration 1354–1464," in *The Government of Medieval York: Essays in Commemoration of the 1396 Royal Charter*, ed. Rees Jones (York: University of York and Borthwick Institute of Historical Research, 1997), 108–40.
33. Fauconnier and Turner, *The Way We Think*, 131.
34. Ibid., 132–3.
35. Ibid., 136.
36. Ibid., 267.
37. For example, *The Temptation* opens with Diabolus saying, "Make rome belyve, and late me gang!" (22.1), suggesting that the actor entered through, or at least physically interacted with, the crowd of spectators. *The York Plays*, ed. Richard Beadle (London: Edward Arnold, 1982), cited by play number and line numbers.
38. Fauconnier and Turner, *The Way We Think*, 83.
39. Bruce McConachie, "Falsifiable Theories for Theatre and Performance Studies," *Theatre Journal* 59, no. 4 (2007): 559.
40. Theodore K. Lerud, "Quick Images: Memory and the English Corpus Christi Drama," in *Moving Subjects: Processional Performance in the Middle Ages and the Renaissance*, eds. Kathleen Ashley and Wim Hüsken (Amsterdam and Atlanta: Rodopi, 2001), 213–37; and *Memory, Images, and the English Corpus Christi Drama* (New York: Palgrave Macmillan, 2008).
41. For instance, *Rhetorica ad Herennium*, by pseudo-Cicero, instructs readers to remember a man accused of murder in order to obtain an inheritance by imagining a man lying ill in bed with the defendant at his bedside "holding in his right hand a cup, and in his left tablets, and on the fourth finger a ram's testicles" (III.xx). *Rhetorica ad Herennium*, ed. and trans. H. Caplan (Cambridge: Harvard University Press, 1954), 215.
42. Thomas Bradwardine, "On Acquiring a Trained Memory," in *The Medieval Craft of Memory: An Anthology of Texts and Pictures*, eds. Mary Carruthers and Jan M. Ziolkowski (Philadelphia: University of Pennsylvania Press, 2002), 208.

43. Ibid., 210.
44. Kimberly Rivers, "Memory and Medieval Preaching: Mnemonic Advice in the Ars Praedicandi of Francesc Eiximenis (ca. 1327–1409)," *Viator* 30 (1999): 253–84. For analysis of performance elements in medieval sermons, see Beverly Mayne Kienzle, "Medieval Sermons and their Performance: Theory and Record," in *Preacher, Sermon and Audience in the Middle Ages*, ed. Carolyn Muessig (Leiden, Boston & Köln: Brill, 2002), 89–124. Significantly, Alexandra F. Johnston's recent work connects the creation and monitoring of the York cycle with the city's Augustinian Friary, whose residents were important members of the community, particularly as preachers to York's laity. Her theory aligns the cycle with preaching culture, which supports the idea that the cycle's creators may have consciously employed mnemonic devices. Johnston, "John Waldeby, the Augustinian Friary, and the Plays of York," in *In Honor of Clifford Davidson: Papers Presented at the 35th International Congress on Medieval Studies, May 6, 2000* (Kalamazoo, MI: Medieval Institute Publications, 2002), 1–15. Fauconnier and Turner mention medieval mnemonic systems briefly when discussing how material structures, such as cathedrals, developed as conceptual structures because they offered accurate material anchors for mental spaces and blends. *The Way We Think*, 206–10.
45. Original: "þe firmament sal nough moue, / But be a mene, þus will I mene, / Ouir all þe worlde to halde and houe, / And be þo *tow wateris betwyne*."
46. Amy Cook, "Interplay: The Method and Potential of a Cognitive Science Approach to Theatre," *Theatre Journal* 59, no. 4 (2007): 589.
47. Original: "For I haue all þis worlde to welde, / Toure and toune, forest and felde: / If þou thyn herte will to me helde / With wordis hende, / 3itt will I baynly be thy belde / And faithfull frende. / Behalde now ser, and þou schalt see / Sere kyngdomes and sere contré; / Alle þis wile I giffe to þe / For euermore, / And þou fall and honour me / As I saide are."
48. Beckwith, *Signifying God*, 100–3; Martin Stevens, *Four Middle English Mystery Cycles: Textual, Contextual, and Critical Interpretations* (Princeton: Princeton University Press, 1987).
49. Original: "I murne, I sigh, I wepe also / Jerusalem on þe to loke."
50. Stanton B. Garner, Jr., *Bodied Spaces: Phenomenology and Performance in Contemporary Drama* (Ithaca and London: Cornell University Press, 1994), 42.
51. Scholars such as Ruth Evans and Sarah Beckwith have examined how York's pageants generate theological meaning through the spectator's presence within the cycle's representational field. Although they recognize the spectator and actor as bodied, these scholars concentrate on how meaning develops through signification rather than on how it develops through the spectator's embodiment explicitly.

Ruth Evans, "When a Body Meets a Body: Fergus and Mary in the York Cycle," in *New Medieval Literatures*, eds. Wendy Scase, Rita Copeland, and David Lawton (Oxford: Clarendon Press, 1997), 193–212; Beckwith, *Signifying God*, 88–9.
52. Simon Shepherd, *Theatre, Body and Pleasure* (London and New York: Routledge, 2006), 76.
53. The ancient story of Simonides, who is credited with establishing the art of memory, is based upon visual order; Simonides was able to identify the bodies of people who had been crushed by a fallen roof from his recollection of the place where each of them had been reclining at table. Cicero recounts this story in Book Two of *De Oratore*, but it also appears in a number of memory treatises from antiquity and the Middle Ages. Theodore K. Lerud draws similar conclusions about how "[p]laces or backgrounds, in the form of key town spaces, themselves became part of the play, incorporating the town itself into the festive pageant" (6) in *Memory, Images*. Sarah Beckwith also analyzes this relationship in *Signifying God*.
54. Mary Carruthers, "The Poet as Master Builder: Composition and Locational Memory in the Middle Ages," *New Literary History* 24 (1993): 881–2.
55. Francesc Eiximenis, "On Two Kinds of Order that Aid Understanding and Memory," in *The Medieval Craft of Memory: An Anthology of Texts and Pictures*, eds. Mary Carruthers and Jan M. Ziolkowski (Philadelphia: University of Pennsylvania Press, 2002), 192.
56. Mary Carruthers, "Rhetorical *Ductus*, or, Moving through a Composition," in *Acting on the Past: Historical Performance Across the Disciplines*, eds. Mark Franko and Annette Richards (Hanover and London: Wesleyan University Press, 2000), 104.
57. Ibid., 101. Given that these compositions were also highly flexible, thus allowing users to develop conversational and personalized ways of working with and through them, Carruthers acknowledges the performance aspect of ductus. She contends that a composed work is "open" and that every reading or "repetition of a work will differ" (112). With respect to York's cycle design, audience members could personalize their viewing experience through various physical choices. At the most basic level, they could begin and end viewing at different times and places, decide to visit multiple stations, watch a pageant more than once, or skip one or more plays entirely.
58. Many scholars have considered how the medieval processional cycle generated social meaning through civic space. The most widely cited article is Mervyn James' "Ritual, Drama and Social Body in the Late Medieval English Town," *Past and Present* 98 (1983): 3–29. James argues that the Corpus Christi procession and play resolved social conflict through ritual action, a claim that many scholars have since refuted. See chapter two of Sarah Beckwith's *Signifying God* and

Benjamin R. McRee, "Unity or Division?: The Social Meaning of Guild Ceremony in Urban Communities," in *City and Spectacle in Medieval Europe*, eds. Barbara A. Hanawalt and Kathryn L. Reyerson (Minneapolis: University of Minnesota, 1994), 189–207. For general work on theatre and processional space, see David Wiles, *A Short History of Western Performance Space* (Cambridge: Cambridge University Press, 2003), 63–91; and Marvin Carlson, *Places of Performance: The Semiotics of Theatre Architecture* (Ithaca: Cornell University Press, 1993).

59. Much work has examined the York cycle's route and staging, including Eileen White, "Places to Hear the Play in York: The Performance of the Corpus Christi Play in York," *Early Theatre* 3 (2000): 49–78; Meg Twycross, "The Theatricality of Medieval English Plays," in *The Cambridge Companion to Medieval English Theatre*, ed. Richard Beadle (Cambridge: Cambridge University Press, 1994): 37–84; and "The Left-Hand Theory: A Retraction," *Medieval English Theatre* 14 (1992): 77–94; David Crouch, "Paying to See the Play: The Stationholders on the Route of the York Corpus Christi Play in the Fifteenth Century," *Medieval English Theatre* 13 (1991): 64–111. Debate about the logistical feasibility of staging all of York's pageants processionally on wagons in a single day at multiple stations has, for the most part, been put to rest in favor of such a possibility. For a summary of this debate, see William Tydeman, *The Theatre in the Middle Ages* (Cambridge: Cambridge University Press, 1978), 114–20.
60. Johnston and Rogerson, *York*, 694 (8).
61. Ibid., 698 (11). For the topography of medieval York, I have referred to the York Archaeological Trust's "Viking and Medieval York" map (1998), which was reconstructed from ordinance survey results.
62. Gervase Rosser, "Communities of Parish and Guild in the Late Middle Ages," in *Parish, Church and People: Local Studies in Lay Religion 1350–1750*, ed. Susan Wright (London: Hutchinson 1988), 35.
63. See Lynette Muir's argument regarding the development of the cycle route out of the Eucharistic processional route in *The Biblical Drama of Medieval Europe* (Cambridge: Cambridge University Press, 1995).
64. Beckwith, *Signifying God*, 23–55.
65. Julia A. Walker, "The Text/Performance Split Across the Analytic/Continental Divide," in *Staging Philosophy: Intersections of Theater, Performance, and Philosophy*, eds. David Krasner and David Z. Saltz (Ann Arbor: University of Michigan Press, 2006), 39.
66. Crouch, "Paying to See the Play," 66–7; Royal Commission on Historical Monuments, *An Inventory of the Historical Monuments in the City of York. Volume Three: Southwest of the Ouse* (London: Her Majesty's Stationary Office, 1972), 68.
67. Sarah Rees Jones and Felicity Riddy, "The Bolton Hours of York: Female Domestic Piety and the Public Sphere," in *Household, Women*

and Christianities in Late Antiquity and the Middle Ages, eds. Anneke B. Mulder-Bakke and Jocelyn Wogan-Browne (Turnhout: Brepols, 2005), 245.
68. Ibid., 239. See also Christopher Dyer, "Work Ethics in the Fourteenth Century," in *The Problem of Labour in Fourteenth-Century England*, eds. James Bothwell and P. Jeremy P. Goldberg (Woodbridge: York Medieval Press, 2000), 21–42.
69. Pamela King, "York Plays, Urban Piety and the Case of Nicholas Blackburn, Mercer," *Archiv für das Studium der neueren Sprachen und Literaturen* 232 (1995): 42.
70. Ibid., 44.
71. Shepherd, *Theatre*, 94.
72. Portions of this section were previously published as "The Material Bodies of Medieval Religious Performance in England," *Material Religion: The Journal of Objects, Art, and Belief* 2, no. 2 (2006): 204–32.
73. P. Jeremy P. Goldberg, "Lay Book Ownership in Late Medieval York: The Evidence of Wills," *The Library* 16, no. 3 (September 1994): 185.
74. Ibid., 189.
75. For a model for the medieval Book of Hours based upon the York Use, see *Horae Eboracenses: The Prymer or Hours of the Blessed Virgin Mary, According to the Use of the Illustrious Church of York, with other devotions as they were used by the lay-folk in the Northern Province in the XVth and XVIth centuries*, ed. C. Wordsworth (Durham: Surtees Society, 1920).
76. Although the basic textual content was fixed, Eamon Duffy notes that "printed editions varied hugely in appearance, decoration and price, ranging from economy paper books half the size of the palm of your hand with few or no pictures, to sumptuous large quarto or octavo volumes printed on vellum, sometimes consciously passing themselves off as substitutes for manuscript, very elegantly and convincingly indeed" (122). Owners also personalized printed editions through annotations, erasures, and other means. *Marking the Hours: English People and their Prayers 1240–1570* (New Haven and London: Yale University Press, 2006), 121–46.
77. Ibid., 38.
78. Amelia Adams, "Evolution of a Manuscript: Text and Image in the Pavement Hours" (MA thesis, University of York, 2004), 1. This manuscript is sometimes referred to as the Pulleyn Hours.
79. Ibid., 52.
80. There are other medieval manuscripts that contain images sewn or pasted onto the pages. See Duffy, *Marking the Hours*, 38–45. Jeffrey Hamburger describes this devotional practice as it relates to Veronica images and badges, arguing that "the [Veronica] images inserted in the margins of missals underscore the Veronica's claims to concrete

physical presence, a presence associated with both the original relic and the consecrated Host." *The Visual and the Visionary: Art and Female Spirituality in Late Medieval Germany* (New York: Zone, 1998), 332. According to Mary Erler, the earliest example of an English printed book that is embellished through pasted images is most likely British Library IA 55038 (STC 16253), a Caxton Psalter (*ca.* 1480). See "Pasted-in Embellishments in English Manuscripts and Printed Books c. 1480–1533," *The Library* 14, Series VI (1992): 185–206.

81. For instance, in their analysis of the Bolton Hours, another Book of Hours from York dated to the same period as the Pavement Hours, Patricia Cullum and P. Jeremy P. Goldberg suggest that it was commissioned by a mother under the assumption that it would be passed down along her family's female line. But the authors also propose that this manuscript may have simultaneously served as a family book. See "How Margaret Blackburn Taught her Daughters: Reading Devotional Instruction in a Book of Hours," in *Medieval Women: Texts and Contexts in Late Medieval Britain*, eds. Jocelyn Wogan-Browne, et al. (Turnhout: Brepols, 2000), 217–36.
82. Adams, "Evolution of a Manuscript," 39.
83. Ibid., 38.
84. Ibid., 41.
85. Alternatively, Adams argues that "it is likely that the owner placed the Agnes image here knowing that the same text appeared earlier in the manuscript. Therefore, covering the text here would not interfere with the use of the text" (ibid.).
86. Alice Rayner, "Presenting Objects, Presenting Things," in *Staging Philosophy: Intersections of Theater, Performance, and Philosophy*, eds. David Krasner and David Z. Saltz (Ann Arbor: University of Michigan Press, 2006), 191.
87. Susan Stewart, *On Longing: Narratives of the Miniature, Gigantic, the Souvenir, the Collection* (Durham: Duke University Press, 1993), 135.
88. Transcription from Neil Ker and A. J. Piper, *Medieval Manuscripts in British Libraries*, vol. 4 (Oxford: Clarendon Press, 1992), 729. As cited in Adams, "Evolution of a Manuscript," 45.
89. For a discussion of "ghosting" in the theatre, see Marvin Carlson, *The Haunted Stage: The Theatre as Memory Machine* (Ann Arbor: University of Michigan Press, 2003).
90. Mark Amsler, "Affective Literacy: Gestures of Reading in the Later Middle Ages," *Essays in Medieval Studies* 18 (2001): 84.
91. Ibid., 96, 97.
92. My conclusions are supported by David Freedberg and Vittorio Gallese's research into aesthetic experiences with art that I discussed in chapter one. Freedberg and Gallese, "Motion, Emotion and

Empathy in Esthetic Experience," *Trends in Cognitive Sciences* 11, no. 5 (2007): 197–203.
93. Adams, "Evolution of a Manuscript," 50.

Five   Pious Body Rhythms

1. As Gail McMurray Gibson notes, the late Middle Ages experienced an "ever-growing tendency to transform the abstract and theological to the personal and concrete." *The Theater of Devotion: East Anglian Drama and Society in the Late Middle Ages* (Chicago: University of Chicago Press, 1989), 7.
2. *The York Plays*, ed. Richard Beadle (London: Edward Arnold, 1982), cited by play number and line numbers.
3. The Chester Banns indicate that the face of God was presented as a "face gilte," which implies either a mask or painted face. Something similar may have been used in York's pageants. See Lawrence Clopper, ed., *Records of Early English Drama: Chester* (Toronto: University of Toronto Press, 1979), 247.
4. Original: "þe heuenes schalle be oppen sene, / The holy gost schalle doune be sente / To se in sight / The fadirs voyce with grete talent / Be herde full riȝt."
5. Original: "ȝe þat haue sene þis sight / My blissyng with ȝo be."
6. Original: "His clothyng is as white as snowe, / His face schynes as þe sonne."
7. Original: "þis brightnes made me blynde"; "Brethir, whateuere ȝone brightnes be? / Swilk burdis beforne was neuere sene. / It marres my myght, I may not see, / So selcouth thyng was neuere sene."
8. Original: "A, lord, why latest þou vs noȝt see / Thy fadirs face in his fayrenes?"
9. Original: "What þe prophettis saide in þer sawe, / All longis to hym."
10. Original: "For I desire to se hym fayne / And hym honnoure as his awne man. / Sen þe soth I see"; "I coveyte hym with feruent wille / Onys for to see, / I trowe fro þens I schall / Bettir man be." Pamela King also identifies the significance of Christ's visual presence and absence in this pageant, and points out that the speeches made by the eight Burgesses after Christ appears "take the form of Elevation lyrics, probably also uttered by the faithful as the Host passes them in its monstrance on the Corpus Christi procession." *The York Mystery Cycle and the Worship of the City* (Cambridge: D. S. Brewer, 2006), 140.
11. Original: "O, my harte hoppis for joie / To se nowe þis prophette appere."
12. Original: "I am gracyus and grete, God withoutyn begynnyng, / I am maker vnmade, all mighte es in me; / I am lyfe and way vnto

welth-wynnyng, / I am formaste and fyrste, als I byd sall it be. / My blyssyng o ble sall be blending, / And heldand, fro harme to be hydande, / *My body* in blys ay abydande, / Vnendande, withoutyn any endyng."

13. Original: "In chastité of thy bodye / Consayue and bere a childe þou sall."
14. For scholarship on this pageant, see Chester Scoville, *Saints and the Audience in Middle English Drama* (Toronto: University of Toronto Press, 2004), 55–80; Rosemary Woolf, *The English Mystery Plays* (Berkeley: University of California Press, 1972), 159–81; Alexandra F. Johnston, "*The Word Made Flesh*: Augustinian Elements in the *York Cycle*," in *The Centre and its Compass: Studies in Medieval Literature in Honor of Professor John Leyerle*, eds. Robert A. Taylor, et al. (Kalamazoo, MI: Medieval Institute Publications, 1993), 241–3.
15. Original: "Thy wombe is waxen grete, thynke me, / þou arte with barne"; "Hir sidis shewes she is with childe."
16. Original: "For trulye her come neuer no man / To waite *þe body* with non ill / Of this swete wight, / For we haue dwelt ay with hir still / And was neuere fro hir day nor nyght. / Hir kepars haue we bene / And sho aye in oure sight, / Come here no man bytwene / *To touche þat berde* so bright."
17. For work on the late medieval culture of surveillance and its relationship to drama, see Claire Sponsler, *Drama and Resistance: Bodies, Goods, and Theatricality in Late Medieval England* (Minneapolis: University of Minnesota Press, 1997), 1–49; and Seth Lerer, "'Representyd now in yower syght': The Culture of Spectatorship in Late Fifteenth Century England," in *Bodies and Disciplines: Intersections of Literature and History in Fifteenth-Century England*, eds. Barbara Hanawalt and David Wallace (Minneapolis: University of Minnesota Press, 1996), 29–62.
18. Original: "Nowe in my sawle grete joie haue I, / I am all cladde in comforte clere, / *Now will be borne of my body / Both God and man togedir in feere*, / Blist mott he be. / Jesu my sone þat is so dere, / Nowe borne is he" (emphasis mine). For the possible staging of this moment, and how it may have recalled liturgical imagery, see King, *The York Mystery Cycle*, 103.
19. Pamela King analyzes how the trial pageants address issues of social and political authority. See *York Mystery Cycle*, 184–203, and "Contemporary Cultural Models of the Trial Plays in the York Cycle," in *Drama and Community: People and Plays in Medieval Europe*, ed. Alan Hindley (Turnhout: Brepols, 1999), 200–16.
20. Alexandra F. Johnston, "'His Language is Lorne': The Silent Centre of the York Cycle," *Early Theatre* 3 (2000): 185, 194; and "*The Word Made Flesh*," 225–46.
21. Original: "But firste schall I wirschippe þe with witte and with will. / This reuerence I do þe forthy, / For wytes þar wer wiser þan

I, / They worshipped þe full holy on hy / And with solempnité sange Osanna till."
22. Original: "þis boy here before yowe full boldely was bowand / To worschippe þis warlowe"; "in youre presence he prayed hym of pees, / In knelyng on knes to þis knave / He besoughte hym his seruaunte to saue."
23. "Trial of Margery Baxter of Norwich," in *Women in England c. 1275–1525: Documentary Sources*, ed. and trans. P. Jeremy P. Goldberg (Manchester and New York: Manchester University Press, 1995), 291.
24. Reginald Pecock, *The Repressor of Over Much Blaming of the Clergy*, ed. Churchill Babington (London: Longman, Green, Longman, and Robert, 1860), 169.
25. Original: "The loke of his faire face so clere / With full sadde sorrowe sheris my harte."
26. Original: "Knele doune here to þe kyng on thy knee."
27. For a related analysis of how tyrants resort to physical violence as a means of controlling Christ, see Ruth Nisse, *Defining Acts: Drama and the Politics of Interpretation in Late Medieval England* (Notre Dame: University of Notre Dame Press, 2005), 40–5.
28. Original: "For me likis noght youre langage so large."
29. Original: "Slike a sight was neuere ȝit sene. / Come sytt, / My comforth was caught fro me clene— / I vpstritt, I me myght noȝt abstene / To wirschip hym in wark and in witte."
30. Pilate's reaction is based on an apocryphal episode that was later embellished in the contemporary medieval narrative poem *The Northern Passion*. See *The Northern Passion*, ed. Francis Foster (Suffolk: Boydell and Brewer, 2002). Richard Beadle notes this connection in "The York Cycle," in *The Cambridge Companion to Medieval English Theatre*, ed. Beadle (Cambridge: Cambridge University Press, 1994), 104.
31. Original: "Thus we teche hym to tempre his tales." I discuss this scourging scene in greater detail in chapter six.
32. Original: "Drawe hym faste hense, delyuere ȝou, haue done. / Go, do se hym to dede withoute lenger delay."
33. Original: "Of japes ȝitt jangelid yone Jewe, / And cursedly he called hym a kyng"; "And worste of all, / He garte hym call / Goddes sonne"; "þou mustered emange many menne; / But, brothell, þou bourded to brade."
34. Original: "þou man þat of mys here has mente, / To me tente enteerly þou take. / On roode am I ragged and rente, / þou synfull sawle, for thy sake; / For thy misse amendis wille I make. / My bakke for to bende here I bide, / þis teene for thi trespase I take."
35. Original: "To þe, kyng, on knes here I knele, / þat baynly þou belde me in blisse."
36. Claire Sponsler analyzes the display of Christ's broken body in York's cycle. See *Drama and Resistance*, 136-60.

37. Patricia Cox Miller, "Visceral Seeing: The Holy Body in Late Ancient Christianity," *Journal of Early Christian Studies* 12, no. 4 (2004): 398.
38. Ibid., 400.
39. Vittorio Gallese, "Embodied Simulation: From Neurons to Phenomenal Experience," *Phenomenology and the Cognitive Sciences* 4, no. 1 (March 2005): 35.
40. Pamela King describes how York's pageants present witnessing as a "process of seeing," specifically when Longinus's sight is restored by Christ's blood. "Seeing and Hearing; Looking and Listening," *Early Drama* 3 (2000): 163. King also discusses the significance of witnessing throughout *The York Mystery Cycle*.
41. Original: "wende we vnto seere contre / To preche thurgh all þis worlde so wide."
42. Original: "turne þame tyte"; "þis lawe þat þou nowe late has laide."
43. Original: "I schall walke este and weste, / And garre þame werke wele were"; "thy selle where þou schalte sitte." According to the Gospel of Nicodemus, from which the harrowing scene is derived, after Hell cast Satan from his dwelling to fight Christ (V.1) "[t]hen the King of Glory seized the chief ruler Satan by the head and handed him over to the angels, saying, 'Bind with irons his hands and his feet and his neck and his mouth'" (VI.2). See the descent episode in "The Gospel of Nicodemus *The Apocryphal New Testament. A Collection of Apocryphal Christian Literature in an English Translation based on M. R. James*, ed. J. K. Elliott (Oxford and New York: Oxford University Press, 1993), 164–204.
44. Stanton B. Garner, Jr., *Bodied Spaces: Phenomenology and Performance in Contemporary Drama* (Ithaca and London: Cornell University Press, 1994), 42.
45. Suzannah Biernoff, *Sight and Embodiment in the Middle Ages* (New York: Palgrave, 2002), 17–39.
46. Alexandra F. Johnston discusses how the use of verbal, and perhaps physical, contrast in this pageant emphasizes the Augustinian notion that "good is stable, tranquil, and harmonious; evil is unstable, restless, and dissonant" (235). "*The Word Made Flesh*," 234–6.
47. Original: "Þat is my comyng for to knawe, / And to my sacramente pursewe, / Mi dede, my rysing, rede be rawe— / Who will noght trowe, þei are noght trewe. / Vnto my dome I schall þame drawe, / And juge þame worse þanne any Jewe. / *And all þat likis to leere / My lawe and leue þerbye* / Shall neuere haue harmes heere, / But welthe, as is worthy" (emphasis mine).
48. Original: "Ensaumpill he gaue þame heuene to wynne."
49. Original: "the tymen is comen I will make ende."
50. Original: "we haue his flesh forsworne"; "may bringe forthe no goode dede."

51. Original: "Allas, þat we swilke liffe schulde lede / þat dighte vs has þis destonye / Oure wikkid werkis þei will vs wreye / þat we wende never schuld haue bene weten."
52. Original: "Oure dedis beis oure dampnacioune"; "Oure wikkid werkis may we not hide, / But on oure bakkis vs muste þem bere –"; "Before vs playnly bese fourth brought / Þe dedis þat vs schall dame bedene / Þat eres has herde, or harte has boght, / Sen any tyme þat we may mene, / Þat fote has gone or hande has wroght, / That mouthe hath spoken or ey has sene—/ Þis day full dere þanne bese it boght; / Allas, vnborne and we hadde bene."
53. Original: "deme folke ferre and nere / Aftir þer werkyng, wronge or right"; "But, aftir wirkyng, welth or wrake."
54. Clifford Davidson, "Space and Time in Medieval Drama: Meditations on Orientation in the Early Theater," in *Word, Picture, Spectacle*, ed. Davidson (Kalamazoo, MI: Medieval Institute Publications, 1984), 80.
55. As I noted in the introduction, this emphasis on deeds is prevalent throughout late medieval devotional and catechetical literature, and in sermons. See John Mirk, *Mirk's Festial: A Collection of Homilies by Johannes Mirkus*, vol. 1, ed. Theodor Erbe (London: Kegan Paul, Trench, Trübner, 1905; Kraus Reprint, 1987). Likewise, artistic representations of the seven Corporal Acts of Mercy, such as the early-fifteenth-century window in York's church of All Saints North Street, usually depict laypeople performing these seven pious acts. These include feeding the hungry, offering drink to the thirsty, providing hospitality to strangers, visiting the sick, clothing the naked, visiting those in prison, and burying the dead.
56. Evan Thompson, *Mind in Life: Biology, Phenomenology, and the Sciences of the Mind* (Cambridge: Harvard University Press, 2007), 386. See also Shaun Gallagher and Dan Zahavi, *The Phenomenological Mind: An Introduction to Philosophy of Mind and Cognitive Science* (London and New York: Routledge, 2008), 183.
57. Edith Stein, *On the Problem of Empathy*, trans. Waltraut Stein (Washington, DC: ICS Publications, 1989), 6–11. Thompson outlines his four processes in *Mind in Life*, 382–411.
58. Thompson, *Mind in Life*, 401.
59. Ibid., 402.
60. Thompson explains, "One of the most important reasons that human mentality cannot be reduced simply to what goes on inside the brain of an individual is that human mental activity is fundamentally social and cultural. Culture is no mere external addition or support to cognition; it is woven into the very fabric of each human mind from the beginning" (ibid., 403).
61. Bruce McConachie, *Engaging Audiences: A Cognitive Approach to Spectating in the Theatre* (New York: Palgrave Macmillan, 2008), 69.

62. For an analysis of charity within this play, see Kate Crassons, "The Challenges of Social Unity: The *Last Judgment* Pageant and Guild Relations in York," *Journal of Medieval and Early Modern Studies* 37, no. 2 (Spring 2007): 305–34.
63. Sponsler, *Drama and Resistance*, 163.
64. Bruce McConachie, "Falsifiable Theories for Theatre and Performance Studies," *Theatre Journal* 59, no. 4 (2007): 566–7.

Six Empathy, Entrainment, & Devotional Instability

1. Alexandra F. Johnston and Margaret Rogerson, eds., *Records of Early English Drama: York*, 2 vols (Toronto: University of Toronto Press, 1979), 728 (43).
2. Ibid., 729 (43).
3. Ibid., 729 (44).
4. Ibid., 62, 777 (109).
5. Suzannah Biernoff, *Sight and Embodiment in the Middle Ages* (New York: Palgrave, 2002), 134.
6. Ibid., 163.
7. *The York Plays*, ed. Richard Beadle (London: Edward Arnold, 1982), cited by play number and line numbers.
8. Original: "I Judeus: Do, do, laye youre handes belyue on þis lourdayne. / III Judeus: We, haue holde þis hauk in þi hend."
9. Original: "That I myght þe take in þe armys of myne / And in þis poure wede to arraie þe"; "The wedir is colde as ye may feele, / To halde hym warme þei are full fayne / With þare warme breth."
10. Original: "Come halse me, the babb that is best born"; "That this sweyt babb, that I in armes hent"; "And yf þou will ought ese thyn arme / Gyff me hym, late me bere hym awhile."
11. Brigitte Cazelles, "Bodies on Stage and the Production of Meaning," *Yale French Studies* 86 (1994): 62, original emphasis.
12. Pamela King, *The York Mystery Cycle and the Worship of the City* (Cambridge: D. S. Brewer, 2006), 103.
13. Ibid., 174, 155, 179.
14. In the *Appearance to Mary Magdalene*, Christ utters the well-known "do not touch me" command; in *The Supper at Emmaus* he eats; in *The Incredulity of Thomas* he invites the disciples to "gropes" his wounds and then agrees to eat with them; and, as King notes, in *The Ascension* "Christ himself makes the point that he has spent forty days eating and spending time with them so that they will be in no doubt of his Resurrection" (ibid., 164–5).
15. Christian Keysers, et al., "A Touching Sight: SII/PV Activation during the Observation and Experience of Touch," *Neuron* 42 (April 2004): 335–46.

16. Vittorio Gallese, "The Roots of Empathy: The Shared Manifold Hypothesis and the Neural Basis of Intersubjectivity," *Psychopathology* 36 (2003): 173.
17. Keysers, et al., "A Touching Sight," 343.
18. Ibid., original emphasis.
19. Original: "Sone, as I am sympill sugett of thyne, / Vowchesaffe, swete sone I pray þe, / That I myght þe take in þe armys of myne / And in þis poure wede to arraie þe." Symeon uses similar language and gesture when he encounters the Christ child in *The Purification* (17.354–410).
20. Chester Scoville argues, "This lifting of the Christ child may have had mnemonic resonances with the Mass...Mary's elevation of the Christ child into visibility may have had an effect reminiscent of that of the elevation of the Host." *Saints and the Audience in Middle English Drama* (Toronto: University of Toronto Press, 2004), 66. Pamela King argues for a similar resonance. See *The York Mystery Cycle*, 103. Gail McMurray Gibson makes a related point about East Anglian drama in *The Theater of Devotion: East Anglian Drama and Society in the Late Middle Ages* (Chicago: University of Chicago Press, 1989), 166–8.
21. V. A. Kolve, *The Play Called Corpus Christi* (Stanford: Stanford University Press, 1966), 182.
22. Ibid., 185. Alexandra F. Johnston describes how the verbal parody and rapid stichomythia in this pageant turns the scourging into a kind of dance. See *"The Word Made Flesh*: Augustinian Elements in the *York Cycle,"* in *The Centre and its Compass: Studies in Medieval Literature in Honor of Professor John Leyerle*, eds. Robert A. Taylor et al. (Kalamazoo, MI: Medieval Institute Publications, 1993), 239.
23. Claire Sponsler, *Drama and Resistance: Bodies, Goods, and Theatricality in Late Medieval England* (Minneapolis: University of Minnesota Press, 1997), 150.
24. Ibid. Sponsler argues that this is especially true in medieval morality plays.
25. Michael H. Thaut, "Rhythm, Human Temporality, and Brain Function," in *Musical Communication*, eds. Dorothy Miell, Raymond MacDonald, and David J. Hargreaves (Oxford: Oxford University Press, 2005), 176. I am employing the traditional definition of entrainment from physics that Thaut uses—when the "frequency of one moving system becomes locked to the frequency of another 'driver' system" (176).
26. Ibid., 185.
27. R. Keith Sawyer, "Music and Communication," in *Musical Communication*, eds. Dorothy Miell, Raymond MacDonald, and David J. Hargreaves (Oxford: Oxford University Press, 2005), 52. Sawyer is citing W. S. Condon and W. D. Ogston, "Sound Film

Analysis of Normal and Pathological Behavior Patterns," *Journal of Nervous and Mental Diseases* 143 (1966): 338–47.
28. Sawyer, "Music and Communication," 52.
29. Ibid.
30. Thaut, "Rhythm," 183. As Thaut explains, experiments also indicate that music can help people recover speech and motor functions in instances of stroke, brain trauma, Parkinson's disease, and cerebral palsy (181–2).
31. Ibid., 181.
32. Sponsler makes a similar point, suggesting that the English cycle plays "seem rather to encourage spectators to enjoy the attacks on Christ's body as moments of undisguised sadistic delight in the inflicting of bodily pain." *Drama and Resistance*, 152.
33. Original: "And þis daye schall his deth be dight—/ Latte see who dare saie naye?"
34. Miri Rubin, *Corpus Christi: The Eucharist in Late Medieval Culture* (Cambridge: Cambridge University Press, 1991), 98.
35. Hans Belting, *The Image and its Public in the Middle Ages: Form and Function of Early Paintings of the Passion*, trans. M. Bartusis and R. Meyer (New Rochelle, NY: Caratzas, 1990), 58.
36. In the case of *The Mirror*, a vernacular adaptation of the early-fourteenth-century Latin text *Meditationes Vitae Christi*, the witness motif is present in the original source. As Michael Sargent explains about the *Meditationes*'s narrative structure, "The purpose of these episodes, as of the imaginative presentation of the events of the gospel narrative, is not to supplant the words of scripture, but rather to increase the devotion of the reader or hearer of the book by presenting not merely the story of Christ's life, but even the basic doctrines of Christianity in such a way that they can be held in the mind's eye and recalled at will." See Sargent's "Introduction" to Nicholas Love's *The Mirror of the Blessed Life of Jesus Christ: A Critical Edition Based on Cambridge University Library Additional MSS 6578 and 6686*, ed. Sargent (New York: Garland Publishing, 1992), xi.
37. Love, *The Mirror*, 179. Original: "Þou also if þou beholde wele þi lorde. Þou maiht haue here matire ynouh of hye compassion, seynge him to tormentede, þat fro þe sole of þe fote in to þe heist part of þe hede. Þer was in him none hole place nor membre without passion."
"Þis is a pitevouse siht & a ioyful siht. A pitevous siht in him. for þat harde passion þat he suffrede for oure sauacion, bot it is a likyng siht to vs, for þe matire & þe effecte þat we haue þerbye of oure redempcion. Soþely þis siht of oure lord Jesu hangyng so on þe crosse by deuoute ymaginacion of þe soule, is so likyng to sume creatours. Þat after longe exercise of soroufull compassion. Þei felen sumtyme, so grete likyng not onely in soule bot also in þe body þat þei kunne

not telle, & þat noman may knowe, bot onely he þat by experience feleþ it."
38. William F. Hodapp, "Ritual and Performance in Richard Rolle's Passion Meditation B," in *Performance and Transformation: New Approaches to Late Medieval Spirituality*, eds. Mary A. Suydam and Joanna E. Ziegler (New York: St. Martin's Press, 1999), 242.
39. *The Book of Margery Kempe* indicates that Kempe spent time in York, perhaps even attending the city's annual Corpus Christi cycle performance. In chapters 10–11, there are references to Kempe journeying to York. And Kempe is in York throughout chapters 50, 51, and 52. *The Book of Margery Kempe*, trans. B. A. Windeatt (New York: Penguin, 1985). For the original language, see *The Book of Margery Kempe*, ed. Lynn Staley, TEAMS Middle English Texts (Kalamazoo, Michigan: Medieval Institute Publications, 1996) available online at: http://www.lib.rochester.edu/camelot/teams/staley.htm.
40. "For some said that she had a devil within her, and some said to her own face that the friar should have driven those devils out of her. Thus she was slandered, and eaten and gnawed by people's talk, because of the grace that God worked in her of contrition, of devotion, and of compassion"; "A good friend of the said creature met the friar who had preached so keenly against her, and asked him what he thought of her. The friar, answering back sharply, said 'She has the devil within her,' not at all shifting from his opinion, but instead defending his error" (ibid., 193, 204–5. Original: I.67.3915–18).
41. The term "tokenys" is used in this way throughout Book One: 18.972, 18.978, 33.1935, 35.2059, 36.2113, 36.2119, 36.2120, 36.2239, and 67.3902.
42. Ibid., 197 (I.64.3734–6). According to Staley, the phrase "token of love" is "enclosed by parallel slash marks that indicate the scribe deleted the phrase and substituted charité, which he wrote above token of love."
43. Ibid., 148 (I.46.2607–12).
44. Evan Thompson, *Mind in Life: Biology, Phenomenology, and the Sciences of the Mind* (Cambridge: Harvard University Press, 2007), 382–411. I discuss these in chapter five.
45. *The Book of Margery Kempe*, 124 (I.35.2042, 2039, 2046–8).
46. Augustine, *Eighty-three Different Questions*, trans. D. L. Mosher. Fathers of the Church 70 (Washington, D.C.: Catholic University Press, 1982), 43 (Q.12). As quoted by Biernoff, *Sight and Embodiment*, 36.
47. Susan Feagin explains that a sympathetic response "does *not* involve simulating the mental activity and processes of a protagonist; it instead requires having feelings or emotions that are in concert with the interests or desires the sympathizer (justifiably) attributes to the

protagonist." *Reading with Feeling: The Aesthetics of Appreciation* (Ithaca: Cornell University Press, 1996), 114, original emphasis.
48. Thompson, *Mind in Life*, 395, original emphasis.
49. Bruce McConachie, *Engaging Audiences: A Cognitive Approach to Spectating in the Theatre* (New York: Palgrave Macmillan, 2008), 97.
50. *A Tretise of Miraclis Pleyinge*, ed. Clifford Davidson (Kalamazoo, MI: Medieval Institute Publications, 1993), 102.
51. Sarah Beckwith, *Signifying God: Social Relation and Symbolic Act in the York Corpus Christi Plays* (Chicago: University of Chicago Press, 2001), 69–70, original emphasis.
52. Stanton B. Garner, Jr., *Bodied Spaces: Phenomenology and Performance in Contemporary Drama* (Ithaca and London: Cornell University Press, 1994), 183.
53. Vittorio Gallese, Morris N. Eagle, and Paolo Migone, "Intentional Attunement: Mirror Neurons and the Neural Underpinnings of Interpersonal Relations," *Journal of the American Psychoanalytic Association* 55, no. 1 (2007): 142. Experiments reveal that the observer's mental attitude determines the degree and quality of the neural activation. As Gallese, Eagle, and Migone explain, "When subjects are required to simply watch the pain stimulation of a body part experienced by some stranger, the observer extracts the basic sensory qualities of the pain experienced by others, mapping it somatotopically onto his or her own sensorimotor system. However, when subjects are required to imagine the pain suffered by their partner out of their sight, only brain areas mediating the affective quality of pain…are activated" (ibid.). This evidence suggests that watching pain onstage will prompt a different neural response than imagining pain inflicted on offstage characters or just hearing it described, a distinction that is relevant to the way York staged Christ's crucifixion.
54. Bruce McConachie, "Falsifiable Theories for Theatre and Performance Studies," *Theatre Journal* 59, no. 4 (2007): 567.
55. *A Tretise of Miraclis Pleyinge*, 102.
56. Original: "For-grete harme haue I hente, / My schuldir is in soundre."
57. Original: "Strike on þan harde, for hym þe boght. / 3is, here is a stubbe will stiffely stande, / Thurgh bones and senous it schall be soght"; "Faste on a corde / And tugge hym to, by toppe and taile"; "Ther cordis haue evill encressed his paynes, / Or he wer tille þe booryngis brought. / 3aa, assoundir are bothe synnous and veynis / On ilke a side, so haue we soughte"; "Latte doune, so all his bones / Are asoundre nowe on sides seere."
58. Gallese, "Roots of Empathy," 174; Vittorio Gallese, Christian Keysers, and Giacomo Rizzolatti, "A Unifying View of the Basis of Social Cognition," *Trends in Cognitive Science* 8, no. 9 (2004): 397.
59. Feagin says that with sympathy we "take on" another person's "interests as our own." *Reading with Feeling*, 114.

60. Robert Sturges argues that this play's action is concerned with achieving Christ's visibility and that by "submitting to the soldiers, Christ allows them to turn him into an object of vision, a spiritual and theatrical icon" (44). He contends that "the spectators are to 'behold' [Christ], and by beholding him, to 'fully feel' his sacrifice, to make an empathetic connection between street and stage, between audience and performer, in an act of affective piety that characterizes the York cycle as a whole...Christ here demands an audience" (43). "Spectacle and Self-Knowledge: The Authority of the Audience in the Mystery Plays," *South Central Review* 9, no. 2 (1992): 27–48.
61. Pamela King also identifies certain control mechanisms operating in *The Crucifixion*. See *York Mystery Cycle*, 149.
62. Original: "Al men þat walkis by waye or strete, / Takes tente ȝe schalle no trauayle tyne. / Byholdes myn heede, myn handis, and my feete, / And fully feele nowe, or ȝe fyne." David Mills argues that Christ's lines from the cross are directed at the audience and only secondarily intended for the characters within the dramatic action. "'Look at Me When I'm Speaking to You': The 'Behold and See' Convention in Medieval Drama," *Medieval English Theatre* 7, no. 1 (1985): 4–12.
63. Original: "My fadir, þat alle bales may bete, / Forgiffis þes men þat dois me pyne. / What þei wirke wotte þai noght; / Therfore, my fadir, I craue, / Latte neuere þer synnys be sought, / But see þer saules to saue."
64. King, *York Mystery Cycle*, 151.
65. Original: "þou man þat of mys here has mente, / To me tente enteerly þou take. / On roode am I ragged and rente, / þou synfull sawle, for thy sake; / For thy misse amendis wille I make. / My bakke for to bende here I bide, / þis teene for thi trespase I take / Who couthe þe more kyndynes haue kydde / Than I? / Þus for thy goode / I schedde my bloode. / Manne, mende thy moode, / For full bittir þi blisse mon I by."
66. This Christ is far more verbose than the Christ in *The Crucifixion*, who only speaks two twelve-line monologues.
67. Original: "on me for to looke lette þou noȝt "; "Manne, kaste þe thy kyndynesse be kende, / Trewe tente vnto me þat þou take, / And treste."

Coda

1. W. J. T. Mitchell, "There Are No Visual Media," *Journal of Visual Culture* 4, no. 2 (2005): 257–8, 262. Using painting as an example, Mitchell explains how materiality, and therefore the sense of touch, is an inextricable feature of this genre: "the beholder who knows nothing about the theory behind the painting, or the story or the allegory, need only understand that this is a painting, a handmade object, to

understand that it is a trace of manual production, that everything one sees is the trace of a brush or a hand touching canvas. Seeing painting is seeing touching" (259). Dominic M. M. Lopes makes a related argument for dispensing with visually oriented genre distinctions in "Art Media and the Sense Modalities: Tactile Pictures," *The Philosophical Quarterly* 47, no. 189 (October 1997): 439. These ideas are substantiated, at least in part, by the research described in David Freedberg and Vittorio Gallese, "Motion, Emotion and Empathy in Esthetic Experience," *Trends in Cognitive Sciences* 11, no. 5 (2007): 197–203.
2. Julie Bloom, "Moved by the Spirit to Dance With the Lord," *The New York Times*, March 4, 2007, Arts section.
3. In the Middle Ages, dance was regularly employed as a part of worship and devotion, and often integrated into religious drama. Records suggest that a wide range of medieval religious dance forms were popular among the late medieval laity. As Walter Salmen explains, throughout late medieval Europe, solo and round dances were common in and around churches, with movements ranging from devout gestures and prayer to more fully choreographed group dances. "Dances and Dance Music, c. 1300–1530," in *Music as Concept and Practice in the Late Middle Ages*, eds. Reinhard Strohm and Bonnie J. Blackburn (Oxford: Oxford University Press, 2001), 162–8. See also Jennifer Nevile, "Dance Performance in the Late Middle Ages: A Contested Space," in *Visualizing Medieval Performance: Perspectives, Histories, Contexts*, ed. Elina Gertsman (Burlington, VT: Ashgate, 2008), 295–310.
4. Bloom, "Moved by the Spirit."
5. N' Him We Move, "About 'N Him," http://www.tpid.org/; Dancing for Him, "Ministry Vision," http://www.dancingforhim.com/.
6. Bloom, "Moved by the Spirit."
7. Bruce L. Shelley and Marshall Shelley, *The Consumer Church: Can Evangelicals Win the World Without Losing Their Souls?* (Downer's Grove, IL: InterVarsity Press, 1992), 14–16; John Fletcher, "Tasteless as Hell: Community Performance, Distinction, and Countertaste in Hell House," *Theatre Survey* 48, no. 2 (2007): 314–16.
8. Naomi Rokotnitz, "'It is required/You do awake your faith': Learning to Trust the Body Through Performing *The Winter's Tale*," in *Performance and Cognition: Theatre Studies and the Cognitive Turn*, eds. Bruce McConachie and F. Elizabeth Hart (New York: Routledge, 2006), 139.
9. For example, in the 1399 list the cycle's sixth station is listed as the "End of Jubbergate in Coney Street," where York's Jewish community lived and worshipped. Alexandra F. Johnston and Margaret Rogerson, eds, *Records of Early English Drama: York*, 2 vols (Toronto: University of Toronto Press, 1979), 698 (11).
10. *Hell House*, DVD, directed by George Ratliff (Cantina Pictures Inc., 2001).

11. This juxtaposition and tonal shift are perhaps most effective in "The Ironists" scene. In this episode, a group of young adults in a coffee shop, speaking in the familiar sarcastic rhythms of "slacker" conversation, discuss making a mockumentary about Christianity. This scene concludes when a bunch of devils interrupt the banter and chase the characters offstage.
12. Matthew Philips and Lisa Miller, "Visions of Hell," *Newsweek* 148, no. 19 (November 6, 2006): 52–3. In Academic Search Premier [database online]. Accessed August 9, 2007. John Fletcher discusses the low immediate conversion rate at Hell Houses: "of the five hundred or so people who had seen the Tallahassee Hell House, only twelve made first-time confessions of faith. Though no comprehensive studies on Hell House efficacy yet exist, my research suggests that Tallahassee's statistics are fairly typical; the people who simply watch the show and leave substantially outnumber those who choose to convert. Keenan Roberts himself estimates that at least 70 percent of attendees at his annual Hell House are simply gawkers uninterested in anything more profound than a few cheap scares. Furthermore, many of the conversions reported by larger Hell House productions turn out in fact to be 'recommitments' by backsliding Christians rather than first-time decisions of brand-new converts." Fletcher, "Tasteless as Hell," 318.
13. As quoted in Barbara Brown Taylor, "Hell House," *Christian Century* 123, no. 24 (November 28, 2006). In Academic Search Premier [database online]. Accessed August 9, 2007.
14. I would echo John Fletcher's view that "the popular dismissal of these events as nothing more than distasteful Grand Guignol proselytizing" constitutes an "impoverished" analytical approach (313–14). Although Fletcher and I consider Hell Houses from different perspectives, his conclusions are consonant with mine, especially his assertion that "Hell House performances are not (or not only) about promoting the love of Christ to unbelievers but (also) about provoking in believers a properly Christian attitude of distaste for the world in general." "Tasteless as Hell," 324.
15. Claire Sponsler, *Drama and Resistance: Bodies, Goods, and Theatricality in Late Medieval England* (Minneapolis: University of Minnesota Press, 1997), 75–103.
16. According to the *Pensacola News Journal*, Hovind "is serving 10 years in federal prison as a result of a tax-fraud conviction for failing to pay more than $470,000 in employee taxes in a long-running dispute with the Internal Revenue Service." In early August 2009, "the nine properties that make up Dinosaur Adventure Land, and two bank accounts associated with the park will be used to satisfy $430,400 in restitution owed to the federal government." Kris Wernowsky, "Feds Can Seize Dinosaur Adventure Land," *Pensacola News Journal*, July 31, 2009, http://www.pnj.com/article/20090731/NEWS01/90731016/1006.

17. Abby Goodnough, "Darwin-Free Fun for Creationists," *The New York Times*, May 1, 2004, final edition.
18. Ibid.
19. Ibid.
20. Dinosaur Adventure Land, "About DAL," http://www.dinosauradventureland.com/aboutDAL.php.
21. Holy Land Experience, "About the Experience," http://www.holylandexperience.com/abouthle/index.html.
22. Holy Land Experience, "Guest Services," http://www.holylandexperience.com/discoverhle/guestservices.html.
23. Creation Museum Souvenir Guide, Answers in Genesis, 36.
24. Creation Museum Souvenir Guide, Answers in Genesis, "Helpful Hints for your day at the Creation Museum," internal page insert.
25. Kenneth Chang, "Paleontology and Creationism Meet but Don't Mesh," *The New York Times*, June 30, 2009, final edition.
26. Creation Museum Souvenir Guide, Answers in Genesis, inside front cover.
27. The Creation Museum, "About Us," http://www.creationmuseum.org/about.
28. "The Scientific Heritage of Christianity," *Joy! Magazine* (January 2009): 50, http://blogs.answersingenesis.org/aroundtheworld/wp-content/uploads/2009/01/article-creation-musuem1-in-joy-mag-jan09.pdf
29. Hovind suggests about Dinosaur Adventure Land: "You're missing 98 percent of the population if you only go the intellectual route." As quoted in Goodnough, "Darwin-Free Fun."
30. Peter W. Williams, "Creation Museum," *Material Religion: The Journal of Objects, Art and Belief* 4, no. 3 (2008): 373.
31. Quoted in Leah Arroyo, "Science on Faith at the Creation Museum," *Museum News*, November/December 2007, http://www.aam-us.org/pubs/mn/scienceonfaith.cfm.
32. Edward Rothstein, "Adam and Eve in the Land of Dinosaurs," *The New York Times*, May 24, 2007, Arts and Leisure section, final edition.
33. Rokotnitz, "Learning to Trust the Body," 138.
34. Anne C. Loveland and Otis B. Wheeler, *From Meetinghouse to Megachurch: A Material and Cultural History* (Columbia and London: University of Missouri Press, 2003), 1, 226.
35. Although I have visited the Brooklyn Tabernacle megachurch, I have not physically engaged any of the megachurches that I discuss here. My analysis is focused on the discourse surrounding megachurches, and is not informed to any great extent by my own experience of these worship spaces.
36. Ibid., 2.
37. Medieval parish churches and megachurches are similar in many respects. Both regularly function as community centers, operate

under a seven-day-a-week "full-service" model, and provide social, recreational, and educational services to the laity. Both also demand a high level of personal and financial commitment from parishioners. Here, I will restrict myself to suggesting how both of these physical spaces construct devotional encounters for worshippers through material enhancements.

38. Ibid., 232–3.
39. Bo Emerson, "Wired for Worship," *The Atlanta Journal-Constitution*, January 26, 2002. In LexisNexis Academic [database online]. Accessed August 9, 2007.
40. Marvin Carlson, *Performance: A Critical Introduction*, second ed. (London and New York: Routledge, 2003), 22.
41. As quoted in Bo Emerson, "Wired for Worship."
42. Jonathan Mahler, "The Soul of the New Exurb," *The New York Times Magazine*, March 27, 2005. In http://select.nytimes.com/search/restricted/article?res=F00613FE3C5B0C748EDDAA0894DD404482.
43. Ibid.
44. "Images and Pilgrimages," in *Selections from English Wycliffite Writings*, ed. Anne Hudson (Toronto: University of Toronto Press, 1997), 84.
45. As quoted in Mahler, "The Soul of the New Exurb."
46. Loveland and Wheeler, *From Meetinghouse to Megachurch*, 257.
47. Mahler, "The Soul of the New Exurb."
48. Ibid.
49. Marcus Bull, *Thinking Medieval* (New York: Palgrave, 2005), 131.
50. Bull defines cognitive assumptions as "the basic conceptual frameworks that we carry around with us all the time in order to make sense of the world as we are bombarded with its sights and sounds" (ibid., 132–3).

Selected Bibliography

Manuscript Sources

York, Borthwick Institute of Historical Research:
Probate Registers of the Exchequer and Prerogative Court of the Archbishop: Regs. 1–13.
Dean and Chapter of York, Original Wills, 1383–1499.
York, Minster Library Archives:
Manuscript XVI.K.6
Probate Jurisdiction, Inventories, L1(17)6, L1(17)17, L1(17)44.
Probate Registers of the Peculiar Jurisdiction of the Dean and Chapter: Regs. 1–3.

Published Primary Sources

Augustine. *On Genesis: Two Books on Genesis against the Manichees and on the Literal Interpretation of Genesis*. Translated by R. J. Teske. Washington, D.C.: Catholic University Press, 1991.
———. *The Confessions*. Translated by Henry Chadwick. Oxford and New York: Oxford University Press, 1992.
Bacon, Roger. *The Opus majus of Roger Bacon*. 3 Vols. Edited by John H. Bridges. London, 1900; Reprint, Frankfurt: Minerva-Verlag, 1964.
The Book of Margery Kempe. Translated by B. A. Windeatt. New York: Penguin Books, 1985.
The Book of Margery Kempe. Edited by Lynn Staley. TEAMS Middle English Texts. Kalamazoo, MI: Medieval Institute Publications, 1996.
Bradwardine, Thomas. "On Acquiring a Trained Memory." In *The Medieval Craft of Memory: An Anthology of Texts and Pictures*. Edited by Mary Carruthers and Jan M. Ziolkowski. Translated by Mary Carruthers, 205–14. Philadelphia: University of Pennsylvania Press, 2002.
[Cicero]. *Rhetorica ad Herennium*. Edited and translated by H. Caplan. Cambridge: Harvard University Press, 1954.
Clopper, Lawrence, ed. *Records of Early English Drama: Chester*. Toronto: University of Toronto Press, 1979.

Collins, F. ed. *Index of Wills in the York Registry, 1389–1514.* Worsop: Robert White, 1891.
———. *Register of the Freemen of the City of York from the City Records, 1272–1558.* London: Surtees Society, 1896.
———. *Index of Wills etc. from the Dean and Chapter of York, 1321–1636.* Worsop: Robert White, 1907.
Collins, F., and A. W. Gibbons, eds. *Index of Wills in the York Registry, 1514–1553.* Worsop: Robert White, 1899.
Cooke, R. Beilby. *Some Early Civic Wills of York.* Vols 1–8. Lincoln: Lincolnshire Chronicle, 1906, 1911, 1913, 1914, 1915, 1916, 1917, 1919.
Davidson, Clifford, ed. *York Art: A Subject List of Extant and Lost Art Including Items Relevant to Early Drama.* Kalamazoo, MI: Medieval Institute Publications, 1978.
Dickens, A. G., ed. "Robert Parkyn's Narrative of the Reformation." *English Historical Review* 62 (1947): 58–83.
Eiximenis, Francesc. "On Two Kinds of Order that Aid Understanding and Memory." In *The Medieval Craft of Memory: An Anthology of Texts and Pictures.* Edited by Mary Carruthers and Jan M. Ziolkowski. Translated by Kimberly Rivers, 189–204. Philadelphia: University of Pennsylvania Press, 2002.
Elliott, J. K., ed. and trans. *The Apocryphal New Testament. A Collection of Apocryphal Christian Literature in an English Translation based on M. R. James.* Oxford and New York: Oxford University Press, 1993.
Gerson, Jean. "Treatise against *The Romance of the Rose.*" In *Jean Gerson: Early Works.* Translated by Brian Patrick McGuire, 378–98. New York: Paulist Press, 1998.
Head, Thomas, ed. *Medieval Hagiography: An Anthology.* New York: Routledge, 2001.
Horae Eboracenses: The Prymer or Hours of the Blessed Virgin Mary, According to the Use of the Illustrious Church of York, with other devotions as they were used by the lay-folk in the Northern Province in the XVth and XVIth centuries. Edited by C. Wordsworth. Durham: Surtees Society, 1920.
"Images and Pilgrimages." In *Selections from English Wycliffite Writings.* Edited by Anne Hudson, 83–8. Toronto, Buffalo, and London: University of Toronto Press in association with the Medieval Academy of America, 1997.
Jackson, Charles, ed. *Yorkshire Diaries and Autobiographies in the Seventeenth and Eighteenth Centuries.* Durham: Andrews and Company, 1877.
Johnson, S. G., ed. *Records of the Borough of Nottingham.* Vol. 3. London and Nottingham: Bernard Quaritch and Thomas Forman and Sons, 1885.
Johnston, Alexandra, and Margaret Rogerson, eds. *Records of Early English Drama: York.* 2 Vols. Toronto: University of Toronto Press, 1979.
Langland, William. *The Vision of Piers Plowman. A Critical Edition of the B-Text Based on Trinity College Cambridge MS B.15.17.* Second edition. Edited by A. V. C. Schmidt. London: J. M. Dent, 1995.

Lay Folks' Catechism. Edited by T. F. Simmons and H. E. Nolloth. Early English Text Society, o.s., 112. London: K. Paul, Trench, and Trubner, 1901.

Lay Folks' Mass Book. Edited by T. F. Simmons. English Text Society, o.s., 71. London: N. Trübner, 1879.

Le livre de conduite du régisseur et le compte des dépenses pour le Mystère de la Passion joué à Mons en 1501 (The Director's Handbook and the Expense Record for the Mystery of the Passion Performed at Mons in 1501). Edited by Gustave Cohen. Paris: Champion, 1925.

Love, Nicholas. *The Mirror of the Blessed Life of Jesus Christ: A Critical Edition Based on Cambridge University Library Additional MSS 6578 and 6686.* Edited by Michael G. Sargent. New York: Garland Publishing, 1992.

Mariken van Nieumeghen: a Bilingual Edition. Edited by Therese Decker and Martin W. Walsh. Columbia, SC: Camden House, 1994.

Mary of Nemmegen. Edited by Margaret M. Raftery. Leiden: Brill, 1991.

Meredith, Peter, and John E. Tailby, eds. *Staging of Religious Drama in Europe in the Later Middle Ages: Texts and Documentation in English Translation.* Translations by Raffaella Ferrari, et al. Kalamazoo, MI: Medieval Institute Publications, 1982.

Mirk, John. *Mirk's Festial: A Collection of Homilies by Johannes Mirkus.* Edited by Theodor Erbe. Early English Text Society, e.s., 96. London: Kegan Paul, Trench, Trübner, 1905.

The Northern Passion. Edited by Francis Foster. Suffolk: Boydell and Brewer, 2002.

Pecock, Reginald. *The Repressor of Over Much Blaming of the Clergy.* 2 Vols. Edited by Churchill Babington. London: Longman, Green, Longman, and Robert, 1860.

The Pricke of Conscience. Edited by Richard Morris. Berlin: A. Asher, 1863; London: Philological Society, 1863.

"A Relation... of the Island of England... about the Year 1500." In *Women in England c. 1275–1525: Documentary Sources.* Edited by P. J. P. Goldberg. Translated by C. A. Sneyd, 283. Manchester and New York: Manchester University Press, 1995.

Royal Commission on Historical Monuments. *An Inventory of the Historical Monuments in the City of York. Volume Three: Southwest of the Ouse.* London: Her Majesty's Stationary Office, 1972.

———. *An Inventory of the Historical Monuments in the City of York. Volume Five: The Central Area.* London: Her Majesty's Stationary Office, 1981.

Skaife, R. H., ed., *The Register of the Guild of Corpus Christi in the City of York.* London: Mitchell and Hughes, 1872.

Testamenta Eboracensia. Vol. 1–5. Edited by James Raine. Surtees Society 4, 30, 45, 53, 79. London: 1836, 1855, 1865, 1869, 1884.

Testamenta Eboracensia. A Selection of Wills from the Registry at York. Vol. 6. Edited by John William Clay. Surtees Society 106. London: 1902.

A Tretise of Miraclis Pleyinge. Edited by Clifford Davidson. Kalamazoo, MI: Medieval Institute Publications, 1993.

"Trial of Margery Baxter of Norwich." In *Women in England c. 1275–1525: Documentary Sources*. Edited and translated by P. J. P. Goldberg, 290–5. Manchester and New York: Manchester University Press, 1995.
"Viking and Medieval York, Map." York Archaeological Trust: York, 1998.
York Civic Records. Vols 1–8. Edited by Angelo Raine. Wakefield: York Archeological Society Record Series, 1938–52.
York Mystery Plays: A Selection in Modern Spelling. Edited by Richard Beadle and Pamela M. King. Oxford: Clarendon Press, 1984.
The York Play: A Facsimile of British Library MS Additional 35290, Together with a Facsimile of the "Ordo Paginarum" Section of the A/Y Memorandum Book, and a Note on the Music by Richard Rastall. Edited by Richard Beadle and Peter Meredith. Leeds: University of Leeds, 1983.
The York Plays. Edited by Richard Beadle. London: Edward Arnold, 1982.
The York Plays. Vol. 1: The Text. Edited by Richard Beadle. Early English Text Society, supplementary series 23. Oxford: Oxford University Press, forthcoming.

Secondary Sources

Amsler, Mark. "Affective Literacy: Gestures of Reading in the Later Middle Ages." *Essays in Medieval Studies* 18 (2001): 83–110.
Anderson, M. D. *Drama and Imagery in English Medieval Churches*. Cambridge: Cambridge University Press, 1963.
Arroyo, Leah. "Science on Faith at the Creation Museum." *Museum News*. November/December 2007. http://www.aam-us.org/pubs/mn/scienceonfaith.cfm.
Ashley, Kathleen. "Contemporary Theories of Popular Culture and Medieval Performances." *Mediaevalia* 18 (1995): 5–17.
———. "Sponsorship, Reflexivity and Resistance: Cultural Readings of the York Cycle Plays." In *The Performance of Middle English Cultures: Essays on Chaucer and Drama in Honor of Martin Stevens*. Edited by James J. Paxson, Lawrence M. Clopper, and Sylvia Tomasch, 9–24. Cambridge: Boydell and Brewer, 1998.
Attreed, Lorraine. "The Politics of Welcome: Ceremonies and Constitutional Development in Later Medieval English Towns." In *City and Spectacle in Medieval Europe*. Edited by Barbara A. Hanawalt and Kathryn L. Reyerson, 208–31. Minneapolis: University of Minnesota Press, 1994.
Badir, Patricia. "Playing Space: History, the Body, and Records of Early English Drama." *Exemplaria* 9 (1997): 255–79.
Barnwell, P. S. "'Four hundred masses on the four Fridays next after my decease.' The Care of Souls in Fifteenth-Century All Saints', North Street, York." In *Mass and Parish in Late Medieval England: The Use of York*. Edited by P. S. Barnwell, Claire Cross, and Ann Rycraft, 57–87. Reading, UK: Spire Books, 2005.
Barnwell, P. S., Claire Cross, and Ann Rycraft, eds. *Mass and Parish in Late Medieval England: The Use of York*. Reading, UK: Spire Books, 2005.

Beadle, Richard. "York Cycle." In *The Cambridge Companion to Medieval English Theatre*. Edited by Richard Beadle, 85–108. Cambridge: Cambridge University Press, 1994.

Beckwith, Sarah. *Christ's Body: Identity, Culture and Society in Late Medieval Writings*. London and New York: Routledge, 1993.

———. *Signifying God: Social Relation and Symbolic Act in the York Corpus Christi Plays*. Chicago: University of Chicago Press, 2001.

Belting, Hans. *The Image and its Public in the Middle Ages: Form and Function of Early Paintings of the Passion*. Translated by M. Bartusis and R. Meyer. New Rochelle, NY: Caratzas, 1990.

Bennett, Judith M. *Ale, Beer and Brewsters in England: Women's Work in a Changing World, 1300–1600*. Oxford: Oxford University Press, 1996.

Biernoff, Suzannah. *Sight and Embodiment in the Middle Ages*. New York: Palgrave, 2002.

———. "Carnal Relations: Embodied Sight in Merleau-Ponty, Roger Bacon and St Francis." *Journal of Visual Culture* 4, no. 1 (2005): 39–52.

Binski, Paul. "The English Parish Church and its Art in the Later Middle Ages: A Review of the Problem." *Studies in Iconography* 20 (1999): 1–25.

Blair, Rhonda. "Image and Action: Cognitive Neuroscience and Actor-Training." In *Performance and Cognition: Theatre Studies and the Cognitive Turn*. Edited by Bruce McConachie and F. Elizabeth Hart, 167–85. New York: Routledge, 2006.

———. *The Actor, Image, and Action: Acting and Cognitive Neuroscience*. London: Taylor & Francis, 2008.

Bloom, Julie. "Moved by the Spirit to Dance With the Lord." *New York Times*, March 4, 2007, Arts and Leisure section.

Boureau, Alain. "The Sacrality of One's Own Body in the Middle Ages." *Yale French Studies* 86 (1994): 5–17.

Boyle, Leonard E., O.P. "The Fourth Lateran Council and Manuals of Popular Theology." In *The Popular Literature of Medieval England*. Edited by Thomas J. Heffernan, 30–43. Knoxville: University of Tennessee Press, 1985.

Bull, Marcus. *Thinking Medieval*. New York: Palgrave, 2005.

Burgess, Clive. "For the Increase of Divine Service: Chantries in the Parish in Late Medieval Bristol." *Journal of Ecclesiastical History* 36 (1985): 46–65.

———. "Late Medieval Wills and Pious Convention: Testamentary Evidence Reconsidered." In *Profit, Piety and the Professions in Later Medieval England*. Edited by Michael Hicks, 14–33. Gloucester: Alan Sutton, 1990.

Burke, Peter. *Eyewitnessing: The Uses of Images as Historical Evidence*. Ithaca: Cornell University Press, 2001.

Bynum, Caroline Walker. *Holy Feast and Holy Fast: The Religious Significance of Food to Medieval Women*. Berkeley: University of California Press, 1987.

Bynum, Caroline Walker. *Fragmentation and Redemption: Essays on Gender and the Human Body in Medieval Religion.* New York: Zone Books, 1991.
———. "Why All the Fuss about the Body? A Medievalist's Perspective." *Critical Inquiry* 22 (August 1995): 1–33.
Camille, Michael. "Before the Gaze: The Internal Senses and Late Medieval Practices of Seeing." In *Visuality Before and Beyond the Renaissance.* Edited by Robert S. Nelson, 197–223. Cambridge: Cambridge University Press, 2000.
Carlson, Marvin. *Places of Performance: The Semiotics of Theatre Architecture.* Ithaca: Cornell University Press, 1993.
———. *Performance: A Critical Introduction.* Second edition. London and New York: Routledge, 2003.
———. *The Haunted Stage: The Theatre as Memory Machine.* Ann Arbor: University of Michigan Press, 2003.
Carruthers, Mary. *The Book of Memory.* Cambridge: Cambridge University Press, 1990.
———. "The Poet as Master Builder: Composition and Locational Memory in the Middle Ages." *New Literary History* 24 (1993): 881–2.
———. *The Craft of Thought: Meditation, Rhetoric, and the Making of Images, 400–1200.* Cambridge: Cambridge University Press, 1998.
———. "Rhetorical *Ductus*, or, Moving through a Composition." In *Acting on the Past: Historical Performance Across the Disciplines.* Edited by Mark Franko and Annette Richards, 99–117. Hanover and London: Wesleyan University Press, 2000.
———. "Sweetness." *Speculum* 81, no. 4 (2006): 999–1013.
Casati, Roberto, and Alessandro Pignocchi. "Mirror and Canonical Neurons are not Constitutive of Aesthetic Response." *TRENDS in Cognitive Sciences* 11, no. 10 (2007): 410.
Caviness, Madeline H. *Visualizing Women in the Middle Ages: Sight, Spectacle, and Scopic Economy.* Philadelphia: University of Pennsylvania Press, 2001.
Cazelles, Brigitte. "Bodies on Stage and the Production of Meaning." *Yale French Studies* 86 (1994): 56–74.
Chambers, E.K. *The Mediaeval Stage.* 2 Vols. London: Oxford University Press, 1903.
Chang, Kenneth. "Paleontology and Creationism Meet but Don't Mesh." *The New York Times,* June 30, 2009, final edition.
Chazelle, Celia. "Pictures, Books, and the Illiterate: Pope Gregory I's Letters to Serenus of Marseilles." *Word and Image* 6, no. 2 (1990): 138–53.
Cheetham, Francis. *Medieval English Alabaster Carvings in the Castle Museum of Nottingham.* Nottingham: Art Galleries and Museums Committee, 1962.
———. *English Medieval Alabasters: With a Catalogue of the Collection in the Victoria and Albert Museum.* Oxford: Phaidon, 1984.

———. *Alabaster Images of Medieval England*. Woodbridge: Boydell Press, 2003.

Clark, Anne L. "Why All the Fuss About the Mind? A Medievalist's Perspective on Cognitive Theory." In *History in the Comic Mode: Medieval Communities and the Matter of Person*. Edited by Rachel Fulton and Bruce Holsinger, 170–81. New York: Columbia University Press, 2007.

Clark, Robert L. A. "Constructing the Female Subject in Devotion." In *Medieval Conduct*. Edited by Kathleen Ashley and Robert L. A. Clark, 160–82. Minneapolis and London: University of Minnesota Press, 2001.

Clopper, Lawrence M. *Drama, Play, and Game: English Festive Culture in the Medieval and Early Modern Period*. Chicago: University of Chicago Press, 2001.

———. "Is the *Tretise of Miraclis Pleying* a Lollard Tract Against Devotional Drama?" *Viator* 34 (2003): 229–71.

Cohen, Jeffrey Jerome, and Bonnie Wheeler. "Becoming and Unbecoming." In *Becoming Male in the Middle Ages*. Edited by Cohen and Wheeler, vii–xx. New York and London: Garland Publishing, 1997.

Coletti, Theresa. "Reading REED: History and the Records of Early English Drama." In *Literary Practice and Social Change in Britain 1380–1530*. Edited by Lee Patterson, 248–84. Berkeley: University of California Press, 1990.

Collins, Patrick J. *The N-Town Plays and Medieval Picture Cycles*. Kalamazoo, MI: Medieval Institute Publications, 1979.

Condon, W. S., and W. D. Ogston. "Sound Film Analysis of Normal and Pathological Behavior Patterns." *Journal of Nervous and Mental Diseases* 143 (1966): 338–47.

Cook, Amy. "Interplay: The Method and Potential of a Cognitive Science Approach to Theatre." *Theatre Journal* 59 (2007): 579–94.

Crane, Mary Thomas. "What was Performance?" *Criticism* 43, no. 2 (Spring 2001): 169–87. In Expanded Academic ASAP [database online]. Cited September 3, 2009.

Crane, Mary Thomas, and Alan Richardson. "Literary Studies and Cognitive Science: Toward a New Interdisciplinarity." *Mosaic* 32, no. 2 (1999): 123–40.. In Expanded Academic ASAP [database online]. Cited September 3, 2009.

Crassons, Kate. "The Challenges of Social Unity: The *Last Judgment* Pageant and Guild Relations in York." *Journal of Medieval and Early Modern Studies* 37, no. 2 (Spring 2007): 305–34.

Cross, Claire, and P. S. Barnwell, "The Mass in its Urban Setting." In *Mass and Parish in Late Medieval England: The Use of York*. Edited by P. S. Barnwell, Claire Cross, and Ann Rycraft, 13–26. Reading: Spire Books, 2005.

Crouch, David. "Paying to See the Play: The Stationholders on the Route of the York Corpus Christi Play in the Fifteenth Century." *Medieval English Theatre* 13 (1991): 64–111.

Crouch, David. *Piety, Fraternity and Power: Religious Gilds in Late Medieval Yorkshire, 1389–1547.* York: York Medieval Press, 2000.
Csikszentmihalyi, Mihaly, and Eugene Rochberg-Halton. *The Meaning of Things: Domestic Symbols and the Self.* New York: Cambridge University Press, 1981.
Cullum, Patricia, and Jeremy Goldberg. "How Margaret Blackburn Taught her Daughters: Reading Devotional Instruction in a Book of Hours." In *Medieval Women: Texts and Contexts in Late Medieval Britain.* Edited by Jocelyn Wogan-Browne, et al., 217–36. Turnhout: Brepols, 2000.
Davidson, Clifford. *Drama and Art: An Introduction to the Use of Evidence from the Visual Arts for the Study of Early Drama.* Kalamazoo, MI: Medieval Institute Publications, 1977.
———. "Space and Time in Medieval Drama: Meditations on Orientation in the Early Theater." In *Word, Picture, Spectacle.* Edited by Clifford Davidson, 39–93. Kalamazoo, MI: Medieval Institute Publications, 1984.
Davidson, Clifford, and Ann Eljenholm Nichols, eds. *Iconoclasm vs. Art and Drama.* Kalamazoo, MI: Medieval Institute Publications, 1989.
De Certeau, Michel. *The Practice of Everyday Life.* Translated by Steven Rendall. Berkeley: University of California Press, 1984.
Del Lungo, Gabriella Camiciotti. "Performative Aspects of Late Medieval Wills." *Journal of Historical Pragmatics* 3, no. 2 (2002): 205–27.
Dobson, R. B. "The Later Middle Ages, 1215–1500." In *A History of York Minster.* Edited by G. E. Aylmer and Reginald Cant, 44–109. Oxford: Clarendon Press, 1977.
———. "Craft Guilds and City: The Historical Origins of the York Mystery Plays Reassessed." In *The Stage as Mirror: Civic Theatre in Late Medieval Europe.* Edited by Alan Knight, 91–105. Cambridge: D. S. Brewer, 1997.
Dox, Donnalee. *The Idea of the Theater in Latin Christian Thought: Augustine to the Fourteenth Century.* Ann Arbor: University of Michigan Press, 2004.
Dronzek, Anna. "Gendered Theories of Education in Fifteenth-Century Conduct Books." In *Medieval Conduct.* Edited by Kathleen Ashley and Robert L. A. Clark, 135–59. Minneapolis: University of Minnesota Press, 2001.
Duffy, Eamon. *The Stripping of the Altars: Traditional Religion in England 1400–1580.* New Haven: Yale University Press, 1992.
———. "Late Medieval Religion." In *Gothic Art for England 1400–1547.* Edited by Richard Marks and Paul Williamson, 56–67. London: V&A Publications, 2003.
———. *Marking the Hours: English People and their Prayers 1240–1570.* New Haven and London: Yale University Press, 2006.
Dyer, Christopher. "Work Ethics in the Fourteenth Century." In *The Problem of Labour in Fourteenth-Century England.* Edited by James Bothwell and P. Jeremy P. Goldberg, 21–41. Woodbridge: York Medieval Press, 2000.

Ehrstine, Glenn. *Theater, Culture, and Community in Reformation Bern, 1523–1555*. Leiden, Boston, and Köln: Brill, 2002.
———. "Framing the Passion: Mansion Staging as Visual Mnemonic." In *Visualizing Medieval Performance: Perspectives, Histories, Contexts*. Edited by Elina Gertsman, 263–77. Burlington, VT: Ashgate, 2008.
Emerson, Bo. "Wired for Worship." *The Atlanta Journal-Constitution*, January 26, 2002. In LexisNexis Academic [database online]. Cited August 9, 2007.
Erler, Mary C. "Pasted-in Embellishments in English Manuscripts and Printed Books c. 1480–1533." *The Library* 14, Series VI (1992): 185–206.
Erler, Mary C., and Maryanne Kowaleski, eds. *Gendering the Master Narrative: Women and Power in the Middle Ages*. Ithaca and London: Cornell University Press, 2003.
Evans, Ruth. "When a Body Meets a Body: Fergus and Mary in the York Cycle." In *New Medieval Literatures*. Edited by Wendy Scase, Rita Copeland, and David Lawton, 193–212. Oxford: Clarendon Press, 1997.
Fauconnier, Gilles, and Mark Turner. *The Way We Think: Conceptual Blending and the Mind's Hidden Complexities*. New York: Basic Books, 2002.
Feagin, Susan. *Reading with Feeling: The Aethetics of Appreciation*. Ithaca: Cornell University Press, 1996.
Fissell, Mary E. "The Politics of Reproduction in the English Reformation." *Representations* 87 (Summer 2004): 43–81.
Flanagan, C. Clifford. "Medieval Liturgical Processions in Semiotic and Cultural Perspectives." In *Moving Subjects: Processional Performance in the Middle Ages and the Renaissance*. Edited by Kathleen Ashley and Wim Hüsken, 35–51. Amsterdam and Atlanta, GA: Editions Rodopi, 2001.
Fletcher, John. "Tasteless as Hell: Community Performance, Distinction, and Countertaste in Hell House." *Theatre Survey* 48, no. 2 (2007): 313–30.
Foister, Susan. "Paintings in Sixteenth-Century English Inventories." *Burlington Magazine* 123, no. 938 (May 1981): 273–82.
———. "Private Devotion." In *Gothic Art for England 1400–1547*. Edited by Richard Marks and Paul Williamson, 334–6. London: V&A Publications, 2003.
Freedberg, David, and Vittorio Gallese. "Motion, Emotion and Empathy in Esthetic Experience." *Trends in Cognitive Sciences* 11, no. 5 (2007): 197–203.
———. "Mirror and Canonical Neurons are Crucial Elements in Esthetic Response." *TRENDS in Cognitive Sciences* 11, no. 10 (2007): 411.
French, Katherine. *The People of the Parish: Community Life in a Late Medieval English Diocese*. Philadelphia: University of Pennsylvania Press, 2001.
Fulton, Rachel. "Praying with Anselm at Admont: A Meditation on Practice." *Speculum* 81, no. 3 (2006): 700–33.

Gallagher, Shaun, and Dan Zahavi. *The Phenomenological Mind: An Introduction to Philosophy of Mind and Cognitive Science*. London and New York: Routledge, 2008.
Gallese, Vittorio. "The Roots of Empathy: The Shared Manifold Hypothesis and the Neural Basis of Intersubjectivity." *Psychopathology* 36 (2003): 171–80.
———. "Embodied Simulation: From Neurons to Phenomenal Experience." *Phenomenology and the Cognitive Sciences* 4, no. 1 (March 2005): 23–48.
Gallese, Vittorio, and George Lakoff. "The Brain's Concepts: The Role of Sensory-Motor System in Conceptual Knowledge." *Cognitive Neuropsychology* 22, no. 3/4 (2005): 455–79.
Gallese, Vittorio, Christian Keysers, and Giacomo Rizzolatti. "A Unifying View of the Basis of Social Cognition." *Trends in Cognitive Science* 8, no. 9 (2004): 396–403.
Gallese, Vittorio, Morris N. Eagle, and Paolo Migone. "Intentional Attunement: Mirror Neurons and the Neural Underpinnings of Interpersonal Relations." *Journal of the American Psychoanalytic Association* 55, no. 1 (2007): 131–76.
Gardiner, Harold C. *Mysteries' End*. New Haven: Yale University Press, 1946.
Garner, Stanton B., Jr. *Bodied Spaces: Phenomenology and Performance in Contemporary Drama*. Ithaca and London: Cornell University Press, 1994.
Gee, E. A. "The Painted Glass of All Saints' Church, North Street." *Archaeologia* 102 (1969): 151–202.
Gelman, Susan. *The Essential Child: Origins of Essentialism in Everyday Thought*. Oxford and New York: Oxford University Press, 2003.
Gertsman, Elina, ed. *Visualizing Medieval Performance: Perspectives, Histories, Contexts*. Burlington, VT: Ashgate, 2008.
Gibson, Gail McMurray. *The Theater of Devotion: East Anglian Drama and Society in the Late Middle Ages*. Chicago: University of Chicago Press, 1989.
Goldberg, P. Jeremy P. "Public and the Private: Women in the Pre-Plague Economy." In *Thirteenth-Century England*. Vol 3. Edited by J. Bothwell, P. J. P. Goldberg, and W. M. Ormrod, 75–89. Woodbridge, Suffolk: Boydell, 1991.
———. *Women, Work and Life-Cycle in a Medieval Economy: Women in York and Yorkshire c. 1300–1520*. Oxford: Clarendon Press, 1992.
———. "Lay Book Ownership in Late Medieval York: The Evidence of Wills." *The Library* 16, no. 3 (September 1994): 181–9.
———. "Craft Guilds, The Corpus Christi Play and Civic Government." In *The Government of Medieval York: Essays in Commemoration of the 1396 Royal Charter*. Edited by Sarah Rees Jones, 141–63. York: University of York and Borthwick Institute of Historical Research, 1997.
———. "Household and the Organisation of Labour in Late Medieval Towns: Some English Evidence." In *The Household in Late Medieval Cities, Italy*

and Northwestern Europe Compared. Edited by Myriam Carlier and Tim Soens, 59–70. Louvain-Apeldoorn: Garant, 2001.

Goodman, Nelson. "Pictures in the Mind?" In *Image and Understanding: Thoughts About Images, Ideas About Understanding.* Edited by Horace Barlow, Colin Blakemore, and Miranda Weston-Smith, 358–64. Cambridge: Cambridge University Press, 1990.

Goodnough, Abby. "Darwin-Free Fun for Creationists." *The New York Times,* May 1, 2004, final edition.

Hamburger, Jeffrey F. *The Visual and the Visionary: Art and Female Spirituality in Late Medieval Germany.* New York: Zone, 1998.

Harvey, John H. "Architectural History from 1291 to 1558." In *A History of York Minster.* Edited by G. E. Aylmer and Reginald Cant, 149–92. Oxford: Clarendon Press, 1977.

Heath, Peter. "Urban Piety in the Later Middle Ages: The Evidence of Hull Wills." In *The Church, Politics and Patronage in the Fifteenth Century.* Edited by R. B. Dobson, 209–34. New York: St. Martin's Press, 1984.

Hickok, Gregory. "Eight Problems for the Mirror Neuron Theory of Action Understanding in Monkeys and Humans." *Journal of Cognitive Neuroscience* 21, no. 7 (2008): 1229–1243.

Hildburgh, W. L. "Folk-life Recorded in Medieval English Alabaster Carvings." *Folklore: Transactions of the Folk-lore Society* 60, no. 2 (June 1949): 249–65.

———. "English Alabaster Carvings as Records of the Medieval English Drama." *Archaeologica* 93 (1955): 51–101.

Hodapp, William F. "Ritual and Performance in Richard Rolle's Passion Meditation B." In *Performance and Transformation: New Approaches to Late Medieval Spirituality.* Edited by Mary A. Suydam and Joanna E. Ziegler, 241–72. New York: St. Martin's Press, 1999.

Holly, Michael Ann. *Past Looking: The Historical Imagination and the Rhetoric of the Image.* Ithaca: Cornell University Press, 1996.

Hope, W. H. St. John. "On The Early Working of Alabaster in England." In *Illustrated Catalogue of the Exhibition of English Medieval Alabaster Work.* Edited by Society of Antiquaries, 1–15. London: Burlington House, 1913.

Husserl, Edmund. *Phenomenology and the Crisis of Philosophy.* Translated by Q. Lauer. 1910; New York: Harper, 1965

———. *Experience and Judgement.* Translated by J. S. Churchill and K. Ameriks. 1939; London: Routledge, 1973.

Jacob, Pierre, and Marc Jeannerod. *Ways of Seeing: The Scope and Limits of Visual Cognition.* Oxford: Oxford University Press, 2003.

James, Mervyn. "Ritual, Drama and Social Body in the Late Medieval English Town." *Past and Present* 98 (1983): 3–29.

Johnson, Mark. *The Body in the Mind.* Chicago: University of Chicago Press, 1987.

———. *The Meaning of the Body: Aesthetics of Human Understanding.* Chicago: University of Chicago Press, 2008.

Johnston, Alexandra F. "The Plays of the Religious Guilds of York: The Creed Play and the Pater Noster Play." *Speculum* 50 (1975): 55–90.

———. "*The Word Made Flesh*: Augustinian Elements in the *York Cycle*." In *The Centre and its Compass: Studies in Medieval Literature in Honor of Professor John Leyerle*. Edited by Robert A. Taylor, et al., 225–46. Kalamazoo, MI: Medieval Institute Publications, 1993.

———. "William Revetour, Chaplain and Clerk of York, Testator." *Leeds Studies in English* 29 (1998): 153–71.

———. "'His langage is lorne': The Silent Centre of the York Cycle." *Early Theatre* 3 (2000): 185–95.

———. "York Cycle 1998: What We Learned." *Early Theatre* 3 (2000): 199–203.

———. "John Waldeby, the Augustinian Friary, and the Plays of York." In *In Honor of Clifford Davidson: Papers Presented at the 35th International Congress on Medieval Studies, May 6, 2000*, 1–15. Kalamazoo, MI: Medieval Institute Publications, 2002.

Johnston, Alexandra F., and Margaret Dorrell. "The Doomsday Pageant of the York Mercers, 1433." *Leeds Studies in English* 5 (1971): 29–34.

———."The York Mercers and their Pageant of Doomsday, 1433–1526." *Leeds Studies in English* 6 (1972): 10–35.

Ker, Neil, and A. J. Piper. *Medieval Manuscripts in British Libraries*. Vol. 4. Oxford: Clarendon Press, 1992.

Kessler, Herbert L. *Seeing Medieval Art*. Ontario: Broadview Press, 2004.

Keysers, Christian. "Mirror Neurons." *Current Biology* 19, no. 21 (2009): R971–R973.

Keysers, Christian et al. "A Touching Sight: SII/PV Activation during the Observation and Experience of Touch." *Neuron* 42 (April 2004): 335–46.

Kienzle, Beverly Mayne. "Medieval Sermons and their Performance: Theory and Record." In *Preacher, Sermon and Audience in the Middle Ages*. Edited by Carolyn Muessig, 89–124. Leiden, Boston & Köln: Brill, 2002.

King, Pamela M. "Contemporary Cultural Models of the Trial Plays in the York Cycle." In *Drama and Community: People and Plays in Medieval Europe*. Edited by Alan Hindley, 200–16. Turnhout: Brepols, 1999.

———. "Seeing and Hearing; Looking and Listening." *Early Theatre* 3 (2000): 155–66.

———. "The York Cycle and Instruction on the Sacraments." In *Learning and Literacy in Medieval England and Abroad*. Edited by Sarah Rees Jones, 155–78. Turnhout: Brepols, 2003.

———. *The York Mystery Cycle and the Worship of the City*. Cambridge: D. S. Brewer, 2006.

Kipling, Gordon. *Enter the King: Theatre, Liturgy, and Ritual in the Medieval Civic Triumph*. Oxford: Clarendon Press, 1998.

Kobialka, Michal. *This is My Body: Representational Practices in the Early Middle Ages*. Ann Arbor: University of Michigan Press, 1999.

Kolve, V. A. *The Play Called Corpus Christi*. Stanford: Stanford University Press, 1966.
Krasner, David, and David Z. Saltz, eds. *Staging Philosophy: Intersections of Theater, Performance, and Philosophy*. Ann Arbor: University of Michigan Press, 2006.
Lakoff, George, and Mark Johnson. *Philosophy in the Flesh: The Embodied Mind and its Challenge to Western Thought*. New York: Basic Books, 1999.
Leder, Drew. *The Absent Body*. Chicago and London: University of Chicago Press, 1990.
Lerer, Seth. " 'Representyd now in yower syght': The Culture of Spectatorship in Late Fifteenth Century England." In *Bodies and Disciplines: Intersections of Literature and History in Fifteenth-Century England*. Edited by Barbara Hanawalt and David Wallace, 29–62. Minneapolis: University of Minnesota Press, 1996.
Lerud, Theodore K. "Quick Images: Memory and the English Corpus Christi Drama." In *Moving Subjects: Procession Performance in the Middle Ages and the Renaissance*. Edited by Kathleen Ashley and Wim Hüsken, 213–37. Amsterdam and Atlanta: Rodopi, 2001.
———. *Memory, Images, and the English Corpus Christi Drama*. New York: Palgrave Macmillan, 2008.
Lindberg, David C. *Theories of Vision From Al-Kindi to Kepler*. Chicago and London: University of Chicago Press, 1976.
Lingnau, Angelika, Benno Gesierich, and Alfonso Caramazza. "Asymmetric fMRI Adaptation Reveals No Evidence for Mirror Neurons in Humans." *Proceedings of the National Academy of Sciences* 106, no. 24 (2009): 9925–9930.
Lipton, Sara. " 'The Sweet Lean of His Head': Writing about Looking at the Crucifix in the High Middle Ages." *Speculum* 80, no. 4 (October 2005): 1172–208.
Lopes, Dominic M. M. "Art Media and the Sense Modalities: Tactile Pictures." *The Philosophical Quarterly* 47, no. 189 (October 1997): 425–40.
Loveland, Anne C., and Otis B. Wheeler. *From Meetinghouse to Megachurch: A Material and Cultural History*. Columbia and London: University of Missouri Press, 2003.
Lumiansky, R. M., and David Mills. *The Chester Mystery Cycle: Essays and Documents*. Chapel Hill and London: University of North Carolina Press, 1983.
Mahler, Jonathan. "The Soul of the New Exurb." *The New York Times Magazine*, March 27, 2005. In http://select.nytimes.com/search/restricted/article?res=F00613FE3C5B0C748EDDAA0894DD404482.
Mâle, Emile. *The Gothic Image*. New York: Harper, 1958.
———. *Religious Art in France, The Twelfth Century: A Study of the Origins of Medieval Iconography*. Princeton: Princeton University Press, 1978.

Mancing, Howard. "See The Play, Read The Book." In *Performance and Cognition: Theatre Studies and the Cognitive Turn*. Edited by Bruce McConachie and F. Elizabeth Hart, 189–206. New York: Routledge, 2006.

Marks, Richard. "An Age of Consumption: Art for England c. 1400–1547." In *Gothic Art for England 1400–1547*. Edited by Richard Marks and Paul Williamson, 12–25. London: V&A Publications, 2003.

Marrow, James H. "Symbol and Meaning In Northern European Art of the Late Middle Ages and the Early Renaissance." *Simiolus* 16 (1986): 150–69.

McConachie, Bruce. "Metaphors We Act By: Kinesthetics, Cognitive Psychology, and Historical Structures." *Journal of Dramatic Theory and Criticism* 8, no. 2 (1993): 23–45.

———. "Approaching Performance History through Cognitive Psychology." *Assaph* 10 (1994): 113–22.

———. "Doing Things with Image Schemas: The Cognitive Turn in Theatre Studies and the Problem of Experience for Historians." *Theatre Journal* 53 (2001): 569–94.

———. "Cognitive Studies and Epistemic Competence in Cultural History: Moving Beyond Freud and Lacan." In *Performance and Cognition: Theatre Studies and the Cognitive Turn*. Edited by Bruce McConachie and F. Elizabeth Hart, 52–75. New York: Routledge, 2006.

———. "Falsifiable Theories for Theatre and Performance Studies," *Theatre Journal* 59 (2007): 553–77.

———. *Engaging Audiences: A Cognitive Approach to Spectating in the Theatre*. New York: Palgrave Macmillan, 2008.

McConachie, Bruce, and F. Elizabeth Hart, eds. *Performance and Cognition*. New York: Routledge, 2006.

McConachie, Stephanie, et al. "Task, Text, and Talk." *Educational Leadership* 64, no. 2 (2006): 8–14.

McKinnell, John. "Producing the York *Mary* plays." *Medieval English Theatre* 12 (1990): 101–23.

McRee, Benjamin R. "Unity or Division?: The Social Meaning of Guild Ceremony in Urban Communities." In *City and Spectacle in Medieval Europe*. Edited by Barbara A. Hanawalt and Kathryn L. Reyerson, 189–207. Minneapolis: University of Minnesota, 1994.

Meredith, Peter. "The Development of the York Mercers' Pageant Waggon." *Medieval English Theatre* 1 (1979): 5–18.

———. "John Clerke's Hand in the York Register." *Leeds Studies in English* 12 (1981): 245–71.

———. "The City of York and its 'Plays of Pageants.'" *Early Theatre* 3 (2000): 23–47.

Merleau-Ponty, Maurice. *Phenomenology of Perception*. Translated by Colin Smith. 1945; New York: Humanities Press, 1962.

Milhaven, J. Giles. "A Medieval Lesson on Bodily Knowing: Women's Experience and Men's Thought." *Journal of the American Academy of Religion* 52, no. 2 (1989): 341–73.

Miller, Patricia Cox. "Visceral Seeing: The Holy Body in Late Ancient Christianity." *Journal of Early Christian Studies* 12, no. 4 (2004): 391–411.

Mills, David. "'Look at Me When I'm Speaking to You': The 'Behold and See' Convention in Medieval Drama." *Medieval English Theatre* 7, no. 1 (1985): 4–12.

———. *Recycling the Cycle: The City of Chester and its Whitsun Plays*. Toronto: University of Toronto Press, 1998.

Mitchell, W. T. J. "There Are No Visual Media." *Journal of Visual Culture* 4, no. 2 (2005): 257–66.

Morgan, David. *Visual Piety: A History and Theory of Popular Religious Images*. Berkeley: University of California Press, 1998.

Muir, Lynette. *The Biblical Drama of Medieval Europe*. Cambridge: Cambridge University Press, 1995.

Mulder-Bakker, A. B., ed. *Seeing and Knowing: Medieval Women and the Transmission of Knowledge*. Turnhout: Brepols, 2004.

Mustanoja, Tauno F. *The Good Wife Taught Her Daughter, the Good Wyfe Wold a Pylgremage [and] the Thewis of Gud Women*. Helsinki: Suomalaisen Kirjallisuuden, 1948.

Nellhaus, Tobin. "Performance Strategies, Image Schemas, and Communication Frameworks." In *Performance and Cognition: Theatre Studies and the Cognitive Turn*. Edited by Bruce McConachie and F. Elizabeth Hart, 76–94. New York: Routledge, 2006.

Nelson, Robert. "Introduction: Descartes's Cow and Other Domestications of the Visual." In *Visuality Before and Beyond the Renaissance*. Edited by Robert S. Nelson, 1–21. Cambridge: Cambridge University Press, 2000.

Nevile, Jennifer. "Dance Performance in the Late Middle Ages: A Contested Space." *Visualizing Medieval Performance: Perspectives, Histories, Contexts*. Edited by Elina Gertsman, 295–310. Burlington, VT: Ashgate, 2008.

Nichols, Stephen G. "Writing the New Middle Ages." *PMLA* 120, no. 2 (March 2005): 422–41.

Nisse, Ruth. *Defining Acts: Drama and the Politics of Interpretation in Late Medieval England*. Notre Dame: University of Notre Dame Press, 2005.

O'Connell, Michael. *The Idolatrous Eye: Iconoclasm and Theater in Early Modern England*. Oxford: Oxford University Press, 2000.

Palliser, D. M. *Company History*. York: The Company of Merchant Adventurers of the City of York, 1998.

Pappano, Margaret Aziza. "Judas in York: Masters and Servants in the Late Medieval Cycle Drama." *Exemplaria* 14, no. 2 (October 2002): 317–50.

Pasnau, Robert. *Theories of Cognition in the Later Middle Ages*. Cambridge: Cambridge University Press, 1997.

Peters, Christine. *Patterns of Piety: Women, Gender and Religion in Late Medieval and Reformation England*. Cambridge: Cambridge University Press, 2003.

Philips, Matthew, and Lisa Miller. "Visions of Hell." *Newsweek* 148, no. 19 (November 6, 2006): 52–3. In Academic Search Premier [database online]. Accessed August 9, 2007.

Potkay, Adam. "Wordsworth and the Ethics of Things." *PMLA* 123, no. 2 (2008): 390–404.

Powell, Sue. "*Pastoralia* and the Lost York Plays of the Creed and Paternoster." *European Medieval Drama* 8 (2004): 35–50.

Ramachandran, V. S., and Sandra Blakeslee. *Phantoms in the Brain: Probing the Mysteries of the Human Mind.* New York: Quill, 1998.

Rayner, Alice. "Presenting Objects, Presenting Things." In *Staging Philosophy: Intersections of Theater, Performance, and Philosophy.* Edited by David Krasner and David Z. Saltz, 180–99. Ann Arbor: University of Michigan Press, 2006.

Rees Jones, Sarah. "York's Civic Administration 1354–1464." In *The Government of Medieval York: Essays in Commemoration of the 1396 Royal Charter.* Edited by Rees Jones, 108–40. York: University of York and Borthwick Institute of Historical Research, 1997.

Rees Jones, Sarah, and Felicity Riddy. "The Bolton Hours of York: Female Domesticity, Piety and the Public Sphere." In *Household, Women and Christianities in Late Antiquity and the Middle Ages.* Edited by Anneke B. Mulder-Bakke and Jocelyn Wogan-Browne, 215–60. Turnhout: Brepols, 2006.

Riddy, Felicity. "Mother Knows Best: Reading Social Change in a Courtesy Text." *Speculum* 71, no. 1 (January 1996): 66–86.

———. "Looking Closely: Authority and Intimacy in the Late Medieval Urban Home." In *Gendering the Master Narrative: Women and Power in the Middle Ages.* Edited by Mary C. Erler and Maryanne Kowaleski, 212–28. Ithaca and London: Cornell University Press, 2003.

Rivers, Kimberly. "Memory and Medieval Preaching: Mnemonic Advice in the *Ars Praedicandi* of Francesc Eiximenis (ca. 1327–1409)." *Viator* 30 (1999): 253–84.

Rizzolatti, Giacomo, Laila Craighero, and Luciano Fadiga. "The Mirror System in Humans," *Mirror Neurons and the Evolution of Brain and Language.* Edited by Maxim I. Stamenov and Vittorio Gallese, 37–59. Amsterdam and Philadelphia: John Benjamins, 2002.

Rokotnitz, Naomi. "'It is required/You do awake your faith': Learning To Trust the Body Through Performing *The Winter's Tale.*" In *Performance and Cognition: Theatre Studies and the Cognitive Turn.* Edited by Bruce McConachie and F. Elizabeth Hart, 122–46. New York: Routledge, 2006.

Rosser, Gervase. "Crafts, Guilds and the Negotiation of Work in the Medieval Town." *Past and Present* 154 (1997): 3–31.

———. "Communities of Parish and Guild in the Late Middle Ages." In *Parish, Church and People: Local Studies in Lay Religion 1350–1750.* Edited by Susan Wright, 29–55. London: Hutchinson 1988.

Rothstein, Edward. "Adam and Eve in the Land of Dinosaurs." *The New York Times*, May 24, 2007, Arts and Leisure section, final edition.
Rubin, Miri. *Corpus Christi: The Eucharist in Late Medieval Culture*. Cambridge: Cambridge University Press, 1991.
Salmen, Walter. "Dances and Dance Music, c. 1300–1530." In *Music as Concept and Practice in the Late Middle Ages*. Edited by Reinhard Strohm and Bonnie J. Blackburn, 162–90. Oxford: Oxford University Press, 2001.
Saltz, David. "Infiction and Outfiction: The Role of Fiction in Theatrical Performance." In *Staging Philosophy: Intersections of Theater, Performance, and Philosophy*. Edited by David Krasner and David Z. Saltz, 203–20. Ann Arbor: University of Michigan Press, 2006.
Sawyer, R. Keith. "Music and Communication." In *Musical Communication*. Edited by Dorothy Miell, Raymond MacDonald, and David J. Hargreaves, 45–60. Oxford: Oxford University Press, 2005.
Scherb, Victor I. *Staging Faith: East Anglian Drama in the Later Middle Ages*. Madison: Fairleigh Dickinson University Press, 2001.
Schleif, Corine. "Hands That Appoint, Anoint and Ally: Late Medieval Donor Strategies for Appropriating Approbation Through Painting." *Art History* 16, no. 1 (March 1993): 1–32.
Schofield, John. "Urban Housing in England 1400–1600." In *The Age of Transition: The Archaeology of English Culture 1400–1600*. Edited by David Gaimster and Paul Stamper, 127–44. Oxford: Oxbow Books, 1997.
Scoville, Chester N. *Saints and the Audience in Middle English Drama*. Toronto: University of Toronto Press, 2004.
Scribner, Robert. "Popular Piety and Modes of Visual Perception in Late Medieval and Reformation Germany." *Journal of Religious History* 15 (1989): 448–69.
Sheingorn, Pamela. "On Using Medieval Art in the Study of Medieval Drama: An Introduction to Methodology." *Research Opportunities in Renaissance Drama* 22 (1979): 101–9.
———. "The Moments of Resurrection in the Corpus Christi Plays." *Medievalia et Humanistica* 11 (1982): 111–29.
———. "The Visual Language of Drama: Principles of Composition." In *Contexts for Early English Drama*. Edited by Marianne G. Briscoe and John C. Coldeway, 173–91. Bloomington: Indiana University Press, 1989.
———. "Medieval Drama Studies and the New Art History." *Mediaevalia: A Journal of Medieval Studies* 18 (1995): 143–62.
Shelley, Bruce L., and Marshall Shelley. *The Consumer Church: Can Evangelicals Win the World without Losing their Souls?* Downer's Grove, IL: InterVarsity Press, 1992.
Shepherd, Simon. *Theatre, Body and Pleasure*. London and New York: Routledge, 2006.

Smith, Darwin. *Maistre Pierre Pathelin-Le Miroir d'Orgueil.* Tarabuste Editions: Saint-Benoît-du-Sault, 2002.
Sofer, Andrew. *The Stage Life of Props.* Ann Arbor: University of Michigan Press, 2003.
Spencer, Brian. *Pilgrim Souvenirs and Secular Badges.* London: Stationery Office, 1998.
Sponsler, Claire. *Drama and Resistance: Bodies, Goods, and Theatricality in Late Medieval England.* Minneapolis: University of Minnesota Press, 1997.
Stafford, Pauline, and Anneke B. Mulder-Bakker, eds. *Gendering the Middle Ages.* Oxford: Blackwell Publishers, 2002.
Stanbury, Sarah. *The Visual Object of Desire in Late Medieval England.* Philadelphia: University of Pennsylvania Press, 2008.
States, Bert O. *Great Reckonings in Little Rooms: On the Phenomenology of Theater.* Berkeley, Los Angeles, and London: University of California Press, 1985.
Stein, Edith. *On the Problem of Empathy.* Translated by Waltraut Stein. Washington, D.C.: ICS Publications, 1989.
Stevens, Martin. *Four Middle English Mystery Cycles: Textual, Contextual, and Critical Interpretations.* Princeton: Princeton University Press, 1987.
———. "The Intertextuality of Late Medieval Art and Drama." *New Literary History* 22, no. 2 (Spring 1991): 317–37.
Stevenson, Jill. "The Material Bodies of Medieval Religious Performance in England." *Material Religion: The Journal of Objects, Art, and Belief* 2, no. 2 (2006): 204–32.
Stewart, Susan. *On Longing: Narratives of the Miniature, Gigantic, the Souvenir, the Collection.* Durham: Duke University Press, 1993.
Stoller, Paul. "Rationality." In *Critical Terms for Religious Studies.* Edited by Mark C. Taylor, 239–55. Chicago: University of Chicago Press, 1998.
Sturges, Robert. "Spectacle and Self-Knowledge: The Authority of the Audience in the Mystery Plays." *South Central Review* 9, no. 2 (1992): 27–48.
Swanson, Heather. *Medieval British Towns.* New York: St. Martin's Press, 1999.
Swanson, Robert N. *Religion and Devotion in Europe, c. 1215–1515.* Cambridge: Cambridge University Press, 1995.
Taylor, Barbara Brown. "Hell House." *Christian Century* 123, no. 24 (November 28, 2006). In Academic Search Premier [database online]. Cited August 9, 2007.
Thaut, Michael H. "Rhythm, Human Temporality, and Brain Function," In *Musical Communication.* Edited by Dorothy Miell, Raymond MacDonald, and David J. Hargreaves, 171–91. Oxford: Oxford University Press, 2005.
Thompson, Evan. *Mind in Life: Biology, Phenomenology, and the Sciences of the Mind.* Cambridge: Harvard University Press, 2007.

Tomaselli, Keyan G., and Arnold Shepperson. "'Speaking in Tongues, Writing in Vision': Orality and Literacy in Televangelistic Communications." In *Practicing Religion in the Age of the Media: Explorations in Media, Religion, and Culture*. Edited by Stewart M. Hoover and Lynn Schofield Clark, 345–59. New York: Columbia University Press, 2002.

Travis, Peter W. *Dramatic Design in the Chester Cycle*. Chicago and London: University of Chicago Press, 1982.

Trexler, Richard. *Church and Community 1200–1600: Studies in the History of Florence and New Spain*. Rome: Storia e Letteratura, 1987.

Twycross, Meg. "The Left-Hand Theory: A Retraction." *Medieval English Theatre* 14 (1992): 77–94.

———. "The Theatricality of Medieval English Plays." In *The Cambridge Companion to Medieval English Theatre*. Edited by Richard Beadle, 37–84. Cambridge: Cambridge University Press, 1994.

———. "The *Ordo paginarum* Revisited, with a Digital Camera." In '*Bring furth the pagants*': *Essays in Early English Drama Presented to Alexandra F. Johnston*. Edited by David Klausner and Karen Sawyer Marsalek, 105–31. Toronto: University of Toronto Press, 2007.

Tydeman, William. *The Theatre in the Middle Ages*. Cambridge: Cambridge University Press, 1978.

Van Os, Henk. *The Art of Devotion in the Late Middle Ages in Europe, 1300–1500*. Translated by Michael Hoyle. Princeton: Princeton University Press, 1995.

Varela, Francisco J. "Neurophenomenology: A Methodological Remedy for the Hard Problem." *Journal of Consciousness Studies* 3 (1996): 330–50.

Vogeley, Kai, and Albert Newen. "Mirror Neurons and the Self Construct." In *Mirror Neurons and the Evolution of Brain and Language*. Edited by Maxim I. Stamenov and Vittorio Gallese, 135–50. Amsterdam and Philadelphia: John Benjamins, 2002.

Walker, Julia A. "The Text/Performance Split Across the Analytic/Continental Divide." In *Staging Philosophy: Intersections of Theater, Performance, and Philosophy*. Edited by David Krasner and David Z. Saltz, 19–40. Ann Arbor: University of Michigan Press, 2006.

Wernowsky, Kris. "Feds Can Seize Dinosaur Adventure Land." *Pensacola News Journal*. July 31, 2009. http://www.pnj.com/article/20090731/NEWS01/90731016/1006.

White, Eileen. "Places to Hear the Play: The Performance of the Corpus Christi Play at York." *Early Theatre* 3 (2000): 49–78.

Wiles, David. *A Short History of Western Performance Space*. Cambridge: Cambridge University Press, 2003.

Williams, Peter W. "Creation Museum." *Material Religion: The Journal of Objects, Art and Belief* 4, no. 3 (2008): 373–5.

Williamson, Beth. "Altarpieces, Liturgy, and Devotion." *Speculum* 79 (2004): 341–406.

Wolska, Aleksandra. "Rabbits, Machines, and the Ontology of Performance." *Theatre Journal* 57, no. 1 (2005): 83–95.

Woolf, Rosemary. *The English Mystery Plays.* London: Routledge and Kegan Paul, 1972.
Yardley, Anne Bagnall. *Performing Piety: Musical Culture in Medieval English Nunneries.* New York: Palgrave Macmillan, 2006.
Zarrilli, Phillip B. "Towards a Phenomenological Model of the Actor's Embodied Modes of Experience." *Theatre Journal* 56, no. 4 (2004): 653–66.
———. "An Enactive Approach to Understanding Acting." *Theatre Journal* 59, no. 4 (2007): 635–47.
Ziegler, Joanna E. *Sculpture of Compassion: The Pietà and the Beguines in the Southern Low Countries c. 1300– c. 1600.* Rome: Institut Historique Belge de Rome, 1992.
Zieman, Katherine. "Reading, Singing and Understanding: Constructions of the Literacy of Women Religious in Late Medieval England," In *Learning and Literacy in Medieval England and Abroad.* Edited by Sarah Rees Jones, 97–120. Turnhout: Brepols, 2003.
Zunshine, Lisa. "Essentialism and Comedy: A Cognitive Reading of the Motif of Mislaid Identity in Dryden's *Amphitryon* (1690)." In *Performance and Cognition: Theatre Studies and the Cognitive Turn.* Edited by Bruce McConachie and F. Elizabeth Hart, 97–121. New York: Routledge, 2006.

Multimedia Sources

Augustine: Confessions. Text and commentary by James J. O'Donnell. New York: Oxford University Press, 1992. For the Stoa Consortium, 1999. http://www.stoa.org/hippo/.
The Creation Museum. "About Us." http://www.creationmuseum.org/about.
Dancing for Him. "Ministry Vision." http://www.dancingforhim.com/.
Dinosaur Adventure Land. "About DAL." http://www.dinosauradventureland.com/aboutDAL.php.
"Eye of the Beholder." April 23, 2007. The Philoctetes Center, New York, NY. Transcript available at: http://philoctetes.org/Past_Programs/Eye_of_the_Beholder.
The Guilds of York. "York Mystery Plays." http://www.yorkmysteryplays.co.uk/.
Hell House, DVD. Directed by George Ratliff. Cantina Pictures Inc., 2001.
Holy Land Experience. "Homepage." http://www.holylandexperience.com/index.html.
N' Him We Move. "About 'N Him." http://www.tpid.org/.
"The Scientific Heritage of Christianity." *Joy! Magazine.* January 2009. http://blogs.answersingenesis.org/aroundtheworld/wp-content/uploads/2009/01/article-creation-musuem1-in-joy-mag-jan09.pdf.

Unpublished Works

Adams, Amelia. "Evolution of a Manuscript: Text and Image in the Pavement Hours." MA thesis, University of York, 2004.
Barnett, Clara. "Memorials and Commemoration in the Parish Churches of Late Medieval York." 2 Vols. PhD diss., University of York, 1997.
Creation Museum Souvenir Guide, Answers in Genesis.
Stell, P. M., and Louise Hampson, eds. and trans. *Probate Inventories of the York Diocese, 1350–1500*. Unpublished typescript, University of York, 1999.
White, E. "Bequests to Religious Gilds in York." Manuscript in the Borthwick Institute of Historical Research, 1983.

Index

actor, 2, 8–9, 12, 16, 19, 24, 26, 39, 54, 56–7, 68, 76–7, 81, 88, 95–9, 118, 124, 126–7, 131–2, 134–6, 140, 146–8, 177 n55, 179 n104, 180 n108, 206 n51
  cognitive research into actor training, 92
  see also players
actuality, 9, 17, 18, 89, 126–7, 132, 135, 149
  material actuality, 12, 33, 38
  rhythmic actuality, 41, 96
Adams, Amelia, xi, 106, 108, 110, 113, 210 n85
aesthetic, 3, 18–19, 39, 69, 138, 146, 155, 157, 160–1, 166 n14, 179 n104, 210 n92
affective, 3, 23, 25, 92, 102, 124, 134, 141, 220 n53
  affective resonance, 144
agency, 18–19, 22–3, 42, 57, 96, 104, 185 n161
alabaster sculpture, 58, 80–6, 88, 97, 104, 105, 210 n54
  Ascension panel, 81, 201 n58
  bequests, 61, 80, 202 n61
  Betrayal panel, 82
  composition, 80–1
  Harrowing of Hell panel, 81–2
  Head of John the Baptist panel, 82–5, 203 n72
  production, 80
  Resurrection panel, 82
al-Haytham, Ibn, 21
alms, 38, 48
altar, 48, 50, 60, 61, 68, 70–2, 74, 76, 198 n24, 198 n26, 199 n35
Amsler, Mark, 113
angels, 54, 55, 63, 71, 72, 82, 83–4, 85, 91, 116, 119, 128–9, 192 n54, 198 n20, 214 n43
Answers in Genesis (AiG), 157–8
anti-image prejudice, 33–7, 38, 40–1
anti-theatrical prejudice, 27–38, 40–1, 145
Aristotle, 21, 22, 180 n105
Arma Christi, 111–12
art, 6, 15–16, 33, 39–41, 45, 80, 184 n156
  borrowed from churches, 78
  claiming space, 67–86
  cognitive studies of, 39–41, 62, 85, 182 n145
  commissioned, 58, 78, 106, 210 n81
  devotional art, 10, 33, 40, 45, 55, 58, 62, 80, 84, 86, 134, 147, 193 n61
  devotional props, 58–64
  domestic, 13, 58, 60, 79–86, 88, 104
  individual art objects

art—*Continued*
  "arras work," 61, 194 n83
  badges, 60, 62, 78, 83, 199
    n41, 209 n80
  beads (rosary), 16, 58, 59, 62,
    77, 78, 172 n7, 197 n3
  decorated pillows, 59
  hammerbeams, 71, 74, 198 n20
  hangings (hallings), 59, 193
    n66, 193 n67
  misericord, 74
  necklaces, 62, 77, 78
  painted cloth, 54, 59–60
  painted images, 35, 58
  painted papers, 59
  pendants, 60, 62
  rings, 58, 59, 60, 62, 77, 78
  roof boss, 68–9, 81
  rosary, *see* beads
  silver plate, 58, 60, 76
  stained glass, 10, 68, 71, 77,
    110, 198 n17
    Bellfounder's window, 68–9,
      74–6
    Corporal Acts of Mercy
      window, 71, 74, 215 n55
    see also Pricke of Conscience
  tapestries, 58, 59, 60
  mass production of, 80
  materiality of 6, 34–7, 50, 53–4,
    57, 69, 76, 85–6, 105–6,
    111, 167 n23, 221 n1
  as performing, 45–66
  relationship to viewer, 17, 37,
    40–2, 45, 56–7, 69, 85,
    121, 132, 166 n14,
    182 n135
  see also alabaster sculpture; anti-
    image prejudice; Books of
    Hours; cross; donations;
    Reformation; stage props;
    "thingness;" wills
artisan, 10, 37, 58, 80, 94, 105
  artisanal ideology, 94
  see also guilds
"as if" response, *see* equivalence

Ascension, 68–9, 81, 201 n58
  see also York Cycle, pageants
Ashley, Kathleen, 186 n164
assimilation, 22, 27, 43, 53, 149
  with city of York, 98–9
Attreed, Lorraine, 89
audience, *see* spectatorship;
  reception
Augustine, Saint, 26, 30–2, 35,
  79, 127, 143, 179 n98,
  180 n107
  Confessions, 30–2
aural, 3, 7
A/Y Memorandum Book, 11, 63,
  64, 65, 94, 100, 101, 133,
  171 n49, 171 n51

Bacon, Roger, 21, 22–3, 26, 175
  n42, 184 n151
baptism, 162
  see also York Cycle, *The Baptism*
Baxter, Margery, of Norwich, 121
Beadle, Richard, 10, 125, 128
Beckwith, Sarah, 3, 12, 94, 102,
  144, 206 n51
bedding, 51, 59, 61, 194 n83
bells, 49, 68, 72, 76, 104, 165 n6,
  199 n41
  see also art, Bellfounder's window
Belting, Hans, 140
Bible, *see* books
biblical history, 57, 91, 125, 130,
  158–9
Biernoff, Suzannah, 21–3, 26, 30,
  127, 134
Binski, Paul, 70
Blair, Rhonda, 92
Blakeslee, Sandra, 45
blending, *see* conceptual blending
blindness, 116–17, 124, 125
bodied forth, 18, 22, 29, 76,
  78, 135
Bolton, Alice, 61
Bolton, John, 61
books, 3, 41, 58, 60, 61, 62, 69, 72,
  76, 104–5, 113, 149, 159

INDEX

Bible, 61, 157, 158
Breviary, 82, 105
primer, *see* Books of Hours
Psalter, 60, 61, 105
see also Books of Hours
Books of Hours, 13, 16, 61, 62, 104–13
   Bolton Hours, 210 n81
   materiality of, 105–13
   Pavement Hours, 106–13
   printed editions, 105, 209 n76, 210 n80
   rhythmic program, 113
   visual layering, 109–10
Bradwardine, Thomas, *On Acquiring a Trained Memory*, 96–7
brain, 9, 25, 98, 137–9, 146, 169 n37, 175 n42, 215 n60, 218 n30
   brain imaging, 23, 39–41, 176 n48, 176 n52
   motor areas, 39–40, 138
   neural, 23–4, 42, 139, 153, 155, 176 n50, 185 n161
   neural mapping, 32, 130, 220 n53
   see also cognition; mirror neurons
Bull, Marcus, 163
Burgess, Clive, 46–7, 49, 188 n11
burial, 47–8, 53, 60, 95, 136, 190 n41
   arguments about, 48
   by daylight, 53, 190 n44
Bynum, Caroline, 6, 185 n163

Camille, Michael, 21
candle, 4, 15, 16, 46, 48, 50, 61, 69–72, 78, 104, 189 n19, 190 n41, 199 n41
   wax, 48, 70, 189 n17
   see also torches
Carlson, Marvin, 161
Carruthers, Mary, 99, 100, 179 n104, 202 n70
catechetical program, 3–4

cathedral, 67–9, 72, 76, 86, 88, 102, 160, 171 n55, 198 n26, 206 n44
   Minster of York, 67–77, 81, 82, 85, 89, 101–2, 106
Cats, 1–3
Cazelles, Brigitte, 136
Chambers, E. K., 10
chantries, 46, 72, 78, 198 n21, 198 n26
chapel, 35, 48, 59, 74, 77, 78, 90
   St. William's chapel, 52
Chazelle, Celia, 33
Cheetham, Francis, 82, 202 n61
Christ's body, 3, 118, 120, 124–8, 133–49
   absence and presence onstage, 117–24, 134, 217 n20, 221 n60
   characters' physical contact with, 135–7, 216 n14, 217 n20
   identification with, 141, 143–9
   violence to, 122, 123, 126–7, 138–40, 141, 145–6
   see also Corpus Christi; Eucharist
churches, *see* parish church; Minster of York
city honor, 51–2, 64
civic identity, 65
Clark, Anne L., 185 n163
Clark, Robert, 7
clergy, 4, 5, 33, 36, 38, 50, 60, 61, 69, 79, 96, 121, 140–4, 149
   anti-clerical, 38
Clopper, Lawrence, 28
clothing, 35, 46, 48, 51–2, 53, 71, 76, 77, 90, 110, 117, 135, 137, 157, 162, 199 n39
   livery, 46
   sumptuary laws, 46, 157
   see also costumes
cognition
   cognitive pattern, 43
   cognitive psychology, 20, 23, 136

cognition—*Continued*
  cognitive science, 8–9, 16–17, 20, 32, 39–42, 130, 132, 139, 145
  cognitive structure, 42
  cognitive template, 41
  cognitive theory, 6, 8–9, 12–13, 16–17, 19–21, 26–7, 32, 42–3, 57, 86, 87, 92, 149, 153
  cognitive unconscious, 24
  see also brain; mirror neurons
Cohen, Jeffrey Jerome, 13
Common Clerk of York, 51, 64, 195 n91
Common Council of York (also Commons), 90, 94, 190 n40, 205 n32
communication practices, 24, 27, 40
conceptual blending, 13, 86–113, 132, 152–9, 183 n150
  being-in-the-biblical-world, 98–99
  with Books of Hours, 105–13
  compression within, 91–2, 204 n21
  decompress, 89
  digging your own grave blend, 95
  double-scope blend, 95, 104
  emergent structure, 95
  framing, 87–9, 94–6, 104, 162
  identity blends, 92, 110
  imaginative addition, 96
  integration networks, 87, 88, 94
  living in the blend, 13, 86, 88–9, 92, 94, 99, 102–6, 113, 115, 130–2, 137, 139, 145, 147, 149, 152–60, 162–3
  living with the dead, 88–9
  material anchors, 87–8, 92, 93, 115, 204 n21, 206 n44
  mental spaces, 87, 163, 206 n44
  relation to suspension of disbelief, 96
  with York cycle route, 100–4
conceptual knowledge, 20, 24, 186 n165
conduct, 4, 7, 51, 53, 94, 127–8, 154, 157
conduct literature, 7, 128
confession, 38, 93, 223 n12
consumption, theory of, 42, 132, 186 n164
  tactics, 42, 45, 108, 132, 186 n164
Cook, Amy, 98, 176 n48
Corporal Acts of Mercy, 71, 74, 215 n55
corporeality, 9, 18, 22, 30–1, 35, 136, 147, 148, 175 n44
Corpus Christi, 50, 118, 133–5, 136, 137, 145, 147
  procession, 11, 50–2, 101–2, 133–5, 207 n58, 211 n10
  disputes over, 190 n40
  shrine, 52
  York guild of, 12, 50–2, 53, 60, 83
  see also Eucharist; York cycle
costumes, 54, 61, 66, 78, 116, 117, 126, 135, 211 n3
Council of Lambeth, 4
creationism, 156–60, 163
Creed play, 11, 12, 60, 89, 171 n53
cross (also crucifix), 4, 5, 13, 15, 33, 34–6, 47, 58, 60–4, 69, 70, 78, 79, 97, 99, 118, 121, 123–5, 136, 140–3, 145–9, 165 n6, 166 n16, 221 n62
  see also York cycle, *The Crucifixion*; York cycle, *The Death of Christ*
crucifix, *see* cross
crucifixion, *see* cross
cycle plays, 10, 195 n95, 218 n32
  see also York cycle

damnation, 29, 126, 129–30, 152–6

INDEX

dance, 1, 151–2, 160, 163, 165 n6, 185 n160, 217 n22, 222 n3
Praise Dance, 151–2
Davidson, Clifford, 10, 130
de Certeau, Michel, 42
de Thoresby, John, 4, 128
decoration, 35, 37, 50, 52, 58–60, 62, 67, 71, 106, 193 n61
decorum, *see* conduct
Descartes, 20–22
design, *see* spectacle; stage design
devil, 29, 143, 153, 219 n40, 223 n11
  see also York Cycle, characters
devotional seeing *see* vision
dinosaur, 156–60
Dinosaur Adventure Land, 156–7, 160, 223 n16, 224 n29
direct address, 97, 130, 147, 221 n62
Dobson, Barrie, 67, 204 n28
domestic art, *see* art
donations, 13, 50, 67, 74, 76–8, 197 n3
  of dramatic texts, 61
  proxy, 74
  to statues, 76–8, 85, 106, 109–10
Dox, Donnalee, 32, 180 n105, 180 n107
ductus, 100, 207 n57
  see also memory; mnemonic
Duffy, Eamon, 11, 16, 46, 49, 72, 105, 193 n65, 198 n24, 198 n26, 198 n27, 209 n76

Early Drama, Art, and Music project (EDAM), 6
ears, 26, 31, 38, 129, 143
Eiximenis, Francesc, 99–100
embodiment, 9, 12, 16, 17, 20–1, 24, 26–7, 58, 61, 87, 91, 94, 124, 127, 132, 144, 152, 158, 168 n35, 175 n42, 178 n80, 206 n51
  Christ's embodiment, 3, 120, 124, 126–7, 135–7, 145–9
  embodied belief, 158–60

embodied mind, 20
embodied schema, 26–7, 32, 38, 41–2, 45, 57–8, 75–6, 84, 88, 99, 103–4, 131, 137, 139
embodied simulation, 25–6, 39–40, 62, 76, 84, 125, 131, 138–9, 141, 143, 145, 149
Emerson, Bo, 160
emotion, 3, 24–6, 32, 49, 53, 76, 84–5, 92, 121, 130–1, 136, 144, 146, 149, 155, 176 n50, 176 n52, 180 n107, 182 n135, 185 n160, 219 n47
emotive coupling, 144
empathy, 25–6, 39, 40, 84, 130–1, 133, 137–48, 155–6, 176 n52, 177 n66, 221 n60
  alterity, 143–4
  moral empathy, 131, 143–4
enlivened images, 16, 82, 116, 144
entrainment, 133, 137–9, 145–6, 149, 152, 155, 217 n25
equivalence, 24, 27
Erler, Mary, 210 n80
Eucharist, 50–2, 70, 72, 74, 82, 101, 102, 133–4, 210 n80, 211 n10
Elevation of the Host, 48, 70, 72, 76, 105, 106–8, 118, 140, 146, 217 n20
  see also Corpus Christi
Evangelical Christianity, 151–2, 155, 157, 159, 162–3
Evans, Ruth, 193 n61, 206 n51
everyday, 2, 7, 19, 88, 104, 128, 138, 147, 163
everyday body, 79–80, 85–6, 88
everyday materialities, 162–3
evolution, theory of, 156–9
excess
  bodily, 38, 139
  material, 38

experiential, 7, 25, 42, 77, 103, 124, 132, 185 n160
eyes, 1, 4, 21–3, 26, 31, 42, 63, 75, 76, 100, 118, 121, 129, 139, 143, 152, 175 n42, 195 n95

Fauconnier, Gilles, 87–9, 91, 95–6, 204 n21, 206 n44
Feagin, Susan, 219 n47, 220 n59
Fissell, Mary E., 78
flesh, 3, 4, 16, 30–2, 34, 35, 37, 55–7, 62, 76, 79–80, 84–5, 105, 113, 118–19, 123, 127, 135–6, 143–4, 149, 162, 175 n44, 179 n104
    control of fleshiness, 4, 28, 30–2, 37, 127–9, 143–4
Fletcher, John, 223 n12, 223 n14
flow, 100, 104, 161
Foister, Susan, 193 n66
Fourth Lateran Council, 3
framing, *see* conceptual blending
Freedberg, David, 39–40, 62, 85, 183 n148
French, Katherine, 69, 74, 78, 199 n35
friar, 4, 15, 48, 60, 100, 133, 189 n20, 206 n44, 219 n40
funerals, 13, 46–54, 57–8, 61, 63, 66, 69, 74, 87, 88, 94, 190 n41, 190 n42

Gallagher, Shaun, 8, 20, 168 n35, 174 n29
Gallese, Vittorio, 23–5, 27, 39–40, 42, 62, 85, 125, 176 n50, 183 n148, 185 n160, 220 n53
Garden of Eden, 158, 159
Garner, Stanton, Jr., 17–18, 42, 54, 99, 127, 145, 179 n104
gender, 6–7
Gerland, Oliver, 43
Gerson, Jean, 26

gesture, 3, 7, 16, 19, 28, 38, 40, 56, 71, 91, 97–8, 120–3, 136, 137, 152, 217 n19, 222 n3
    proper use, 7, 120–5
    spontaneous, 120–4
    see also kneeling
ghosting, 111
Gibson, Gail McMurray, 211 n1
girdle, 55–7, 61–2, 77–8, 93, 101, 142, 192 n54, 193 n61, 193 n62, 197 n3
    see also props
Goldberg, Jeremy, xi, 47, 93–4, 105
The Golden Legend, 192 n54
Gréban-Michel, *Mystère de la Passion*, 196 n101
guilds of York, 11, 48, 53, 63–5, 77, 85, 92–4, 102, 104, 133, 190 n40, 205 n32
    disciplinary tactics, 93–4
    fines, 92–3, 100
    values, 94, 104
    Specific guilds
        Armourers, 133
        Coopers, 63
        Cordwainers, 190 n40
        Corpus Christi guild, 12, 50–3, 60
        Girdlers, 61, 93
        Glaziers, 102
        Goldsmiths, 65
        Guild of Jesus Christ and the Blessed Virgin Mary, 190 n45
        Latteners, 63–5
        Lorimers, 93
        Masons, 65, 102, 196 n99
        Mercers (also Merchants), 53, 80, 103, 110, 191 n45
        Painters, 63–4
        Parchmentmakers, 204 n26
        Pater Noster, 11
        Pinners, 63–5
        Plasterers, 204 n26
        Saddlers, 92–3
        St. Christopher, guild of, 60

Stainers, 64
Tailors, 204 n24
Weavers, 93, 190 n40

hagiography, 124, 193 n61
Ham, Ken, 157, 159
Hamburger, Jeffrey, 209 n80
Harrowing of Hell, 81–2, 125–9, 214 n43
Hell Houses, 153–6, 163, 223 n12, 223 n14
documentary *Hell House*, 153, 154
heresy, 121
Hodapp, William, 141
Holy Land Experience theme park, 157
Holy Trinity Priory of York, 100, 101
home, 16, 59, 78, 79–86, 99, 100, 104, 163
homly, 79, 86
see also everyday
Host, *see* Eucharist; Corpus Christi
Hovind, Kent, 156, 160, 223 n16, 224 n29
Husserl, Edmund, 17–18, 20, 173 n16, 174 n29

iconography, 6, 16, 30, 36–7, 68–70, 81, 106, 116, 146
see also art
ideology, 2, 12, 56, 94, 186 n164
imaginative addition, 96
Imago Pietatis (Man of Sorrows), 82, 85, 140
incarnational theology, 3
indulgence, 4, 49, 111, 133
infiction, 41–2, 45–6, 57
integration networks, *see* conceptual blending
intentionality, 25, 39–41, 45–6, 54, 81, 84, 95, 104, 130
intentional attunement, 25, 40
interactivity, 5, 24–7, 41–2, 45, 53, 58, 134, 136–8, 144, 153, 159, 179 n104

with objects, 3, 27, 37, 39, 42, 45, 54–5, 57–8, 70, 201 n57
of spectatorship, 8, 41, 43, 45, 134, 136–8, 144–9, 153
inventories, 57, 58–60, 80, 193 n66
conventions, 58–9, 193 n68
Specific individuals
Carter, John, 59
Collan, John, 59
Duffield, William, 60
Gryssop, Thomas, 59
Morton, Thomas, 60

James, Mervyn, 207 n58
jews
in medieval York, 222 n9
references in cycle, 63, 122, 123, 128, 135
John the Baptist, *see* Saints; York Cycle, characters
Johnson, Mark, 8, 24, 26–7
Johnston, Alexandra F., 10, 60, 120, 171 n53, 206 n44, 214 n46, 217 n22

Kempe, Margery, 4–5, 15, 142–3
Kessler, Herbert, 85–6, 167 n23, 182 n131
kinesthetic, 46, 49, 92, 187 n3
King, Pamela, 10, 78, 103, 136, 147–8, 214 n40, 221 n61
Kipling, Gordon, 91
kneeling, 50, 56, 75, 82, 121–2, 124–5
Kolve, V. A., 138–9

Lakoff, George, 23–4
language, 24, 33, 51, 52, 98, 115–19, 122–3, 126, 135–6, 141, 152, 184 n156, 195 n95
laughter, 65, 138
Lay Folks' Catechism, 4, 10, 128
Lay Folks' Mass Book, 10
Leder, Drew, 50
Leiblichkeit, 18, 20

Lerer, Seth, 196 n101
Lerud, Theodore K., 33–4, 96, 207 n53
Les Freres Corbusier, 153–5
Lindberg, David C., 22
Lipton, Sara, 36
literacy, 113, 185 n159, 186 n165
 liturgical literacy, 41
 see also performance literacy
liturgy, 3, 16, 49, 69–72, 74, 76, 78, 105, 107–8, 110, 140, 147, 22 n18
 liturgical drama, 28
 liturgical literacy, 41, 49
 see also Eucharist; worship
lived experience, 26, 42, 125
liveness of objects, 46, 81, 140
living in the blend, *see* conceptual blending
Lollard, 33
Lopes, Dominic M. M., 222 n1
Lord's Prayer, *see* Pater Noster
Love, Nicholas, *The Mirror of the Blessed Life of Jesus Christ*, 5, 140–1
Loveland, Anne C., 160

Mahler, Jonathan, 161–2
make-up, 1, 54, 116, 117, 2212 n3
 see also costumes
manuscript, 11, 17, 34, 63, 105–13, 170 n44, 171 n48, 209 n76
 see also books; Books of Hours
Marks, Richard, 80
Marrow, James, 15–16
Mary, the Virgin, *see* Saints; York Cycle, characters
mass, 10, 41, 48–50, 61, 68–70, 72, 74, 140, 172 n7, 189 n20, 190 n41, 198 n21, 198 n26, 217 n20
material anchors, 87–8, 92–3, 115
material culture, 10, 86–8
material piety, 16, 44

McConachie, Bruce, 8–9, 25, 39, 96, 131–2, 144, 186 n165
McFarland, Lee, 161–2
media, 3, 5, 12, 40, 43, 46, 77, 81, 88, 141, 149, 151–2, 159, 163
 devotional media, 6, 9, 13, 41–2, 45–6, 132, 141, 149, 163
medievalism, 163
meditation, 5, 29, 100, 113, 128, 147, 175 n43
megachurch, 159–63
 Radiant Church, 161–2
Melton, Friar William, 133
memorials, in churches, 46, 62, 74, 104
memory, 12, 27, 34–5, 37–8, 46, 49–50, 53, 58, 61–3, 66, 87, 90, 113, 139, 169 n37, 187 n4, 190 n44
 bodily memory, 27, 37–8, 48–9, 58, 128
 communal memory, 47, 66
 locational memory system, 99–100
 medieval treatises, 96–100, 202 n70
 remember, 1, 12, 33–4, 48, 62, 74, 76, 88, 126
 sense memory, 48, 66, 76–7, 92
 see also memorials; mnemonic; pilgrimage
mental images, 5, 16, 20, 30, 96–9, 151 175 n42
merchant, 47, 80, 103, 110, 202 n61, 204 n28
 see also guilds of York, Mercers
Meredith, Peter, 10, 186 n169, 195 n95
Merleau-Ponty, Maurice, 18, 20, 23, 174 n31, 175, n44
Mickelgate, 71, 100, 101–4, 131
Milhaven, J. Giles, 37–8
Miller, Patricia Cox, 124–5
Mills, David, 221 n62
Minster of York, *see* cathedral

miraclis pleyinge, 27–30, 34–5, 38, 79, 144, 145, 149
Mirk, John, 48
mirror neurons, 23–6, 39–40, 53, 130, 132, 146
   disputes surrounding studies, 176 n52
   responses to touch, 62, 98, 136–7
   see also brain; cognition; simulation
Mitchell, W. J. T., 151
mnemonic, 49, 50, 53, 61–2, 68, 92, 96–7, 99, 102, 137, 139, 206 n44, 217 n20
   see also memory
mode of becoming, 2–3, 12, 43, 58, 62, 88, 149, 153
monarchs of England
   Edward IV, 203 n11
   Edward V, 89
   Edwin, 67
   Henry IV, 67, 91
   Henry VI, 91, 203 n11
   Henry VII, 89–92, 94, 203 n11
   Henry VIII, 203 n11
   Mary, 70
   Richard II, 203 n11
   Richard III, 89, 203 n11
monetary values, 193 n68
moral perception, 142
   see also empathy
Morgan, David, 2, 5, 20, 66, 173 n11
mortality of objects, 38–41, 57
motor system, 24, 39–40, 95, 138, 153, 183 n148, 218 n30
   see also sensorimotor
Muir, Lynette, 208 n63
museum, 111, 156–60, 163
music, 6, 26, 46, 49, 76, 138–9, 160, 184 n158, 218 n30
   see also rhythm

Nellhaus, Tobin, 27
Nerve-Wracking Ball, 156
neural, *see* brain; cognition

neuron, *see* brain; mirror neurons
The Northern Passion, 213, n30

objectness, 36–7, 56, 69, 76
Olson, Glending, 28
openness of spectator, 19, 158–9, 177 n69
Ordo paginarum, 55, 63
ornamentation, 52, 60, 104, 193 n62
   see also decoration
Ouse bridge, 52, 60, 100
Ouse River, 71, 97, 100, 103

pageants, *see* York Cycle
pain, spectator respones to, 29, 31, 136, 144–6, 154, 220 n53
Palm Sunday, 78, 98–9, 121
parish church, 10, 13, 35, 47–8, 50, 60–1, 69–79, 81, 85–6, 88, 101, 104, 105, 110, 121, 160, 224 n37
   lay control, 69–71, 77–9
   as material anchor, 88
   as medium, 70
   seating arrangements, 74
   on York Cycle route, 100–2
   Selected parish churches
      All Saints North Street, 71–6
      All Saints Pavement, 100, 101, 106, 110, 198 n17
      St. Michael-le-Belfry, 102, 198 n17
Parkyn, Robert, "Narrative of the Reformation," 70
Passion of Christ, 4–5, 15, 29, 34, 36, 37, 55, 81, 98, 108, 111, 120, 135, 136, 138, 141–9
   textual control, 36, 141
Pater Noster (Lord's Prayer), 11, 61, 171 n55
   Pater Noster play, 11
patronage, 37, 58, 84
Pavement in York, 100–1, 106, 110, 198
Pavement Hours, *see* Books of Hours

Pecham, John, 21, 22
Pecock, Reginald, *The Repressor of Over Much Blaming of the Clergy*, 33–4, 121
penance, 38, 93
perception, 12, 17–27, 30–43, 45, 50, 58, 85, 96, 98, 104–5, 125, 131, 138, 142, 144–5, 167 n23, 169 n37, 177 n69, 182 n145, 186 n168
  medieval theories, 21–3, 26–7, 30–7, 45, 58, 145, 186 n168
performance, definition of, 2–3, 42–44
performance literacy, 9–10, 12–13, 15, 41–3, 45–6, 49, 54, 57, 67, 69, 71, 76, 79, 113, 120, 130, 132, 149, 152, 186 n165
  instability, 132, 144–9, 155–6
performing objects, 39
  see also art; props; "thingness"
phenomenology, 6, 7–9, 12, 16–21, 23, 34, 54, 56, 85, 130
  naturalized phenomenology, 8–9, 20–1, 23
  neurophenomenology, 20, 174 n29, 174 n31
pietà, 15, 37–8, 59
piety, 4, 7, 15, 47, 58, 67, 70, 85, 103, 104, 121, 124, 142, 167 n24, 172 n7, 221 n60
  female piety, 6–7
  sensual piety, 151–2, 156, 163
  visual piety, 2, 3, 5–6, 12–13, 16, 17, 20, 42, 45, 66, 68–9, 80, 113, 115, 117, 124, 132, 134, 137, 151
pilgrimage, 4, 15, 38, 111
  badges, 62, 78, 111
  by proxy, 49, 189 n24
Plato, 21
players, 29, 64–5
  see also actor

plays
  Creed play, 11–12, 60, 89
  Pater Noster play, 11
  Play about Saint James the Apostle, 60
  see also York Cycle
pleyinge, *see* miraclis pleyinge
Pope Gregory the Great, 33
Pope Urban IV, 50, 133
Praise Dance, *see* dance
prayer, 11, 38, 48, 49, 50, 55, 61, 62, 72, 75, 78, 86, 104–6, 108–10, 121, 137, 154, 198 n18, 198 n21, 222 n3
preaching, 3, 36, 40, 48, 55, 83, 97, 99, 125, 133, 140, 142–3, 147, 160, 215 n55
Pricke of Conscience window, 71, 72–6, 82, 88
priest, 4, 29, 38, 50–1, 61, 72, 80, 197 n10, 198 n21
primer, *see* Books of Hours
procession, 3, 11, 46, 48–52, 70, 78, 94, 100–2, 133–4, 221 n10
  see also royal entry
props, 19, 39, 54–8, 61, 66, 77, 78
  devotional props, 58–63
  Virgin's girdle, 55–8, 61–2, 142
  see also art; stage design
proselytize, 152–3, 223 n14

Ramachandran, V. S., 45
Ratliff, George, 153–4
Rayner, Alice, 38–9, 56–7, 111, 195 n85, 199 n38
reading, 5, 7, 17, 33, 43, 78, 113, 132, 140–1, 153, 163, 172 n7, 186 n165, 207 n57
  misreading, 36
  reader, 4, 36, 105, 110, 113, 124, 141
  see also books; Books of Hours
reception, 8, 18–19, 89, 115, 137
Records of Early English Drama (*REED*), 10, 170 n45

Rees Jones, Sarah, 103
Reformation, 33, 70, 72
    see also Parkyn, Robert
relics, 16, 60, 78, 106, 193 n61,
    197 n3, 209 n80
    therapeutic powers, 78
Revetour, William, 60–1
Rhetorica ad Herennium, 205 n41
rhythm, 19, 39, 41, 44, 46, 50–4, 58,
    62, 69, 72, 75, 76, 84–6,
    94, 104, 151, 153, 163
    auditory rhythm, 138–9, 146
    of Books of Hours, 104–5, 111–13
    of performance, 19, 32, 54, 57, 63,
        66, 85, 96–7, 99, 120, 126,
        127, 131, 138–9, 145–6,
        149, 152–5, 223 n11
    of space, 60, 68–9, 72, 75–80,
        88, 96, 104, 155, 156, 158
    see also music
Riddy, Felicity, 79, 103, 200 n48
ritual, 1, 3, 4, 12, 28, 42, 43, 72, 78,
    86, 103, 105, 121, 124,
    140, 142, 149, 207 n58
    posthumous rituals, 46–54, 74,
        88, 94, 104
Roberts, Pastor Keenan, 153, 155
Rogerson, Margaret, 10
Rokotnitz, Naomi, 9, 159
rood screen, 72, 198 n27
Rosser, Gervase, 102
Rothstein, Edward, 159
royal entry, 11, 89–94
    specific characters
    Ebrauk, 90–1
    King Solomon, 91
    King David, 91
    Mary, the Virgin, 91
Rubin, Miri, 82–3, 140

sacraments, 3, 4, 16, 29, 51–2, 70,
    74, 128, 136, 140
saints, 30, 35, 36, 47, 48, 49, 60,
    61, 105, 108–9, 110, 124,
    136, 192 n54, 193 n61,
    199 n39, 199 n41
    Agnes, 108
    Anne, 48
    Anthony, 106–8, 110
    Catherine, 60
    Christopher, 60, 108–10
    Clare, 106–8, 110
    Clement, 60
    George, 59, 61, 106–8, 110
    James, 48, 60, 72, 90
    John of Bridlington, 77
    John the Baptist, 48, 82
        head of, 82–5, 203 n72
    John the Evangelist, 48, 60, 81,
        192 n54
    Leonard, 101
    Mary Magdalene, 201 n54
    Mary, the Virgin, 15, 37–8, 47,
        48, 59, 60, 68, 71, 77, 79,
        81, 91, 105, 121, 142, 189
        n19, 190 n45, 192 n54,
        200 n43
    Michael, 60
    Nicholas, 48, 72
    Peter, 60, 77, 82, 196 n1
    Richard Scrope, 67, 77, 106,
        197 n3
    Roch, 106–8, 110
    Thomas, 72, 192 n54
    Thomas Becket, 82
    William of York, 52, 77, 82
    see also Augustine; parish church;
        relics; York cycle,
        characters
Salmen, Walter, 222 n3
Saltz, David, 16, 41
salvation, 11, 49, 84, 99, 119, 124,
    127–8, 130, 141, 147–8,
    152–3
Sargent, Michael, 218 n36
Satan, 154, 214 n43
    see also York cycle, characters
Sawyer, R. Keith, 138
scourge, 34, 123, 136, 138–9, 154
Scoville, Chester, 217 n20
Scribner, Robert, 167 n24
Scrope, Richard, *see* saints

sculpture, *see* alabaster sculpture; art
seeing, *see* vision; visual
semiotics, 8, 54
sensation, 1, 25–6, 142, 160, 185
 n160, 187 n2
senses, 17, 30, 57, 92, 96, 111, 124,
 142–3, 149, 151–2, 155,
 157, 179 n104
 concerns about senses, 30–2, 35,
  143, 162, 184 n151
 sense organs, 21, 26
 sense to history, 57–8, 62,
  66, 77
sensorimotor, 23–6, 57, 98, 125,
 136, 144, 146, 220 n53
sensual, 2–3, 18–19, 31–2, 50, 53,
 57, 62, 66, 72, 76, 78, 86,
 88–9, 104, 111, 113, 149,
 151–2, 155–8, 160–1,
 163, 180 n105
 sensual culture, 151–2
 sensual piety, 151–2, 156, 163
sermons, *see* preaching
Sheingorn, Pamela, 6, 166 n18,
 201 n56
Shepherd, Simon, 17, 19, 54, 85,
 99, 103–4
sight, *see* vision; visual
signify, 3, 12, 33–4, 39, 46, 47, 50,
 54, 57, 93, 111, 195 n85,
 199 n38, 206 n51
silence, 120, 122, 138, 139,
 146–7
simulation, 23–5, 32, 39–40, 42,
 53, 57, 62, 76, 84–5, 125,
 130–2, 137–9, 141,
 143–6, 149, 153–5,
 219 n47
sin, 26, 29, 30, 36, 56, 124, 127–8,
 143, 145, 148, 153–5
singing, 1, 38, 48, 49, 55, 68, 91,
 152, 160–1
 see also music
slippage, 77, 106, 134, 137, 145, 147
Sofer, Andrew, 55–6
souvenir, 78, 111

space, 10, 12–13, 38, 39, 41–4,
 59–60, 67–86, 88–106,
 123, 132, 140, 141, 149,
 151, 156, 159–63
 bodied space, 85
 city space, 10, 12, 88, 96, 99,
  100–3
 performance space (stage space;
  theatrical space), 10, 17,
  18, 19, 57, 64, 95, 102
 spatial assimilation with city,
  89, 96–9, 100, 102
species, 21–2, 40–1
spectacle, 1, 46, 53, 64–6, 72,
 90–1, 93, 136, 139, 157,
 159, 160
 see also stage design; technological
  enhancement
spectatorship, 16, 27, 42, 65, 117,
 120, 134, 145, 152
 actor-audience relationship, 12,
  118, 124, 136
 participatory, 83, 95–9, 116,
  125–6, 128–30,
  138–40, 148
 viewing positions, 102, 145–6,
  148–9
Sponsler, Claire, 7, 28, 132, 155,
 169 n39, 175 n43, 186
 n164, 213 n36, 218 n32
St. Leonard's Hospital, 101
St. Mary's abbey, 77
stage design, 1, 6, 63, 77, 81, 90–2,
 96, 117, 155–6, 196 n101
 The Last Judgment indenture,
  53–4, 78, 202 n59
 see also props; costumes; spectacle
stained glass, *see* art; *Pricke of
  Conscience* window
Stein, Edith, 130
Stewart, Susan, 111
Sturges, Robert, 221 n60
subjectivity, 18, 26, 131, 177 n69,
 220 n53
suffering, 4, 31, 34, 79, 145, 148,
 154, 156

of Christ, 4, 15, 123, 130, 134, 141–3, 145, 147–9
surveillance, 119, 212 n17
suspension of disbelief, 96
sympathy, 13, 25, 130–1, 139, 141–4, 147–8
synesthetic, 46, 50, 162
   synesthetic memory, 48, 76
   synesthetic worship, 160, 162

tactility, 37, 56, 76, 111, 195 n85
Taylor, Barbara Brown, 155
technological enhancement, 160–1
Ten Commandments, 4, 34
testator, *see* wills
Thaut, Michael, 138–9
theme parks, 156–7, 160, 162, 163
theology, 3, 12, 36, 38, 54–5, 83–4, 115, 127, 130, 137, 149, 152, 162, 206 n51, 211 n1
Theory of Mind, 24–5, 131
   standard simulation theory, 25
thingness, 38–42, 57, 62, 75, 78, 80
Thompson, Evan, 8, 20, 25, 130–1, 142, 144, 173 n16, 175 n46, 177 n69
Thumma, Scott, 161
tombstone, 88
torches, 11, 48, 50–2, 74, 76, 78, 104, 190 n40, 197 n3
   see also candles
touch, 16, 23, 33, 57, 97, 113, 134–6, 152, 221 n1
   neural responses to, 137
   in performance, 57, 62, 84, 119, 124, 135–7, 216 n14
A Tretise of Miraclis Pleyinge, 27–32, 34, 35, 38, 79, 144–5
Tretyse of Ymagis, 34–8, 69, 79, 199 n39
Trinity images, 33, 34, 48, 59
Trinity Church (Assemblies of God), 153

Turner, Mark, 87–9, 91, 95–6, 204 n21, 206 n44
Twycross, Meg, 10, 171 n51

Van Os, Henk, 84
Veronica images, 209 n80
vestments, 61, 71, 76
Vie de Saint Jehan Paulus, 136
violence in performance, 138–9, 146
   as game, 138
visceral, 1, 32, 41, 76, 78, 100, 102, 124–5, 141, 145, 155, 185 n163
vision, 4, 7, 16, 23, 52, 134, 159, 225 n50
   cognitive theory, 23–7, 32, 39–40, 125, 136–7, 145
   devotional seeing, 9, 15–16, 41–3, 110, 134
   hierarchy of vision, 30–1, 35
   interpretive strategies, 9, 45
   medieval theories, 13, 16, 21–3, 26–7, 30–7, 40–1, 45–6, 53, 134, 149, 151, 187 n3
   optical illusions, 45
   regulation of, 5, 6, 36, 51–2, 134, 137, 141
   sight in the York cycle, 63, 115–19, 121–5, 133–7, 146, 148, 221 n60
   visceral seeing, 124–5
visuomotor, 23, 39, 182 n145
see also cognition; perception; senses; visual
visual, 2–3, 5–6, 21, 27, 39, 46–7, 51–4, 62–6, 68–74, 76–82, 86–91, 94, 108, 111, 117–18, 122, 127, 134, 145, 152–3, 157–8, 160
   cycle's visual arrangement, 94, 100–4
   interactivity, 8, 24, 26–7, 58
   juxtaposition, 74, 111, 117
   visual anticipation, 115–18, 134
   visual culture, 2, 5–6, 13, 17, 70, 151, 177 n59

visual—*Continued*
visual devotion, 2, 6, 15, 46, 159
visual layering, 74, 77, 85, 106, 110, 162
visual metaphors, 115–16
visual performance encounter, 2–3, 12, 17, 18, 29, 32, 39, 43, 45, 63, 66, 103–4, 115, 117, 125, 130, 134, 140, 145–9, 152
visual piety, 2–3, 5–6, 12–13, 16–17, 20, 42, 45, 66, 68–9, 80, 113, 115, 117, 124, 132, 134, 137, 151
visual theory, *see* vision
visuality, 2, 46, 70
visualize, 29, 80, 127, 130
see also spectacle; stage design

wagons, *see* pageants
Walker, Julia A., 102
wax, *see* candles
wealth, medieval interpretations of, 37, 47, 103
weeping, 4, 15, 29, 97, 98, 142, 144–5
Wheeler, Bonnie, 13
Wheeler, Otis B., 160
White, Eileen, 170 n46
Williamson, Beth, 16
wills, 46–9, 52–3, 57–63, 65, 74, 80, 82, 105, 197 n1, 197 n10, 199 n39
bequests, 47–9, 58–62, 67, 77, 80, 88, 191 n45, 193 n62, 197 n3
customs, 47, 49, 52–3
problems of interpretation, 46–7, 52–3
testators, 46–54, 61–2, 77, 80, 188 n11, 189 n20
Specific testators
Bawtre, Reginald, 74
Blackburn family, 74
Bracebrig, Thomas, 47–9, 52–3, 65, 88

Carter, John, 59
clergy, 60–1
de Craven, Katherine, 77
Dautre, John , 48
Duffield, William, 60
Gryssop, Thomas, 59
Henryson family, 74
Hessle family, 74
Katheryne the Countes of Northumberlande, 62
Morton, Thomas, 60
Revetour, William, 60–1
Santon, Beatrix, 193 n62
Thomson, Annas, 59
Wod, Thomas , 61
witness, 29, 68–9, 77, 81–2, 84, 93, 116–18, 121–2, 125–6, 128, 137, 141, 144, 147–8, 152–3, 214 n40, 218 n36
bere wittenesse (bodily witness), 85, 125–6, 168
eyewitness, 55
relationship to belief, 128
visual witness, 81–2, 116, 141
Wolska, Aleksandra, 2, 43
worship, 3, 28–9, 38, 50, 67–8, 70–2, 78, 104, 110, 121, 123, 151–2, 160–2, 175 n43, 222 n9

Yardley, Anne Bagnall, 49
York cycle, 10–13, 17, 28, 53, 54, 63, 66, 77, 80, 81, 83, 85, 90, 92, 95, 106, 115–49, 219 n39
as artisanal ideology, 94
assimilation within, 97–9, 102–4, 145–9
characters
Adam, 63
Andrew, 56
angels, 54, 55, 63, 83–4, 91, 116, 119, 128–9
Annas, 122–3, 147
Barabbas, 123

INDEX

Bedellus, 120–1, 125
Belliall, 126
burgess, 117, 211 n10
Caiaphas, 122–3, 147
Centurion, 125
Christ, 54, 55, 63, 64, 81, 84, 97–9, 115–49
   Deus, 54, 63, 67, 117–19, 128
   devils, 54, 126
   disciples, 55–7, 116–17, 125, 135–6, 147–8, 216 n14
Elizabeth, 119
Eve, 63
Fergus, 65, 191 n50
Herod, 118, 122–3
Jacobus, 56
James, 56, 117
jews, 63, 122, 123, 128, 135
John the Baptist, 83–4, 116
John the Evangelist, 56, 63, 81
Joseph, 54, 79, 115, 119, 136
Joseph of Arimathea, 124–5
Judas, 135
Lazarus, 116
Longinus, 124, 214 n40
Mary, the Virgin, 55–7, 61–3, 79, 119–20, 135–7, 142, 147–8, 191 n50, 193 n61, 217 n20
Peter, 56, 117, 121, 125
Pilate, 120, 122–5, 139, 147
porter, 117
Satan, 126–7
soldiers, 97, 115–16, 118, 120–1, 123–4, 135, 138–9, 145–6
Symeon, 115, 126, 136, 217 n19
Thomas, 55–6
Vice characters, 155
waiting women, 119
Zaché, 118
disputes over, 64–5, 133–5
dramatic structure, 96–7, 99–100
as memory system, 95–7, 99–100
pageants by title

The Agony in the Garden and the Betrayal, 115–16, 135, 138
The Annunciation and the Visitation, 119
Appearance to Mary Magdalene, 216 n14
The Ascension, 63, 68, 81, 84, 97, 117, 125, 216 n14
The Assumption of the Virgin, 55–7, 61, 142, 192 n54, 202 n59
The Baptism, 83–4, 116
Christ Before Annas and Caiaphas, 121
Christ Before Herod, 118, 120, 122
Christ Before Pilate I: The Dream of Pilate's Wife, 120
Christ Before Pilate II: The Judgment, 120, 122–3, 138
The Coronation of the Virgin, 191 n50
The Creation, 63, 97–8
The Crucifixion, 54, 97, 118, 124–5, 140, 144–9, 220 n53
The Death of Christ, 123–5, 136, 147–9
The Death of the Virgin, 191 n50
The Entry into Jerusalem, 98, 117–18
The Fall of the Angels, 97, 118–19
The Fall of Man, 63
The Flight into Egypt, 136
The Funeral of the Virgin ("Fergus" play), 65, 191 n50
The Harrowing of Hell, 125–9
The Incredulity of Thomas, 55, 216 n14
Joseph's Trouble about Mary, 119
The Last Judgment, 54, 78, 125, 128–30, 137, 154, 191 n46, 191 n50
indenture, 53–4, 78, 202 n59

York cycle—*Continued*
   The Last Supper, 116, 136
   The Nativity, 54, 115, 119–20, 135–7
   Pentecost, 125
   The Purification, 115, 136, 217 n19
   The Road to Calvary, 139–40, 146
   The Supper at Emmaus, 216 n14
   The Temptation, 98, 116, 205 n37
   The Transfiguration, 116–17
   The Women Taken in Adultery/ The Raising of Lazarus, 116
   as penance, 93–4
   processional route and stations, 11, 94–5, 100–4, 208 n59, 208 n63
   regulation, 11, 64, 93–4, 100
   relationship to Corpus Christi procession, 133–5
   wagons, 11, 81, 95, 97, 100, 146

Zahavi, Dan, 8, 20, 168 n35, 174 n29
Zieman, Katherine, 41
Zunshine, Lisa, 183 n150

GPSR Compliance

The European Union's (EU) General Product Safety Regulation (GPSR) is a set of rules that requires consumer products to be safe and our obligations to ensure this.

If you have any concerns about our products, you can contact us on

ProductSafety@springernature.com

In case Publisher is established outside the EU, the EU authorized representative is:

Springer Nature Customer Service Center GmbH
Europaplatz 3
69115 Heidelberg, Germany

www.ingramcontent.com/pod-product-compliance
Lightning Source LLC
LaVergne TN
LVHW011808060526
838200LV00053B/3705